TRAVELS

with

TED & NE

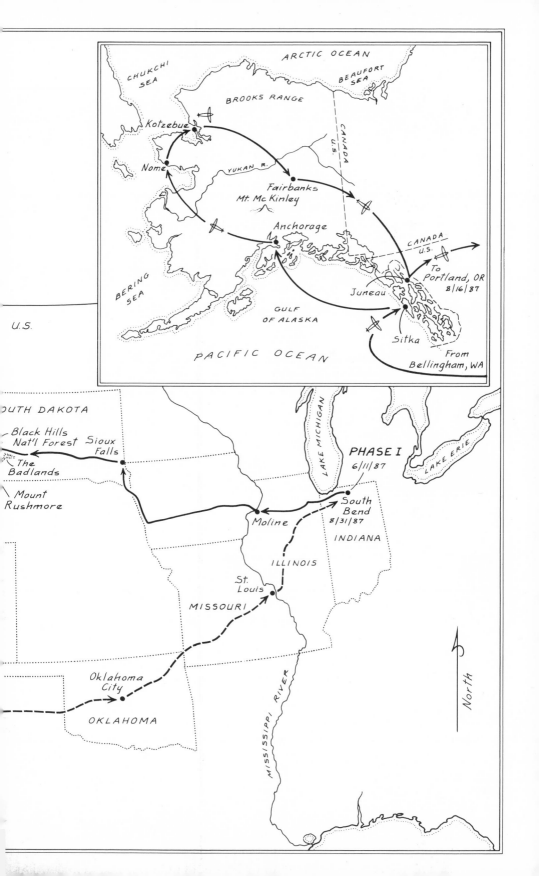

TRAVELS
with
TED & NED

Theodore M. Hesburgh, C.S.C.

Edited by Jerry Reedy

DOUBLEDAY

New York   London   Toronto   Sydney   Auckland

PUBLISHED BY DOUBLEDAY

a division of Bantam Doubleday Dell Publishing Group, Inc.
666 Fifth Avenue, New York, NY 10103

DOUBLEDAY and the portrayal of an anchor with a dolphin
are trademarks of Doubleday,
a division of Bantam Doubleday Dell Publishing Group, Inc.

Book design by Richard Oriolo

Endpaper maps by Aher/Donnell Studios

Library of Congress Cataloging-in-Publication Data

Hesburgh, Theodore Martin, 1917–
Travels with Ted and Ned / Theodore M. Hesburgh : edited by
Jerry Reedy.
p.   cm.
Includes index.
1. Hesburgh, Theodore Martin, 1917—Journeys.   2. Voyages and
travels—1981–   I. Reedy, Jerry.   II. Title.
[G465.H485   1992]
910.4—dc20   92-26432
CIP

ISBN 0-385-26681-2

Printed in the United States of America

November 1992

First Edition
1   3   5   7   9   10   8   6   4   2

CONTENTS

To the University of Notre Dame, a special place, because of the patronage of a very special Lady. This book is dedicated to the Lady, Notre Dame, and to the place, with love and gratitude for a happy life, spent here for half a century.

The year recounted in this book was a year away from Notre Dame but never that far away, as we encountered wonderful Notre Dame alumni and alumnae everywhere we went, from Alaska to Antarctica.

ACKNOWLEDGMENTS

This book began with a daily diary I dictated describing Ned's and my travels during our first year of retirement. Dick Conklin, associate vice president of Notre Dame's University Relations staff, and his colleague, Dennis Moore in Public Relations, gave the transcripts their excellent editorial critique.

When I decided to turn the diaries into a book, I had the help of travel writer Jerry Reedy, who collaborated with me on *God, Country, Notre Dame*, my autobiography. Deftly wielding his red pencil, Jerry further streamlined the transcripts, reducing them to about half their original length.

For these essential services I am truly grateful to Dick, Dennis, and Jerry. I also owe much to my secretary of thirty-eight years, Helen Hosinski, who typed the original diaries amid myriad other tasks. Her successor, Melanie Chapleau, generously took up the task when Helen retired.

Books never get published without the unsung work of publishers and their supportive and professional staffs. In this case, kudos to Bill Barry of Doubleday and his associates, especially Mike Iannazzi.

I am also grateful to my religious community, the Congregation of Holy Cross, for making such a wonderful year possible. Both Ned and I came back refreshed, renewed, better informed, and very ready to go to work again in a different yet challenging context.

Finally, my gratitude to Ned Joyce, my companion in all of these travels. Always affable and agreeable, he put up generously with my deficiencies as we deepened a friendship that is now more than four decades old.

I also thank those who in reality and through this book have traveled with us.

INTRODUCTION

This is obviously a book about travel and two seventy-year-old Holy Cross priests who did the traveling. It was the way we chose to begin our retirement after working together for thirty-five years as president and executive vice president of the University of Notre Dame. Our friends call us Ted and Ned.

We began in June 1987 by traveling throughout the West and Far Northwest of the United States in a recreational vehicle or RV. Sandwiched between legs of this motor trip was a journey to Alaska in a small two-engine Cessna airplane. We flew all over this enormous state, from Sitka in the south to Kotzebue, just north of the Arctic Circle.

After a scant week or so back at Notre Dame, our home base, we were off to Central and South America, from Mexico to Patagonia and most countries in between. This segment, mostly done by commercial airliner, also included a month-long, 2,000-mile trip down the Amazon on the *Society Explorer* from Iquitos, Peru, near the Pacific Ocean, to Belém, Brazil, on the Atlantic coast. Later, in southern Chile, we boarded the *Evangelista* at Puerto Natales on the Pacific coast and cruised the Chilean fjords all the way to Puerto Montt.

We were back at Notre Dame in mid-December for a week or so before sailing on the *Queen Elizabeth 2*'s Caribbean Christmas cruise, earning our passage as chaplains. We returned in January and then left again immediately to take care of other business, I at The Hague in Holland, Ned at Notre Dame. We then shipped out together on the *QE2* on January 13 for the second time in a month, this time to serve as chaplains on an around-the-world cruise. When we returned in May, we had sailed for more than a hundred days and visited some forty countries.

The around-the-world cruise on the *QE2* was to have been the final segment of our year of travel, but our friends on the *Society Explorer's* "Little Red Ship" decided they wanted us back as chaplains for their Christmas cruise to Antarctica. So off we went again—this time from the Strait of Magellan due south across the Drake Passage. It is 600 miles of the roughest ocean in the world, but once you've completed the passage you're rewarded with some of the world's most glorious (and iciest) scenery.

So there it is: a curious combination of travels that marked the beginning of our retirement years. Looking back, we can say that it was a great way to begin what has now lengthened into almost five years away from those jobs that we held for such a long time.

We were long gone and far away all year, which is the best way to start retirement. We told our successors, Father "Monk" Malloy and Father Bill Beauchamp, both of whom are good friends, "Be yourselves and forget us. It's now your show. Do it your way." They took us at our word, and we didn't bother them. Hardly a postcard passed back and forth for the whole year. That was good for them and good for us too.

We made a clean break from the old to the new. We did it happily, with joy at the prospect of the first sabbatical we had ever had, after long years of very demanding service, of always being on call, of always being up front. The whole year was full of new sights and sounds, new friends made almost daily, old friends and alumni encountered everywhere. And with all that newness there was a strong link to the past, especially at our daily Masses and during the daily prayers we offered together. We also had more opportunities for pastoral services along the way, so we never felt useless. We prepared and delivered homilies every day, even on those occasions when the only listeners were ourselves.

There were wonderful free swatches of time, especially aboard ship, for reading all the good books that enticed us. Imagine reading Robert Massie's *Peter the Great*, as I did, while floating down the Amazon. There were hundreds of good conversations that we never had time for during the hustle and bustle of our past lives, conversations with each other and with all of our new friends. "Never a dull moment" is a trite phrase, but it was indeed true of this enchanting year of living and learning in a wide variety of new circumstances.

Why did we decide to spend our first year of retirement traveling all over the world? The best answer I can give is that during our final year as president and executive vice president, a lot of people asked us what we planned to do when we retired. We hadn't given it much thought, so we often just said that we planned to do some traveling, some reading and writing. From those casual responses, the travel idea gradually took on a life of its own. And almost before we knew it, we were heading west on Interstate 80 in a large motor home with an automobile hooked on behind. We hadn't a clue as to what was in store for us.

Each night I dictated my diary, which explains why this book is in diary form. While it is my book, Ned Joyce is very much part of it, even when he isn't mentioned specifically. He also kept his own diary, somewhat briefer than mine. Because there is more about me than I care to contemplate in my recent autobiography, *God, Country, Notre Dame* (Doubleday, 1990), it seems fitting in this place to say something about Ned Joyce. He will blush at the thought, but this book will make more sense if you know something about both of us.

Father Ned Joyce was my right-hand man for the entire thirty-five years that I was president of Notre Dame. It would be impossible to recount, even in cursory fashion, all the great things he did for Notre Dame during his thirty-five years as executive vice president. Without him, both the university and I would have been much diminished.

In a very real sense Ned was the anchor of the executive echelon during those years. Many vice presidents came and went, but Ned was always there. And up until 1970, when we created the position of provost, he was always the number two man in authority. When I was away, he was acting president, the man in charge. I traveled a lot, often for weeks at a time, but I never worried for a moment about how the university was doing in my absence. With Ned Joyce in charge, I knew I had nothing to worry about. He was, and is, a man of impeccable moral character, shrewd judgment, rocklike fidelity, and unfailing dependability.

The first time I met Ned Joyce was the day he was ordained, June 8, 1949, the same year I became executive vice president. The ordination ceremony was over and Ned was on his way to the office of Notre Dame's president, Father John Cavanaugh, to give him a blessing, something young priests still do for relatives and close friends on ordination day. The friendship between Ned and Father John had started during Ned's student days when he worked as Father John's secretary. I also had some business with Father John that day, and just as I was on my way into his office, out came Ned. I remember being struck by his vitality and ebullience as we met in the hallway and introduced ourselves to each other. I could tell immediately that there was something special about him.

Cavanaugh later told me that Ned had majored in accounting and had been graduated from Notre Dame with high honors. He had passed the CPA exam, worked in the business world for five years, then had come back to Notre Dame to study for the priesthood. He was just three months older than I was. We had overlapped at Notre Dame in 1934–35 and 1936–37, but had not known each other.

On his return to Notre Dame after ordination, Ned's first job was not much different than what mine had been. They made him an assistant rector of Morrissey Hall and assigned him to teach theology. He'd been at it barely one semester when Father John Burke, who was financial vice president at that time, became sick with nephritis and had to go to Arizona, where the climate was drier. Cavanaugh immediately tapped Ned to fill in for Burke, and in a couple of weeks Ned had everything running smoothly.

When Burke came back at the end of the summer, I went to see Cavanaugh and told him how impressed I had been with the way Ned had come into that department cold and yet had done such a superb job. I then recommended to Father John that he send Ned over to Oxford for a degree in PPE (Philosophy, Political Science, and Economics). That, with his CPA, would put him on an equal footing with the Ph.D.s in the administration, were he to become a permanent member of it after returning from Oxford. The degree would also expose Ned to a lot of things he probably hadn't read when he was studying business and accounting.

Father John took to the idea immediately. He liked Ned as much as I did, and he could see that the additional degree would be beneficial for him. To no one's surprise, Ned took Oxford by storm. He excelled in the classroom, made all kinds of friends, played on a world championship Oxford basketball team, assisted the famous Father Ronald Knox on Sundays, and was unofficial chaplain to the American Rhodes Scholars at Oxford. Among them was John Brademas, the future Indiana congressman, House Whip, and president of New York University. Other well-known people whom Ned came to know at Oxford were the author Robert Massie and the present director of the Library of Congress, Jim

Billington. Ned also knew all the Jesuits at Oxford because he lived with them in Campion Hall.

Despite all the success and enjoyment Ned had at Oxford, I suspect his fondest memory was the basketball championship. Ned had played high school basketball in South Carolina, and he had looked forward to trying out for the Notre Dame team. His hopes were dashed, though, when he failed to make the cut. One reason, I imagine, was that he was about a year younger than his classmates and had not yet reached his full growth. By the time he reached Oxford, of course, he was fully grown. He stood more than six feet tall, and his height, combined with his playing skills, was all he needed to make the All-America team at Oxford. In the finals, it was Ned's team against another All-America team fielded by the U.S. Air Force. Oxford won, and all of a sudden the fellow who couldn't make the team at Notre Dame fifteen years earlier found himself on a world championship team in England. Ned also won an Oxford blue, or rather half blue. (In America we give varsity letters; in Oxford they give blues.) They don't rate basketball at Oxford as highly as cricket or rowing.

About a year and a half after Ned arrived at Oxford, Father Burke's nephritis flared up again, this time fatally. We summoned Ned back to Notre Dame, and he took over the financial vice presidency once more. I'm sure Ned would have preferred to stay at Oxford and finish his degree, but good soldier that he's always been, he came back to Notre Dame and went to work. By the time Cavanaugh appointed me president, a year or so after Ned's return, I already knew whom I wanted for number two—Ned Joyce. Not only was he an extremely capable administrator, and just an all-around first-class fellow, but he also knew and cared about athletics. This was an area that had never much interested me, but I considered it to be very important because it gave national visibility to the university. The athletic department also had a tradition of enforcing academic integrity that I knew Ned would maintain and even strengthen. The provincial had to appoint him, of course, because in those days the school was run by the order. But they had already told me that I could pick my own team, so the appointment was pretty much a formality.

Over the years Ned and I have worked extraordinarily well together, no doubt because we balance each other so nicely. That's another way of saying we're quite different from one another. For that reason, those who know us well consider us rather strange boon companions. Ned is a

Southerner from Spartanburg, South Carolina; I am a Yankee from Syracuse in upstate New York. He is good with numbers; I am better with words. He is patient and methodical; I am impatient and impulsive. He is a good athlete; I have two left feet. And to be completely honest, I should admit that he has more virtue than I.

We are also characterized by some in liberal and conservative terms, I being the liberal, Ned the conservative. I've always felt that "liberal" is a label that doesn't fit me all that neatly. For example, I think I'm rather conservative when it comes to values. Ned, on the other hand, tends to take a conservative stance about most things, especially in the area of finance. Given his accounting and business background, that's not surprising.

Ned also likes to take his time making a decision. He looks ten ways at everything, and always makes sure all the *t*'s are crossed and the *i*'s dotted. He's a meticulous planner. I, on the other hand, tend to jump right in. I like to take financial chances, and I get impatient with planning. It's the same way when we give talks. He'll work on a talk for a long time, thinking about it, organizing it, writing it out, making sure it's just the way he wants it. My talks are more spontaneous. My former assistant John Wilson, in referring to my speaking style, once said it was only a matter of "standing him up and turning him on." I freely admit that I don't like to speak from a carefully prepared text, and I rarely do, a habit that hasn't made me terribly popular with some of the people in our public relations area.

But different as we are, Ned and I, we have worked closely together for thirty-five years and there's never been a bad word between us. Nor have we had a single serious disagreement on anything that I would consider fundamentally important. When we did disagree on various decisions, I felt I was wrong about half the time and I deferred to him. While we disagreed occasionally on policies, procedures, and projects, we never disagreed on the goals or the philosophy of the university.

We trust one another implicitly, and we have enormous respect and admiration for one another. There's nothing I wouldn't do for him, nor he for me. But I have to give Ned more than half the credit for our compatibility, because it's much more difficult to be the number two man than it is the number one. You just normally have to be more accommodating when the fellow you're working with is your boss. I knew that, because I worked as executive vice president under Father Cavanaugh for three years.

It could be argued that the reason Ned and I got along with one another so long and so well was that we really weren't around each other that much. There's some truth in this. When I was traveling, he covered for me. When he was traveling, I covered for him. It wasn't often that we went anywhere together. This may explain why, when we decided to travel together for a full year, a lot of people wondered how long it would be before we couldn't stand each other.

Then there was the matter of living on our own, far away from the Holy Cross community at Notre Dame. Neither of us knew how to cook, much less how to do laundry. Living in the community is much easier. The bell rings and you go down to eat. On Sunday night you toss out your laundry and it comes back clean on Thursday. On this trip, we enjoyed none of these conveniences. We were completely on our own. High time, some undoubtedly said. Now the young priests at Notre Dame all know how to cook and do laundry.

We didn't spend as much money on this trip as you might think. The RV was supplied to us by a Notre Dame Trustee, Art Decio, who is chief executive officer of the Skyline Corporation. For this segment of the trip, our only real cost was gasoline. We were guests of Ollie Cunningham on the Alaskan segment. He not only accompanied us but also supplied the plane and the pilot. Latin America was all economy-class air fares, with a friend picking up the cost of the month on the Amazon. On the QE2 and the Society Explorer to Antarctica, as I mentioned earlier, we worked for our passage by serving as chaplains each day. We also received some generous gifts at retirement that helped a lot.

Some might say, what do you do for an encore? Well, as I write these words it is Easter Sunday, and I am aboard the Seaborne Spirit on the Amazon. We had full Holy Week services for all Christians aboard, Mass and a homily each day since we left Fort Lauderdale, and a lecture on the history of the Amazon this morning with a replay this afternoon on the cabin TVs. And last night we had special Easter Vigil services for the crew—mostly Filipinos—at midnight.

When we dock in Manaus this Friday, I'm off to Rio, New York, and Washington for a Saturday wedding, and must be in Boston Saturday evening for a two-day meeting of Harvard's Board of Overseers. The next day I fly to Johns Hopkins for eye treatment and then back to Notre Dame.

Ned goes directly back to Notre Dame from Manaus for ten days of annual alumni meetings from New York City to Pocatello, Idaho. He has ten meetings in ten days, plus travel.

When we returned to the University of Notre Dame after the year of sabbatical, we settled into new adjoining offices on the thirteenth floor of the library. We have absolutely no administrative duties, thank God, but we both keep very busy at other activities, both at the university and with many other organizations around the world that correlate with our work here. I do hope we are pulling our weight, and I think we are, because we turn down many new invitations each week, simply because we are overcommitted and short of time.

I mention these activities not to brag but to assure men and women approaching retirement that it is not a fate worse than death. Rather, it can be both rewarding and exciting. Ned and I are probably overdoing it, accepting too many new tasks, but we can always retrench when some of the present projects, like mine on the Knight Commission on reforming intercollegiate athletics, are completed. Anyway, we'd much rather be overcommitted than undercommitted. Too many people take retirement too seriously. They shut off the lights, lock the door, and vegetate. Others may drink too many martinis or play too much gin rummy. That isn't retirement; it's quitting while still having much to give, much to enjoy, much to love, much living yet to do.

This book, therefore, isn't just about travel, as much fun as travel can be. Fundamentally it's a book about totally changing one's ordinary, lifelong way of living without coming apart at the seams. It's a book about enjoying, not dreading retirement. And yes, it's about stopping—stopping, at long last, to smell the roses. We've done just that.

Part I

OUT WEST

This Great Adventure, unlike many others, began precisely on time. We had planned to leave the University at 9:15 A.M. from the back gate in our Skyline motor home. Around 9:05, Father Ned, dressed in his coveralls, put the last touches on the Kaddy Kar, a trailerlike rig that would enable us to pull a small Chevy behind the RV. For the next twelve weeks, it would follow us like a dingy lifeboat following a yacht.

At 9:10, as about a hundred faithful souls gathered around, Gene Corrigan, Notre Dame's athletic director, broke a bottle of champagne over our front bumper. Then Ned and I gave the RV a blessing, christening it the Lindy, the name of Art Decio's daughter. At 9:15 sharp we climbed in and, with Ned at the wheel, headed for the exit. The smart money at Notre Dame said we wouldn't get past Gary, Indiana, about seventy-five miles to the west; so as we pulled away I held a sign to the window. It said, "Gary or Bust."

A university security car, its siren blaring, preceded us until we reached the entrance to the Indiana Toll Road (Interstate 80) and headed west. Never had two more innocent persons taken to the road in an RV. Although Ned had been given some instructions by the Skyline people in nearby Elkhart, I had seen the vehicle only once or twice before and knew absolutely nothing about it. That explains in part why Ned was driving. Not wanting to be completely useless, I prayed the Breviary—out loud so it counted for both of us. We decided that we would make this a regular practice each morning and afternoon throughout the trip. Whoever wasn't driving did the praying.

As we continued heading west on Interstate 80 in this large motor home with our automobile in tow, we hadn't a clue as to what was in store for us. But as Gary came and went, we couldn't resist congratulating each other. Even if disaster were to strike us before we reached Hammond, Indiana, we had at least proved the skeptics wrong.

At an interstate service station about 125 miles west of Notre Dame, we learned our first lesson in RV fuel consumption. It took twenty-two gallons of gasoline to fill our tank, which meant we were burning fuel at about the same rate as a small airplane. Of course, the RV was new and fairly heavily laden, and we were dragging that Chevrolet, full of odds and ends and excess baggage.

The first night out we decided to play it safe. We pulled into Moline, Illinois, and checked in at the home of our trustee Jerry Hank and his wife, Joyce. As might be expected, we not only had a wonderful evening with cocktails and dinner but also comfortable beds and a good night's sleep. I was so fatigued after the past couple of months of goodbyes that I went to bed and slept ten hours without moving. Or maybe it was the Moline air. Or the first full day of freedom.

FRIDAY, JUNE 12
Moline, Illinois

We had Mass with the Hanks; it is always a wonderful experience when we can pray for the whole family in a friend's home. Then Joyce gave us what had to be the best breakfast we'd have in the next two or three months.

I began thinking of how the early immigrants picked up their Conestoga wagons at Studebaker's in South Bend back in the last century and then traveled west toward St. Louis, where they crossed the Mississippi River and headed out to the Oregon Trail. Here we were one day out in Moline and already crossing the Mississippi River into Iowa. We picked up more fuel before leaving and found that we had gone through another twenty-two gallons. We're averaging about

5.8 miles per gallon, but we expect to do better after Lindy is a bit more broken in and we master some of the tricks of economy driving.

By the end of the day, we made it across Iowa and decided to try our luck at a campground in the Wilson Island Recreation Area near the town of Missouri Valley, Iowa, on the Missouri River. It's a beautiful place with spacious grounds and beautiful river oaks, and our particular parking place allows us to get out without backing up. This is a real blessing, as backing up means having to spend five to twenty minutes disconnecting the rig that links us to the Chevy.

We hooked up the Lindy's systems to the water and electricity shortly after 5 P.M. Then it was time for a pleasant walk to get the kinks out of our legs and have a try at cooking dinner. Fortunately, Joyce Hank froze what was left of the meal we had the night before, beef tips and rice with green peppers. I had read up on the microwave as we rolled along in the afternoon, so we felt quite confident about our first solo attempt at a meal. The directions said six minutes to defrost, but after fifteen minutes the beef and rice were just beginning to get a little soft. The directions say you can always reset the microwave for additional minutes so that's what we did—several times, in fact. But dinner, once we got it properly warmed, was delicious. Coffee was easier. We had to warm the water only three times before it was hot enough.

Our next challenge was the TV, which surprised us by providing a better picture than we get in our offices at Notre Dame. We watched a couple of old reruns until 11:30 P.M. and then decided to check on the technology again. To our surprise, the gray water (which, to put it nicely, is all of the sewage, apart from the solid waste) was almost a full tank, so we would have to dump it in the morning somewhere in the campground where they have a place for this sort of thing. Also, although we didn't think we were using much water, we had gone through half of the forty gallons we picked up from Jerry Hank's garden hose. This without any showers and not very much washing either, except dishes. We also had picked up a gallon of drinking water.

Now we were really getting our minds focused, thinking about important things that had eluded us all of these years, such as water and sewage. With all kinds of ingenuity, neither of us has used the bathroom on the RV yet. That's the only advantage of having to stop so many times for fuel. Here we also solved the mystery of the RV's radio, a complicated Japanese model, but wonderful once one learns how to use it. It's surprising how many good FM stations there are along the way, even though one runs out of range of them rather quickly.

As we settled in for some rest, the air conditioning was working well. We have a dual system, one up front where we drive, and one in the back where we live. So far, so good with both systems, even though it was over 95 degrees today in Iowa. As for sleeping, Ned insisted on taking the bunk over the cab. This is in keeping with his usual virtue and generosity, but I was prepared to argue about taking turns, since it requires some acrobatics to get up there and it's not the most commodious place in the world. However, it turns out that it's longer than the bunk in the back, which is simply too short for Ned, who is a couple of inches taller than I am. So this terminated the argument. It's almost impossible to make up these bunks, especially the one over the cab. Our solution was to get a couple of sleeping bags. Tonight was a bit too warm for them. We had thrown in a couple of afghans before we began, and they worked just fine as the temperature dropped along the Missouri River. We both were asleep about three minutes after hitting the pillow. Maybe the nightcap helped. It's hard to believe we have survived two days so far.

SATURDAY, JUNE 13
Missouri Valley, Iowa

Ned was up an hour before me and went out walking on a nature path in the woods, where he promptly got lost. He arrived back breathless just as I was setting up our little table in the middle of the van for Mass. We concelebrate each day. Today it was his turn to be principal celebrant. We agreed on a simple breakfast: orange juice, coffee, and bran flakes. Ned had probably not eaten dry cereal in fifty years, but he seemed to enjoy it. Shopping for food has been easy, because many of the service stations have little commissaries attached to them. We also did the usual housekeeping chores, like disposing of the garbage and cleaning up the van. The van is almost like a ship, with cupboards everywhere, and everything tidily stacked away so that

it won't fall out while we're moving. We have plenty of things to read
and often read to each other from things we find particularly interesting. Light reading was fun after plowing through a whole series of
technical manuals that came with the Lindy. It seems every hour we
discover something new about this vehicle, which is marvelous in its
ingenuity of design. Not a square inch of space is wasted.

We were back on the road at nine o'clock and soon afterward
crossed into South Dakota. That makes four states in three days, so
we are making some progress. We also took advantage of the long
straight stretches to put the van on cruise control at about 60 miles
an hour. That raised our average fuel consumption to almost seven
miles a gallon, considerably better than yesterday. So far, Ned has
been doing all of the driving, but I'll be easing into that as we get
away from heavy traffic. Driving on long stretches of interstate is no
problem, but the Chevy we're pulling can make off-road maneuvers
fairly complicated.

The weather has been great so far, with bright sunny skies and
temperatures mainly in the 80s. We have passed a few million acres of
corn, which gives every indication of being well on its way to knee-
high by the Fourth of July. This agricultural land out here has to be
one of the greatest boons of our nation, and the world too, since
we've been feeding the hungry everywhere these past years. We've also
noticed that the people look healthier and more wholesome as one
moves west.

We arrived in Sioux Falls, South Dakota, around noon. With
around 100,000 population, it is the largest city in the state. We
checked into a Holiday Inn for the first time. The president of the
chain has given us passes that are good for a year, so they'll enable us
to enjoy an occasional respite from sleeping in the RV. Also, a hotel
brings the added joy of a good hot shower and a full-size bed.

We've both been out this way once before. Ned drove across the
country with his family following his graduation from Notre Dame in
1937. In 1950, when I was executive vice president under Father John
Cavanaugh, I drove as far as Aspen, Colorado, to take part in a
seminar with Mortimer Adler and Jacques Barzun on William James's
Pragmatism. Father Cavanaugh thought the seminar might be enliv-
ened by having five of us young priests, mainly theologians, come to
participate. It gave us a chance at least to drive from Notre Dame to

Aspen, when it was just being born as a cultural center. Those two trips were the only basis of comparison we have for this one. We're agreed that these interstate highways are infinitely better than what we drove on back then.

We have a good friend and classmate in Sioux Falls, Monsignor Frank Sampson, a retired major general in the paratroopers and former Chief of Chaplains for the Army. Until quite recently he was serving very effectively as my special adviser and chaplain for the ROTC detachments at Notre Dame, but now he, too, is retired from Notre Dame. Frank picked us up at 4:30 this afternoon. We went to his house for a drink and then, with a friend of his, Father John McEneaney, to the Elks Club for dinner. In these smallish towns it's advantageous for the priests to belong to organizations like the Elks and Rotary because that is where they meet the local citizens. That's a bit different than the University Club in Chicago, the Century Club in New York City, or the Metropolitan or Cosmos in Washington. At least twenty people visited our table while we were there. A Notre Dame alumnus who was dining at another table wanted to pay for our dinner, but someone else had already picked up the tab. We never found out whether it was a friend of the two local priests or someone who recognized us from Notre Dame.

After dinner, we did a quick tour of the city. St. Joseph's Cathedral, done in Indiana limestone, overlooks the whole area from a commanding hill. We also saw the falls that give the place its name. They are on the Big Sioux River and stretch out with smaller and smaller waterfalls for a mile or two. The Sioux called it the Winding River because it takes a big S-turn before flowing into the Missouri. After the tour, we visited Father Mac's parish, Christ the King. At the entrance it has a marvelous stained-glass window that was designed by the Notre Dame art department's Bob Leader.

As the day came to a close, I thought back to when I was praying the Breviary today. I thought about how life, the transit from time to eternity, is so often referred to as a journey. As we live, we are constantly getting new insights, surmounting new difficulties, suffering some defeats, and rejoicing in a few victories as the journey continues and we work our way toward God and eternity. One has to develop a capacity for enjoying surprises, facing new challenges, growing in a lot of little ways, and not being discouraged if some things aren't always perfect. Anyway, this is an interesting way to start retirement, and I guess we don't really retire until we get home. By that I mean all the way home to heaven.

Just before we turned in, Frank Sampson called to say that I'd had a call from Notre Dame. The news was sad. Father Mike McCafferty, a wonderful young priest and an outstanding professor in the Law School, had died that day. He will be sorely missed. May he rest in peace.

SUNDAY, JUNE 14
Sioux Falls, South Dakota

We were up at 6:30 A.M. and began a Requiem Mass for Father Mike McCafferty about seven o'clock. The thought of losing such a young and promising priest filled us both with sadness. Since it was Trinity Sunday, I also said a few words on the Trinity. It's a central mystery, but one runs out of words very quickly when theologizing about God the Father, Son, and Holy Spirit. But I did my best, relying heavily on a religion textbook I'd written for Notre Dame students many years ago.

Until today, Ned had done all the driving. This morning, I thought it was high time I found out whether or not I could drive this contraption. As we headed out of Sioux Falls I discovered, much to my surprise and relief, that the rig didn't present much more difficulty than driving a car on the interstate, and soon I was quite comfortable in the driver's seat. At 2 P.M. we reached the Badlands National Park in the western part of the state and called it a day. The odometer showed that we had traveled about 300 miles since leaving Sioux Falls and a little over 1,000 since leaving South Bend.

South Dakota is really two states, divided into nearly equal halves by the Missouri River. Much of the eastern half is a continuation of the corn belt. In the western half, the flat land and the corn give way to rolling hills, grazing land, and fields of durum wheat, barley, and other grains. We crossed the Missouri at Chamberlain. The river was the natural highway into this region when it was first opened by fur trappers. There were ancient Indian tribes here originally, but around the middle of the eighteenth century, the Sioux took over. Ultimately, they were done in, as were the buffalo, by the railroads, the hide hunters, fur traders, cattlemen, and farmers. These changes led to a number of very unhappy events, such as the massacre at Wounded Knee and Custer's disastrous defeat at the Little Big Horn. A whole culture was fundamentally changed, and the face of the land changed with it.

There was plenty of daylight left when we reached the Badlands, so we unhitched the Chevy for the first time since leaving home—a task that turned out to be, happily, far less daunting than we had anticipated—and took a drive around. The Badlands proved to be unlike any place we had ever seen before. A guidebook we bought provided this description: "Out of the rolling Dakota prairie, rain and wind and frost have carved steep canyons, sharp ridges, gullies, spires and knobs, providing a glimpse into the relentless pace of geological change, for not only has erosion created a new landscape, it has also bared rocks laid down as sediment during the Oligocene Epoch between 23 and 37 million years ago, revealing the record of the past to us."

The Badlands were once covered by a salt sea. After it dried up, there was an upthrust of earth and much flow of waters from rivers running eastward from the Rockies. These waters washed out the sea sediment that had formed the bottom of the ocean here. At the beginning of the Oligocene the land was a broad marshy plain crossed by sluggish streams. The Badlands are also a giant boneyard of prehistoric animals, including the mammoth brontosaurus. Today this 250,000-acre geological phenomenon is surrounded by a verdant prairie. In the previous century, 60 million buffalo grazed here, and a few still do.

The Badlands got their name from the Indians. They called them Macosica, the literal translation of which is Land Bad. Accounts of the early pioneers contained many references to the difficulty they had in making their way across the region. So, at least where the Badlands were concerned, Indians and whites were in complete agreement.

We are now sitting here in our Lindy enjoying air conditioning, a scotch, and the anticipation of a quiet dinner. Then we'll attend an outdoor movie about the Badlands. An aside before we head for the restaurant: Retirement is not all that bad, but I hate the term "golden age." However, when we arrived at this, the first of our national parks, we found out that if one is over sixty-five, he or she qualifies for a free pass to all of the national parks in America. As soon as I learned this, my aversion to "golden age" disappeared, and Ned and I immediately applied for and received our free passes.

We ate tonight at the park restaurant—Indian tacos, served by Indian waitresses. Then we listened to a lecture which we thought would be on geology but turned out to be an account of various grasses on the prairies. We learned that in addition to the native buffalo grass, there is now a Russian grass, and even golden clover which blankets the hills in yellow. This was not Ned's idea of a good show, but we did learn a few things. Before retiring for the night, we called back to Notre Dame to send our sympathy to the parents and sisters of Father Mike McCafferty.

MONDAY, JUNE 15
Badlands National Park, South Dakota

Up at seven and off to a lazy start this morning. After Mass and breakfast in the RV, we planned the day's activities, then plunged into our housekeeping chores. We filled our fresh water tank, reattached the Chevy, emptied our waste water, paid our bill, and were on the road by eleven. About three this afternoon, having finished the Breviary for the day, we reached the Black Hills of South Dakota, the highest range of mountains east of the Rockies. The tallest peak is Mount Harney, at 7,242 feet, the highest spot in the state. But the best-known mountain here is Mount Rushmore, where the famous heads of Washington, Jefferson, Lincoln, and Theodore Roosevelt have been carved out of the face of the mountain. They are a spectacular sight, no matter how often you may have seen them in pictures. We learned that the project was authorized by the federal government and begun by Gutzon Borglum, the son of Norwegian immigrants, in 1927, the same year that Lindburgh flew across the Atlantic. The head of Washington was dedicated in 1930. Next came Jefferson in 1936, then Lincoln in 1937, and finally Teddy Roosevelt in 1939.

The Black Hills are so named because they are covered with dark pine trees, and the crests of the hills are characterized by large upthrusts of pink granite in various shapes. Among the most spectacular formations are the Needles. These granitelike spires thrust upward much like the Dolomites in northern Italy. I have loved the Dolomites ever since I spent a vacation there in 1938 after my first year of study in Rome. I have never seen anything resemble them so closely as the Needles here in the Black Hills National Forest and adjacent Custer State Park.

We ate out that night, then viewed the illuminated Mount Rushmore around 9:30 P.M. We have to get off reasonably early in the morning, because we have a fairly long run from here to Cheyenne, Wyoming, well over 300 miles away. It may not sound like very much, but with our 49-foot rig—plus the Chevy—and these twisting mountain roads, it's a good day's drive. It's very cool here in this wooded park, the kind of weather that makes sleep come easily. So we take advantage of that.

TUESDAY, JUNE 16
Black Hills National Forest, South Dakota

We left our Mount Rushmore campsite about 8:15 A.M. Again, it was a beautiful sunny day, with a perfect blue sky flecked with wonderful, pure white cumulus clouds. They contrasted nicely with the towering pine-clad hills, most of them capped with stone palisades. For the first hour or so en route to the Wyoming border, we drove the narrowest, hilliest roads we had yet seen. The omnipresent pines grew practically down to the roadside.

As we crossed into Wyoming, the land began to change right away. The hills flattened out to rolling prairies that stretched all the way to Cheyenne, the state capital and the place where we planned to spend the night. We didn't stop for lunch, but rather made sandwiches as we rolled along. The trees became fewer and fewer and then the grass-covered rolling hills reminded me of the country we went through in Outer Mongolia last summer. We saw large herds of cattle, but few people. And there aren't many people here in Wyoming either. We thought South Dakota was sparsely populated with its population of 690,000, but Wyoming has only 450,000. The lowest spot in the state is over 3,000 feet high. We noticed the altitude as the RV strained on the hills and dropped back at times to 40 miles an hour from the 60 we had been traveling. We drove on single-lane highways through the rest of South Dakota and into the first 100 miles or so of Wyoming, then took Interstate 25 into Cheyenne. The capitol is rather modest, but it has a gold dome quite similar to ours at Notre Dame. Though somewhat smaller, the dome made us feel right at home. We will check in at a Holiday Inn here, have a quiet dinner, and start off early in the morning for Vail, Colorado, where we'll stay at my brother Jim's condominium.

By now we've learned a few things about the RV. We know it can go all day at 60 or 65 miles per hour. But it is definitely not made for climbing mountains—at least not fully loaded and pulling a car. On the other hand, it is a marvelously versatile machine with almost everything one could possibly need and a few more things besides. Each day it becomes more comfortable for us, and we are more at ease with it. And as we get better at driving it, our gas mileage improves.

WEDNESDAY, JUNE 17
Cheyenne, Wyoming

Everything has been going so well so far, we were bound to encounter a bad day. This one was it. We left the Holiday Inn in Cheyenne around nine in the morning, gassed up a block away, and headed out on Interstate 25 to Denver. We were through Denver in a breeze, connecting with Interstate 70, which runs straight out to Vail. About twenty miles out of Denver on that first long climb up to Idaho Springs, we were laboring along at about 25 miles an hour when suddenly, pow! It sounded like a giant firecracker had gone off beneath us. The engine stopped. The power brakes and power steering went off. Luckily, we had enough forward speed to pull over and get out of the way of the three lanes of traffic climbing that hill behind us—but just barely. No sooner had we made it to the shoulder than we simply stopped rolling. Now what to do? We had discussed the wisdom in dragging that Chevy behind us, but now it became our lifeboat. As the traffic shot by, we unhooked it from the wounded RV. Then Ned drove it uphill to the nearest cutoff, where he dialed the AAA number. But nothing happened. The 800 numbers we had with us were good only in Illinois and Indiana. And Ned had left his glasses back in the RV, so he couldn't check the phone book for the AAA in Colorado.

I stayed with the RV, and decided to make the best of the wait. I got a cold beer and a couple of chocolate chip cookies that Ann Sexton, the wife of our vice president for university relations, had given us as we departed. Then I grabbed one of our folding chairs and Parkman's *Oregon Trail* and walked up the hillside a bit. When I found a nice, sunny spot I sat down with the beer and the chocolate chip cookies and started reading.

Pretty soon Ned was back for his glasses. On his second trip to the phone he managed to reach George Grimes, who heads Skyline's RV Division back in Elkhart, Indiana. George had several things to check on. As he received each piece of information, he called Ned, who was still standing in the phone booth. After a few calls, George told Ned that he had arranged for a tow truck to come out from the Mountain States Ford Truck Agency in Denver. We were lucky. We could have broken down many miles from the nearest help, but the truck agency was only twenty-five miles away. And if we'd broken down an hour later, we would have been coming out of the Eisenhower Tunnel on one of the worst hills in the West. It's six miles long and slopes downward at seven degrees. With no power brakes or steering, we could have been in real trouble. The Lord must have been looking out for us.

We followed the tow truck back to Denver in the Chevy. When we arrived at the agency, the luck of the Irish was with us again. The general manager was Pete O'Meara, whose father and uncle had graduated from Notre Dame. Also, the garage was open until 9:30 P.M. If the problem wasn't serious we could be out of there before closing time.

While they were unhitching the RV we went off and had an early supper, shrimp and catfish. We arrived back at the agency about 5:30 P.M. The verdict was a lot better than it might have been. Two main cables, one positive and one negative, going from our auxiliary battery to our generator (which is alongside the back door of the RV) had been strung on the underside of the body too close to the exhaust pipe. The exhaust had completely melted the insulation and burned through the clip that was holding the cable to the body. When the two wires met, we had a monumental short, which, in turn, burned out the cutoff circuit on our main ignition wire, thereby causing a total electrical blackout. Replacing the main ignition wire was simple enough, but we had to remove both main cables between the battery and the generator (each was about eight feet long) and realign them along a different route on the other side of the van away from the exhaust. Then we put extra insulation on them and strung them through another heavily insulated tube. Everybody pitched in, including the two of us whenever possible. In addition to helping the mechanics with the electrical work, Ned and I changed the oil. For the first time in a long time, I finished the day with grease under my fingernails. That hasn't happened to me since I worked in a gas station many years ago when I was in high school.

By 9:30 P.M. we were rolling again along Route 70 where we had broken down just ten and a half hours ago. Having spent several hours reworking the entrails of our machine, a veritable ganglia of wires, we felt much more at home with it now. Interstate 70, like all of these interstates, is a marvelous road, a real feat of engineering as it passes through the mountains. Once again we found ourselves traveling only 25 miles an hour, but we didn't worry, because we had now figured out the gears. We keep it in drive until we get down to 30 miles an hour, then we put it in second gear. If that gear drops below 15 miles an hour, we put it in low. Actually, because the night was cool, and not sizzling warm like this morning, we never dropped below 20 miles an hour, although we climbed to 11,000 feet to enter the Eisenhower Tunnel and then down to 5,000 and up to 11,000 again coming into Vail through the Vail Pass. Vail itself is about 8,600 feet above sea level.

Ned drove the night shift because his eyes are better at night than mine, and, if it must be admitted, he's a better driver too. It was about 2:30 A.M. when we came out of the pass at Vail. We found my brother's condo, parked the van lengthwise in the parking lot behind it, and, miracle of miracles, I found the key to the condo in the secret compartment of my shaving kit. We stretched out, heaved a sigh of relief, and had ourselves a nightcap. Thus ended our first week on the road. With an extra day here, we'll redo our luggage, buy our groceries, reorder the packing (we have about thirty different compartments in the RV to stash things away), and generally relax before moving on. The odometer in the RV shows that we've traveled 1,655 miles. In addition, we've done a couple of hundred in the Chevy, so we've traveled fairly close to 2,000 miles for the week.

Up till now, it's really been a week of firsts: no serious business appointments; our first experience of shopping for groceries (over $100 worth); our driving the RV; getting towed through Denver traffic; working several hours with the mechanics; using public showers in the washrooms in the campsites; fixing about half our meals; cooking with the microwave; seeing wild buffalo; running into Notre Dame connections almost every day; and, best of all, every day enjoying sunshine, wonderful scenery, leisure, and the carefree spirit of settling into a completely new routine and way of living. Ned and I are gradually arranging our separate duties and collaborating as we have in a variety of tasks during the past thirty-five years. At 3:15 A.M., we decided to close out the week and turn in.

THURSDAY, JUNE 18
Vail, Colorado

W e slept for more than nine hours, awakening to another sunny day, with a marvelous view of the ski runs down the mountain. Skipping breakfast, except for a glass of orange juice and a spot of coffee, we unhitched the Chevy and the Kaddy Kar so we could back up the van to put it in a less obtrusive spot. The parking lot bulged outward, so we could park it facing out.

As I had visited here before, I spent most of the day showing Vail to Ned. We had lunch at a little outdoor cafe facing the chapel where I've had Holy Week and Christmas services with my brother. It's an interdenominational chapel shared by the Lutherans, Episcopalians, Presbyterians, Methodists, Christian Scientists, and Catholics. A beautiful little building, it fits Vail like a glove. We then wandered about the streets on foot, which is the only way you can wander here. I had my camera fixed. No big deal, since I had managed to put the batteries in wrong. We bought a USA *Today* for Ned and a *Time* magazine for me and then drove the length of Vail, which stretches out for about five miles from East Vail to West Vail, with the longest golf course in the world, simple fairways, end to end.

Everything here seems to be named after Gerald Ford, who lives up the road at Beaver Creek. Next we ran the Chevy through a car wash, something it desperately needed. Later in the afternoon, we drove up one of the lateral valleys here for about twenty miles to a piney lake where we walked a couple of miles to limber up our legs. After all that time in the RV we really needed the exercise. About 8 P.M. we went back to Vail, scouted the restaurants, and picked one out. I had osso buco and Ned had grilled tuna. We haven't had a dessert since we left Notre Dame, except, of course, an occasional chocolate chip cookie. We have those in abundance because in addition to the three sacks that Ann Sexton gave us, we have another big tin from Joyce Hank.

Our horarium is gradually changing. For years, I've been turning in at about 3 A.M., but ever since we started this trip, we've been going to bed between 11 and 12 P.M. and getting up seven or eight hours later, both sleeping soundly in the van or in the Holiday Inns and, curiously, waking up almost every morning within a few minutes of each other. Ned turned in a bit earlier tonight and I stayed up to finish *Time* magazine. This was the first news I've had in a week.

FRIDAY, JUNE 19
Vail, Colorado

Today was another relatively quiet day. I caught up on the diary, and Ned put some order into our accounts, checked the maps, and pulled out some correspondence with a couple of people we hope to see along the way. I thought back to our RV's breakdown and realized that Francis Parkman had his own problems as he moved this way. His horse kept running away at night, and that really put a crimp in his transportation too. Old or modern, the problems seem to be the same, although in different versions. We had a simple lunch of soup in town today and then went up 10,500 feet on the mountain in the gondola. Another "golden age" surprise. While the normal fee would have been $16, we went for free since we're over seventy. This business of being over seventy is looking better all the time.

Tonight was my turn to cook, so I made corned beef hash with three poached eggs on top of each plate. Since it all disappeared from both Ned's plate and mine, I guess it must have been O.K. But I had a bit of a problem with the frying pan afterward because I couldn't find a scouring pad. Live and learn. We're turning in early tonight because tomorrow will bring a 6 A.M. reveille. We've packed our duffels for a four-day trip in the Chevy, leaving our RV behind. And so to bed. It's a nice cool night here, although when making our first weekly Friday call to Helen Hosinski, my secretary, we learned that it has been very hot and humid in South Bend, but then, who ever defended South Bend weather?

SATURDAY, JUNE 20
Vail, Colorado

Up at 6 A.M., Mass at 6:30, then orange juice and coffee and off in the Chevy. Splendid is too mild a word for the sights we saw today. We drove 400 miles and I've never seen more dramatic scenery in my whole life, although I've seen a good deal of scenery around the world. The first part of our trip was down the Vail Valley past the place where Gerald Ford lives, then along a roaring river into Glenwood Springs. From there we continued on for another 100 miles or so to Grand Junction. A few miles beyond that, we entered Utah. Instead of taking the best road to Moab, we followed the road that parallels the Colorado River and its spectacular canyon, stopping from time to time to watch the tourists go by in their rubber rafts. It's hard to believe that this river, which was a hundred yards or so wide as we followed it today, was capable of creating the Grand Canyon in Arizona.

We left the river to head south a few miles at Moab, which was a town founded by Mormons back in the 1840s. There were four earlier founders, but they left when two of their number were massacred by the Indians. Today just happened to be the 50th anniversary of Moab. As we were finishing lunch here, we saw the anniversary parade as it proceeded down the main street. It consisted of people in Western costume riding horses, Model T Fords, the fire department, and all the rest. We watched the parade for a few minutes, then started off to

Arches National Park, which has within it more than two hundred arches ranging in size from a one-foot opening to a span of 291 feet. One enters the park from the main road north out of Moab across the Colorado River. It's about a forty-mile round trip, with the road climbing up to the tops of the mountains, at their highest over 6,000 feet. There are a lot of side roads leading to different formations of arches—eroded stone in about as many sizes, shapes, and forms as one could possibly imagine. Besides the arches there are palisades and mesas and buttes, canyons, and balanced rocks. They were formed over 100 million years ago, when erosion of this red sandstone took place. As I've mentioned before, originally, all of this part of the world was a salt ocean. When the ocean dried up, it left several thousand feet of salt, which makes a very poor base. On top of it, sandstone rocks were formed from the sand foundation. With wind, temperature change, and water, the softer stone began to erode. Thanks to this process, we have these marvelous formations to admire today.

The sea that covered the region goes back 300 million years, but the erosion of the current sandstone was about 100 million years in the making. Today, this country would be classified as high desert. It's quite barren, mainly pinyon and juniper forest, along with tumble-weed and other sorts of desert bushes. For the past century, it's been ranching and range land. One fact I find curious is that the federal government owns about 70 percent of the land here and, of course, all of the national parks. The state owns about another 20 percent. The Ute Indians, after whom Utah was named, own about 6 percent. The roughly 5 or 6 percent that is left is owned by private individuals.

From Arches National Park, we moved on a few miles south into Canyonlands National Park. To get there, one has to traverse Dead Horse State Park. The park is so immense that there are three entrances, one from the south, one from the west, and the one we entered from the east. The center of the park is a canyon as deep as the Grand Canyon, but ten times wider. There is really a canyon within a canyon here. From our lookout, we could see the confluence of the Colorado and Green rivers. Each of those rivers has formed its own canyon several hundred feet deep.

The land is indescribably rugged and negotiable only by jeep trails or packhorses. We tried to arrange an airplane flight over the whole Canyonlands Park because it can best be seen from the air, even though the lookouts are over 6,000 feet high. We failed to get an airplane because of the wind conditions over the canyon. Pilots, seeing these conditions, had quit for the day. However, when Ned was making inquiries, he was told about a wonderful boat trip, which we took tonight after dinner. Just beyond the bridge that leads into Moab, we joined seventy other people on a boat about forty-five feet long and twelve feet wide. The people were seated eight abreast and about nine rows deep.

The sound-and-light show that accompanied the ride was one of the most spectacular I'd ever seen. First, we went up the river for about an hour in the gathering twilight and dusk. As soon as it became dark, we turned around and came down the river. Accompanying us, on the road we had traversed this morning along the riverside, was a truck with a generator and three high-powered searchlights. For the better part of ten miles or so, we slowly drifted with the current while searchlights from the truck played on the fantastic stone walls.

It's difficult to describe the effect as the lights roamed the 500- or 600-foot palisades, revealing their colors and textures so dramatically. The text began with Genesis, "let there be light," and went on through the history of this land, geologically and anthropologically, since the first humans arrived here from Asia some 12,000 years ago. All of this was accompanied by beautiful music, some of it from the Mormon Tabernacle Choir in Salt Lake City. The whole experience was truly exhilarating.

Thanks to a lucky break we got the last room in the Ramada Inn. In addition to several conventions, a rodeo and a softball tournament were going on, but someone canceled out and we got the room. It was 95 degrees here this afternoon and tonight it was chilly enough to wear a sweater or a jacket on the boat. The final reflection of the day: Too bad more Americans can't see the variegated beauty of this wonderful country. It took both of us seventy years to see this southeast corner of Utah, and we still haven't seen the southwest beauty of Bryce and Zion, which we hope to visit later on.

SUNDAY, JUNE 21
Moab, Utah

We woke at 7:30 A.M. to another beautiful day. Standing on the balcony outside our second-floor room, I could see a brown palisade of rugged rock several hundred feet high and, above that, a flawless blue sky and, below, some wonderfully big and fluffy cottonwood trees. Off in a corner was the inevitable Pizza Hut. Ned presided at Mass this morning. After the Gospel, we both sat down for a while and meditated on it. As the trip has progressed, Ned has begun to give homilies as long as or longer than mine. It's a great way to start the day.

Our driving today took us almost 300 miles. First, we headed south to Monticello, Utah, and then east past Cortez, Colorado, to Mesa Verde. The land flattened out as we drove, but to the east we could see the snowcapped mountains of Purgatory, in Colorado, where we will be tonight. Shortly after leaving Cortez, we turned into the Mesa Verde National Park. We climbed to about 8,000 feet, had lunch at the guesthouse, and then began our explorations for the day. The mesa, really a flat-topped mountain, extends about twenty or thirty miles. It is intersected in the middle by Cliff Canyon and an offshoot of this called Fewkes Canyon. On the east side of this canyon are a whole series of cliff dwellings and on the west side, a profusion of early human settlements going back to the time of Christ. This is probably the only national park given over to anthropological, rather than natural, phenomena.

We did the east side of Mesa Verde first. To get to the place the cliff dwellers had inhabited, we had to go down over the cliffside, negotiating a series of ladders, paths, and tunnels along with endless natural stairs that had been hewn out of the rock. There are two major cliff dwellings. Cliff Palace is the classic village one sees in the *National Geographic* articles on Mesa Verde. It was discovered by cowboys in 1888 and is the largest cliff dwelling in North America. It contains 217 rooms and 23 kivas, which are community rooms for ceremonial purposes. The people who lived in Mesa Verde are called the Anasazi, a Navajo Indian word meaning "the ancient ones" or "ancient foreigners." While they came to this part of the world around the time of Christ, they moved into the cliff alcoves around

500 A.D. and into the Cliff Palace around 1200. Across the canyon, one sees their earlier housing, which were pit houses, formed by a hole in the ground with a bit of wood roofing erected above it. By 1300, most of the Anasazi had left this area for reasons unknown. Most of them moved south and east into the Rio Grande Valley and mixed with the other tribes there.

The other large dwelling we visited on the east side of the canyon was Balcony House. Just getting down there was quite a feat, and getting up was an even greater challenge, since it involved a rigorous series of ladders, tunnels, and stairways. We then moved over to the west side of the canyon, where we saw the earliest and most primitive of the dwellings that the Anasazi occupied and where they began their slow but steady progression as a civilization. As they moved from basket making to clay pots they became artists and their pots grew more beautiful as the generations passed.

They also progressed from hunters and gatherers to farmers who knew how to grow corn, beans, and squash. Then, after thirteen centuries here, they passed into oblivion. Perhaps as their numbers grew they outstripped the land's ability to provide for their needs, or perhaps their numbers required a political organization that simply was not needed in the earlier days when they were organized in clans. In any event, they moved out en masse and lost their identity for all time. There may be a lesson in all of this for our generation, which is squandering natural resources and really has no other place to move to beyond our planet.

As the sun was setting, we drove on to Durango and then north to Purgatory, where we are now ensconced in a condominium belonging to Joe and Jan O'Neill, who live in Midland, Texas. Joe's a Notre Dame alumnus who, with Vince Duncan, another Notre Dame grad, is trying to make the ski runs here at Purgatory equal to those at Vail and Aspen.

MONDAY, JUNE 22
Purgatory, Colorado

After fixing our breakfast, we went up on the ski lift to get a look at the ski runs in this resort. The top of the run is 10,000 feet above sea level and, of course, the scene was spectacular. After coming down, we were off on another day's adventure. The story of this day is like Dickens's *A Tale of Two Cities*, except now we are telling the tale of two old mining towns, Silverton and Ouray. Both are north of here, and to get to them, one has to go over a pass about 11,000 feet high. The pass on the way to Silverton is called Molas Lake Pass, with spectacular scenery all the way and with much snow on the mountains, even though it's late June.

Silverton is about thirty miles from here, but it seems like three times as long because of all the twisting and turning roads and the high climbs. We arrived in Silverton in time to see the only narrow-gauge steam-engine train left in America arrive from Durango. It takes three hours to make the forty-five-mile run, a spectacular passage through the mountains. We also found a St. Patrick's Catholic Church in Silverton. If you wonder about the name Silverton, here's how it purportedly came about: When they first found silver here, they said, "There's a ton of it." From there, we went over Red Mountain Pass, again over 11,000 feet high, and into Ouray, which is another classic mining town. It has a population of 700 persons—100 fewer than Silverton.

Silver was first found here in 1875. The most famous mine was the Camp Bird mine of Tom Walsh. In a six-year period, from 1896 to 1902, the mine produced what at the time toted up to $24 million worth of gold and silver. Walsh bought his wife the Hope diamond. His daughter, Evelyn Walsh McLean, became a society queen in Washington, D.C. All told, these two towns turned out about a quarter of a billion dollars in gold and silver during the heyday of mining early in the century. One major problem the miners confronted was that they couldn't get over the mountains between Ouray (named after a Ute Indian chief) and Silverton, except by mule train. Then along came Colorado pioneer Otto Mears, who built a toll road across Red Mountain Pass. It cost $10,000 a mile and was called the Million Dollar Road because Mears used the tailings from the gold and silver mines in Ouray as ballast for the road. The road we passed over today was constructed on his roadbed and is a magnificent feat of engineering.

After lunch in Ouray, we went out north of the town to the Bachelor-Syracuse mine. A little donkey railroad took us 3,200 feet into the center of the mountain to the mine shaft. There we saw the actual vein of silver and gold that was being worked. We also heard from a real miner about how they go about this business of mining. He convinced me that the last thing in the world I would want to be is a miner. It was, however, a fascinating visit. And so went the tale of two old mining towns.

Lest I forget, some of the best-known bad guys and other characters of the Wild West frequented these parts. Butch Cassidy and the Sundance Kid hung out in Moab and returned there after their biggest bank robbery. Local historians in Ouray say that at the height of the mining industry here, the miners used to frequent Blair Street every Saturday night and made the words "wide open" seem the understatement of the year. The citizenry decided to do something about it, and they brought in Bat Masterson, the famed sheriff of Dodge City, to tame the town.

TUESDAY, JUNE 23
Purgatory, Colorado

We were up at 6:30 A.M., concelebrated Mass, and were on the road before eight. If one phrase could describe our 300-mile drive from here to Pueblo, it is "changing topography." We began the journey driving down through mountain passes into Durango with snowcapped mountains on both sides. Out of Durango, we soon came into rolling wooded hills and meadowland. We saw practically no agriculture all day, except a bit of hay harvesting. This seems to be horse country. We even saw an Arabian horse farm just outside of Durango. Off to the north as we traveled east across southern Colorado, were the Rockies. After Pagosa Springs, one of the few towns we passed on the road we traveled today, the Rockies dipped down to us and we went over a 10,000-foot pass at Wolf Creek.

Most of these passes are about five miles up and five miles down, with gorgeous scenery on both sides. The trees also changed with the topography. We began, of course, with ponderosa and ridgepole pines and then came into the drier country, where cottonwoods came up along the rushing mountain streams. The closer we got to New Mexico, the drier the landscape became. Trees gave way to great upthrusts of granite and sandstone and sparse forage. Navaho has been replaced by Spanish on the car radio, drums by guitars. I must say I prefer the latter.

We arrived in Pueblo around 3 P.M., got badly needed haircuts, showered, dressed up for the first time since leaving Notre Dame almost two weeks ago, and went out to dinner at the country club with John and Barbara Walsh. John used to be academic vice president at Notre Dame. He is an old friend of ours and a classmate of Ned's. Both of us were very glad to see him again.

WEDNESDAY, JUNE 24
Pueblo, Colorado

John came over for Mass at 7:30 A.M. and breakfast following. We then drove west to the new lake created by a reservoir on the Arkansas River outside of Pueblo. Believe it or not, although it was a bit cloudy when we got up, by 8:30 it was another bright and sunny day with clear blue skies. How long can we be so fortunate? We said goodbye to John and headed west again to Canon City, where there is a Benedictine Abbey. Driving along, we could see Pikes Peak about fifty miles off to the north. Right outside of Canon City, we turned off to Royal Gorge on the Arkansas River. The Arkansas is one of the five longest rivers in America. Its headwaters are at Leadville, Colorado, about 100 miles north of here. It flows through the mountains and then across the flatlands into the Mississippi. Eventually its waters end up in the Gulf of Mexico, about 1,400 miles away. We took a miniature train ride on Royal Gorge out to the edge of the gorge, where we could see the largest suspension bridge in the world. It spans the gorge at its narrowest point. Below, you can see the 1,200-foot-deep canyon that the Arkansas River has carved down through the granite over millions of years.

After the train ride, which took about thirty minutes, we went across the gorge and back in a gondola. It's quite a feeling to swing out over those 1,200 feet suspended only by a cable. We left the gorge around 12:30 P.M. and headed west again and then north along the Arkansas River through a whole series of gorges with low granite hills, spotted by mesquite brush and scrub trees and dotted with huge boulders. It was a beautiful ride. We stopped at Salida for a quick lunch, a sandwich and iced tea, and then quickly turned north again toward Leadville. Just below Leadville, we cut off to Twin Lakes and over Independence Pass, which is over 11,000 feet high with much snow around, plus a horrendous wind coming over the top of the pass. However, climbing up to Independence Pass is one of the most beautiful drives in the world. Driving down the pass was long and not quite so beautiful, as the road narrows and you have relatively little room between the solid rock walls on the right and the canyon on the left. I was glad that we were in the Chevy and not the RV.

We arrived in Aspen about four o'clock. One of our Notre Dame alumni and a good friend of Father Ned, Nestor Weigand, had offered Ned his condo here. We showered quickly, put on clean clothes, and headed off to visit the Aspen Institute for Humanistic Studies. Beginning in 1950, I attended several summers here. That first one was a discussion of William James's book *Pragmatism*, with Mortimer Adler and Jacques Barzun. That was the very beginning of the Aspen seminars, but I spent many other happy weeks in this delightful place, mostly conducting seminars on the Great Books for business executives.

I vividly remember one of those seminars. During a break, some of us, including the Israeli ambassador to London, decided to take a raft trip down the Little Colorado River. In the course of the trip the raft that the ambassador and I were helping to paddle struck an underwater boulder and we were all hurled into the river. Fortunately, we made it out safely, and the ambassador jokingly accused me of trying to baptize him. He kept yelling, "Only in the Jordan! Only in the Jordan!" Tragically, however, a man in a raft some distance ahead of us wasn't so lucky. He drowned.

At the Aspen Institute we ran into Tom and Tanya Cronin. I'd teamed up on a seminar with Tom about ten years earlier. Currently he is a Distinguished Professor at Colorado College and continues to write on the American presidency. We had a drink out on the

Cronins' veranda, caught up on old times, and had a great discussion about a wide variety of intellectual subjects. When I told them that the following day I would be celebrating the forty-fourth anniversary of my ordination to the priesthood, they offered their apartment for the Mass and said they'd invite the members of the current seminar to help mark the occasion.

THURSDAY, JUNE 25
Aspen, Colorado

We woke up around 7 A.M. to another beautiful sunny day and I suddenly realized that we lost a day somewhere along the line. I should have celebrated my forty-fourth ordination anniversary yesterday instead of today. We drove over to the Cronins' this morning to celebrate Mass. About twenty-five people came to the Mass, roughly half of whom were Catholic and the rest Protestant and Jewish. After Mass, we had breakfast with the group and then joined them for their seminar around 9:15 in the seminar room of the Institute. The subject of the day was Machiavelli's *The Prince*, a book I had taught over thirty-five years ago when I had led a seminar in jurisprudence in our Law School. Tom Cronin asked one of the members of the seminar, Celio Franca of Brazil, to conduct the seminar with me. It was a wonderful experience, as seminars always are here, and we went on until after 11:30. We then drove to town to pick up some sandwiches, a *Time* magazine, and a new ice container to replace the one we broke. Next we changed into some old clothes for an afternoon hike.

There are two lateral valleys going out to the south from Aspen. We drove to the end of the first one, a distance of about ten or fifteen miles, and ate our picnic lunch beside a roaring stream. Then we drove up the next one, which goes all the way to Maroon Lake. There, we climbed from about 9,000 to more than 11,000 feet up to Crater Lake. It was a tough climb and there were times when I felt like I was on a stress machine, but we made it in about an hour.

The lake is filled with pure, cold water from melted snow and ice. We slaked our thirst with it, splashed some more in our faces, which were dirty and dripping with perspiration. Then we rested, all the while admiring the Maroon Bells, three bell-shaped mountains that give the area its name. The scenery, both going up and coming down, was absolutely fabulous, particularly the wildflowers that grow in such variegated profusion here.

Later on we had dinner in a small outdoor cafe, where we were entertained by a group of young musicians from the Aspen Music Institute playing classical music. They study and practice during the day and at night break up into quartets to entertain the visitors.

FRIDAY, JUNE 26
Aspen, Colorado

After Mass and a quick breakfast we were off to Vail to reunite ourselves with the RV and prepare it for the Utah leg of our journey. We arrived before noon, picked up our laundry and several other things we needed, had an outdoor lunch of vealburgers at a German restaurant, and made our weekly call back to Notre Dame to catch up on the news with our secretaries, Helen and Pat.

I know this must be getting monotonous, but today was another wonderfully sunny and bright day with the temperature ranging from the 70s to the high 80s. We faced another problem when we came back to my brother's condo and unlocked the RV. When we opened the door, the step below the door didn't come out. That could mean only one thing: the battery was dead. We tried the generator, but it wouldn't start either. In fact, it didn't even turn over. Fortunately we found a good young mechanic on duty at the Vail Amoco station. Though he was anxious to join his teammates for a baseball game they were playing in Eagle, he delayed his departure to find the cause of our trouble. He quickly discovered that we weren't getting enough gas into the generator, so he blew out the line, tightened the gasket, and soon had it running again. While he was doing this, we had the battery recharged.

Neither of us felt like going out for dinner tonight, so I quickly cooked up some clam chowder, which was all we really needed. By now, we've both lost a little weight and we're happy about that. Our hopes are to take off about ten pounds each on this trip.

The university seems miles and miles away and, of course, it is. The former life of hustle and bustle seems miles away too. When the mechanic at the garage said today that it would take forty minutes to recharge our battery, we simply said, "No problem." Ned went off to mail a letter and I collected the second batch of laundry.

SATURDAY, JUNE 27
Vail, Colorado

We were on the road about 8 A.M. The RV odometer registered 3,600 miles as we left Vail. We chalked up 1,402 on the Chevy during the past week in our run about Utah and southern Colorado. Many of those miles were driven in six national forests: San Juan, San Isabel, Sangre de Cristo, White River, Uncompahgre, and the Rio Grande. We have about five more coming up in the next week or so.

Our first objective today was Richfield, Utah, where we arrived about 4 P.M. The trip was fairly uneventful because central Utah is a vast desert, looking very much like the landscape of the moon. There are large rock upthrusts of red sandstone and gray granite. They stretch out as mesas in every direction from about one to five miles long and about 2,000 feet high. All afternoon as we went across central Utah, we were climbing about eight miles to go over the pass between the mesas and then down another eight miles. In the middle of the afternoon, while Ned was catching a catnap and I was driving, we had our first rain of the trip. Purely by coincidence, the tape we were playing was Lena Horne singing "Stormy Weather." That brought back ancient memories. I remember dancing to that tune while a senior in high school. I still remember the words.

There were practically no cities on our route today, Grand Junction near the border of Colorado and Salina halfway across Utah being the exceptions. We stopped in the middle of the desert for gas, at a town called Green River. The proprietors said it was the only station for 100 miles in either direction. We saw practically no agriculture along the way and even the range land looked very poor, not much more than scrub brush and an occasional stand of miniature pines. We didn't see many animals, and since there were no towns, the only exits from Interstate 70 were ranch exits.

As we neared the edge of the desert, we did see our first sheep grazing. Utah has about 1.4 million inhabitants, but I think most of

them must live in and around Salt Lake City and Provo. About 4
P.M., as we neared Richfield, which is across the state to the west of
Moab, where we were traveling this time last week, Ned came up with
a great idea. Instead of staying here overnight, why not park the van
and continue on in the Chevy for another 111 miles to Cedar City,
the gateway to Bryce and Zion national parks? The additional miles
would be easier and more relaxing in the Chevy, and we could get an
early morning start on our tour of the two parks. So that's what we
did.

As we continued south, there were more trees and more rolling
hills, but again no agriculture, except for a few alfalfa fields that were
under irrigation. All day, every hour on the hour, we tried to get
some news on the radio, but there simply was no news being broadcast
in Utah. Fortunately we had plenty of tapes along. Today it was
Johann Strauss's "Tales from the Vienna Woods" and Viennese
waltzes. They reminded me of those fifteen years when I spent part of
each September in Vienna at the International Atomic Energy
Agency. Around seven o'clock, we pulled into Cedar City, checked
into a Holiday Inn, showered for the second time today, and poured
ourselves scotches. Someone once asked Graham Greene what was
the best thing one could carry with him on his trips around the world.
One might think he'd have said soap or penicillin or a raincoat, but
he said scotch. I tend to agree with him.

During dinner at the motel, we were introduced to Utah's
peculiar drinking laws, which Greene wouldn't have cared for one bit.
We asked the waiter if we might have some red wine with our beef.
He said, "I can't sell it to you here in the restaurant, but if you go to
the front desk, you can buy a bottle there." I went to the desk and
got half a bottle of California Burgundy. He then had to charge us
each $1.25 for a glass and another fee to open the bottle. I guess they
are trying to discourage drinking, which is against the Mormon creed.

SUNDAY, JUNE 28
Cedar City, Utah

Another bright, sunny day. Yesterday we traveled 527 miles, today 416, giving us over 1,000 for the last two days. Leaving Cedar City, we went up through Cedar Canyon, which is a most beautiful drive. The canyon climbs very steeply through rugged rock walls studded with juniper, the tallest I have seen. As it twists and turns upward, gaining 10,000 feet in a matter of a few miles, you pass one glorious vista after another. Incidentally, Cedar City and Cedar Canyon are misnomers because the trees one sees are junipers, not cedars. The Mormons had them mixed up, I guess. Before I leave the matter of trees, let me say that today we went through Dixie National Forest, for which Ned gave a cheer. In the past week we have added four more national forests to our list: Dixie, Fishlake, Manti–La Sal, and Arapaho. Many more are yet to come.

Bryce Canyon reminded us of Mesa Verde. It's part of an 8,000-foot mesa, but it's not really a canyon. Rather, it's an enormous amphitheater eroded into the side of the mesa. When I say enormous, I mean about ten miles long and about five miles wide. There are, of course, smaller ones as well. The canyon is filled with stone monoliths hundreds of feet tall. They resemble everything from the Turkish army on the march, to a sinking ship, to Thor's hammer. As with many other places we have explored so far in the West, all of this used to be the bottom of a shallow sea with various layers of sediment laid down millennia after millennia. What we're seeing now is the work of time and water in the form of streams, rain, ice, and snow. The profusion of forms and figures have been executed in a wide variety of colors— mostly brown, pink, white, and yellow. In the early morning sun, the shapes and colors are mesmerizing. Ebenezer Bryce, one of the earliest settlers, lived here for five years, trying to raise cattle. In his immortal words, "It's a hell of a place to lose a cow!"

The first high plateau we reached today, 10,000 feet up at the top of Cedar Canyon, is called Markagunt. The plateau that rises to Bryce Canyon is called Paunsaugunt. They are both Paiute Indian names. One also notices, along these plateaus and up into the mesa into which Bryce Canyon has encroached, a continual change of trees from junipers to blue spruce to ponderosa pine to white pine and all varieties of fir. These are the tallest trees of their kind that we have seen so far and they add a certain grandeur to the whole area. The color of the rocks contrasts dramatically with that of the trees. The reds, yellows, purples, and whites of the rocks are produced by iron and manganese oxides. On the way out of the park, we stopped for a quick lunch and had buffalo burgers. They are a little tangier than beef hamburgers, but, all in all, very tasty.

The entrance into Zion National Park is the most spectacular we've seen so far. I'm running out of adjectives, so you will have to excuse the overuse of "spectacular" and "unbelievable." This is a real canyon with sheer monoliths rising several thousand feet in every direction, leaving narrow confines between them. The centerpiece of the park is a deep canyon filled with all sorts of seemingly religious figures of monumental size. Some of them were named by Frederick Vining Fisher, a young Methodist minister who came here toward the end of the century. Among his many contributions are: the Great White Throne, Angels Landing, the Organ, the Pulpit, and the Altar of Sacrifice. All of the huge formations are the results of millions of years of work by the Virgin River. Looking at them, one can't help but feel undersized; some of these rocks are over 3,000 feet high, and the tallest of them, West Temple, soars to a height of 3,805 feet. As many persons have experienced, from the Paiutes who once lived here to Fisher and thousands of latter-day visitors, there is truly a religious sense to this place. Before the Paiutes, members of the same Indian tribe, the Anasazi, who inhabited Mesa Verde lived here. They left very suddenly around the year 1300 A.D., just as their cousins in Mesa Verde had. I should note that much of the information we have regarding the parks comes from useful booklets they hand out at each entrance. The parks are enormously well organized. We also used extensively two books published by Reader's Digest: America from the Road and Our National Parks: America's Spectacular Wilderness Heritage.

At the end of the canyon drive we parked and climbed to Weeping Rock. Water resulting from rain and snow on the top of the plateau has seeped down through the sandstone over the course of centuries, reaching the slate strata slanting downward. Since the water can't penetrate the slate, it travels along the surface of it and seeps through the sandstone on the face of this several-thousand-foot cliff, a veritable waterfall with no visible river.

As we headed back to Richfield, we encountered several showers and some flashes of lightning. It was raining hard when we got to the campsite in Richfield. It was good to get back to the comforts of the RV. We quickly transferred our gear from the Chevy, then came happy hour and a simple stew accompanied by coffee and some of Joyce Hank's cookies. Then, wonder of wonders for this 3 A.M. go-to-bedder, I was in bed by ten. Ned beat me by about five minutes. We both slept about nine hours.

MONDAY, JUNE 29
Richfield, Utah

Mass of Saints Peter and Paul today. It was Ned's turn to be principal celebrant. He gave a fine homily on Peter and Paul and the papacy today, as well as Paul's advice to Timothy from the second reading, which has a certain relevance to us on the occasion of retirement. Paul tells Timothy that he (Paul) has lived a difficult life, "poured out like a libation," and that death cannot be all that far away. However, Paul is glad that thus far he has "finished the race and kept the faith." Paul is sure that the Lord will "keep him from future harm and bring him to his heavenly kingdom."

We performed two more culinary experiments this morning. We broke out our toaster and made toasted English muffins, and we tried cooking bacon in the microwave. Both successful!

Today, we drove to Park City, where we met Jack Gallivan, the publisher of the Salt Lake City *Tribune*. Jack is a classmate of Ned's, and his son Mickey also graduated from Notre Dame. Jack had invited us to spend a couple of days on his ranch and we had accepted. From the interstate exit he took us down the road halfway to Park City and then up through a beautiful aspen forest that we hardly got through because the road was so narrow. The ranch house can accommodate twenty guests. It's nestled against the hills that rise up to a ridge about 10,000 feet above us. We had cocktails and a wonderful dinner cooked by Jack's wife, Grace Mary. We talked about our trip, this country of ours, and the interplay between Mormons and the "gentiles," which is what the Mormons call everyone else. It's good to have a couple of days to relax after all of our traveling. We're at 8,000 feet and the air is cool. About ten o'clock I felt wiped out. I went to bed and slept ten hours.

TUESDAY, JUNE 30
Park City, Utah

A number of the Gallivan clan gathered for Mass this morning. Then Jack, Mickey, and Jim Ivers III from next door took Ned and me on a jeep tour of the backcountry. We went up a wild road through White Pine Valley behind the house and on up to the ridge leading to Scott Peak, just over 10,000 feet high. Our average speed was about three miles an hour as we went up through the forest to the tree line. These old mining roads were built in the 1880s and used until the turn of the century to carry supplies up to the mines and bring the ore down. Not only do they go up at a steep grade but they also are full of rocks and deep cuts made by the rushing flow from the spring melt of snow and ice on top. At times we had to simply leave the road and rumble through the woods and meadows off to the sides of the road.

Jack and Jim, friends since childhood, roamed this mountain as thirteen-year-olds, staking out many of the mines that we passed on the way. There are over 1,000 miles of what they call "drifts," holes that the miners punched in the side of the mountain to find the veins of ore. Near the top of a ridge, around 10,000 feet, we came upon a marvelous area of wildflowers: Indian paintbrush, blue-purple lupine, miniature yellow buttercups, and a white flower I couldn't identify. These were nature's flower beds at their best and it was hard to believe that this same spot was under six to ten feet of snow just a few months ago.

The story of mining here began when a young man named Tom Kearns, who had not even graduated from grammar school but had learned mining, arrived here and made a discovery. He joined up with a chap named David Keith and Jim Ivers I, grandfather of Grace Mary. When Jim was first invited to join the group, he didn't have the $1,500 capital required. As he was lamenting this to wife, Grace Mary's grandmother, she disappeared into the backyard and came back carrying two tin cans full of money. Between them, the cans contained more than $1,500, enabling Jim to make his investment.

When he asked her where she got the money, she said, "I've been picking your pockets for years."

This mine was the King Silver, one of the two big original mines in this area. Most of the ore here was lead carrying silver and, at times, zinc and manganese. It is calculated that the miners took about half a billion dollars' worth of ore from these hills, which at today's prices would be probably more than three billion dollars.

Not a single mine is operating here today, but two other industries are very visible—namely, skiing and tourism. As we jeeped up and down the valleys of Park City and Brighton, we kept thinking of Aspen and Vail because the hillsides are dotted with very expensive condominiums. In Park City itself, there are the less expensive hotels and hostels for young skiers. Park City has the oldest Catholic church in Utah, St. Mary's, which was built in 1884. Jack Gallivan's mother and father were baptized in this church, as were the parents of Grace Mary Gallivan, the Iverses. In the early days, most of the pastors were from Ireland, as is the present one, Father Pat Carley of Tipperary.

We were back at the ranch about five, had a shower, and then went over to Jim's house, a few hundred yards from here in a grove of aspens and pines, for drinks. We returned here to the Gallivan house, where Mickey grilled us some wonderful hamburgers.

WEDNESDAY, JULY 1
Park City, Utah

The same blue sky greeted us today with the same beautiful cumulus clouds drifting across the top of the ridge that we had visited yesterday. Just before Mass, a deer with a wonderful six-point set of antlers pranced across the meadow right behind the house. As he delicately picked his way across the meadow, I could understand why one of Santa's reindeers is called Dancer.

After breakfast, Jack, Grace Mary, Ned, and I had a long talk about the history of this part of the world. The Holy Cross nuns were a large part of it for a while. They ran Holy Cross Hospital, St. Mary of the Wasatch School, orphanages, and several elementary and secondary schools, including Judge High School, the only Catholic secondary school in the diocese. There were well over a hundred

Sisters here at that time, but now there are only two grade schools and a few Sisters at the hospital. The state's population of 1.4 million includes only about 50,000 Catholics.

In the afternoon Ned was interviewed by John Mooney, the sports editor of the Salt Lake City *Tribune*, and I was interviewed by Pete Scarlet, who was mostly interested in education and world affairs. Tonight, Ned and I went to dinner with Jack and Grace Mary at Adolph's in Park City. We came back to the ranch house to watch our first news broadcast in about two weeks and then went to bed.

THURSDAY, JULY 2
Park City, Utah

We had Mass at 9 A.M. with our hosts, then breakfast and more exploring, this time to a canyon called Little Cottonwood. This was one of the earliest ski developments out here. It has two centers close to each other: the older one, Alta, at the end of the canyon, and Snowbird, a brand-new development a mile or so from Alta. Snowbird has the world's largest gondola up the mountainside. It's a really marvelous machine that holds 125 people and it goes up beyond 11,000 feet, where it provides a great view. I concluded after today's drive up the third canyon that one doesn't have to go to Europe anymore to see the scenes that the Alps offer. These mountains are just as good if not better.

We returned to the ranch at 4:30 P.M. to change clothes, finish the Breviary, and catch up on the diary. Tonight, dinner with some more Notre Dame friends, Phil and Noreen Purcell. We wanted to thank them for helping to make the Campaign for Notre Dame a success. Their son is a Notre Dame Trustee.

FRIDAY, JULY 3
Park City, Utah

We had a bit of a problem maneuvering out of Jack's ranch because the entrance is such a narrow road with birch and aspen trees on both sides. We were on the road by about 10:45 A.M., following Interstate

80 to the east until we came to Evanston, Wyoming. Then we went north for a while, drifting into Utah and back into Wyoming, where we met the rolling hills that seem so characteristic of that state. Along the way, we passed through three national forests—Bridger, Targhee, and finally, Teton, which led us to our destination. It was a beautiful drive as we came up the Snake River Canyon with high, rocky, pine-studded hills on both sides. Below, of course, was the Snake River, still relentlessly cutting its way through the rocks. Today the river seemed to be full of people who were paddling rafts and kayaks. Along the way, we went over a nameless pass where the Lindy slowed to 25 miles an hour again. This is really big sky country. It's hard to describe how the sky seems to go out in all directions forever and ever. About 4 P.M. we came into Jackson, Wyoming, the center of Grand Teton National Park.

Our final destination was the Biolchini home, just outside the nearby town of Kelly. Our directions required us to count some gravel driveways and turn into the third one. Unfortunately, a new driveway had been added since the directions had been written. The first house we pulled up to, therefore, was the wrong one. We found the right house soon enough, but then we couldn't find the key. The Biolchinis wrote that they would attach it to a lamp at the side of the door, but we couldn't find it, despite doing everything but disassemble the lamp. Finally Ned went back to the house where we had stopped first. They called around town and finally found the architect who had designed the house. He had an extra key and brought it out to us, but it didn't work. With his help, however, we finally managed to find the hidden key. It had been in the lamp all along.

It didn't take us long to make ourselves at home and soon we were relaxing with a scotch. Then I whipped up a dinner that Noreen Purcell had sent along with us—haddock with rice. By nine o'clock we were sitting out on the veranda with coffee and cigars, watching the sun drop behind the silhouetted peaks of the Tetons. This must sound terribly sybaritic, but after all, this is supposed to be a change and a vacation. Still, it's almost too much. Anyway, we did cook our meal and wash our dishes, so we probably felt a little less guilty. The Biolchinis can't be here until about the eleventh of July, but we may stick around, since this is a good base from which to explore Grand

Teton and Yellowstone, as well as Cody, where we would like to look in on the Buffalo Bill Museum.

It's difficult to describe the serenity and peace of this place. We're on a high hill looking directly across the Grand Teton peaks, mountains that rise straight up without warning from a high plateau. That's what makes them so spectacular. The moon is now rising and the sun is just reddening the sky to the west. We're surrounded by elk and moose and quaking aspen trees and a quiet stream meandering below us, the Gros Ventre. For those interested in altitude, we are perched here at 7,000 feet and right across the way the highest of the Grand Tetons is over a mile higher.

SATURDAY, JULY 4
Jackson, Wyoming

The Biolchinis called us from Tulsa to welcome us to their house. They will be here next Friday night, so we will probably stay over Saturday to have a visit with them and to thank them for their hospitality.

Later on, we had lunch with John and Mary Kay Turner at their Triangle X guest ranch, just a dozen or so miles from here. John's a Notre Dame grad. He and Mary Kay operate rafting and horseback-riding concessions from the ranch. Each day they raft 300 people down the Snake and put another 30 on horseback for trail rides. Besides running the ranch, Jack is the president of the Wyoming Senate.

After a great hamburger lunch, we went to visit Grand Teton National Park, the eighth national park since we began this journey. Right in the middle of the park is Jackson Lake, shaped like a giant arrowhead. Six miles up the road from the Jackson Lake Lodge is Colter Bay Visitors' Center, which has a long beach and a lot of aquatic activity, including swimming. The lobby of the lodge looks directly out across the lake to the Tetons, surely one of the greatest views of any hotel in the world. Just below the lodge we visited a little church called Sacred Heart Chapel. We then followed a one-way road around the shore of the lake. It passes Lay Lake and Jenny Lake, both of which are beautiful and give a new perspective of the Tetons, since the shores of these lakes go right to where the mountains soar up another 7,000 or 8,000 feet. On a calm day, the lakes mirror the jagged peaks and broad canyons of the mountains.

Like several other places we have visited, this region, too, was covered by a succession of oceans. They receded. Then, about 70 million years ago, the mountains thrust up, carrying with them bands of sedimentation laid down millions of years earlier by the oceans. Today you can see the same sandstone sedimentation at the top of Mount Moran as you would 25,000 feet below the surface here. One can still see glaciers on most of these mountains, so the work of erosion and formation is still taking place. Another great creator of much of the splendor and beauty we see here is the Snake River, which originates near the south boundary of Yellowstone just north of here and passes through the dam at the end of Jackson Lake and on through the original canyon that was made by glaciers moving south. Each year, for millions of years, the Snake River carved the canyon deeper.

Later in the evening we enjoyed a cookout on the banks of the Buffalo River with the Turners and some friends of theirs from Houston. We cooked an authentic Mexican dinner alongside the swift-flowing river, then built a big campfire and sat around singing songs appropriate for the Fourth of July. It was a very pleasant evening to end another great day.

SUNDAY, JULY 5
Jackson, Wyoming

After Mass was had a phone call from the Biolchinis in Tulsa. They wanted to instruct Ned in the complicated art of getting the Jacuzzi to work. I have long been of the opinion that two people shouldn't worry about the same thing, so I let Ned worry about the Jacuzzi. He soon had it running and, appropriately, was the first one to enjoy it. The Jacuzzi, by the way, is out on the deck facing the Tetons. What a place to take a bath! I look forward to immersing myself in it tomorrow—if we get back from fishing on time.

Bob Biolchini had told us to be sure to visit the Great American Wildlife Museum, which opened only forty days ago. He's the chairman of the board. There we particularly enjoyed an exhibition of the wildlife paintings of Carl Rungius, especially the moose, bear, mountain sheep, wolf, elk, and buffalo. The museum also had paintings by George Catlin, Charles Russell, and Herman Herzog.

Following our tour of the museum we kept a date to meet Jerry Brady, who had come down from Idaho Springs with his wife, Ricci. Jerry was Notre Dame's student body president in 1957–58 and traveled with me to Africa after graduation. He now runs the family TV and cable business. We took the Bradys back to the house, had a wonderful visit, then saw them off.

This evening we put together a meal of turkey stew with carrots and peas. We couldn't get the microwave in the Biolchinis' kitchen to work, so we turned on the generator to the Lindy and did the defrosting there, returning to the house for the cooking. The stew was wonderful by itself, and tasted even better with white wine. Tomorrow reveille is at 4:30 A.M. John Turner is going to take us fishing at Lake Yellowstone.

MONDAY, JULY 6
Jackson, Wyoming

Today was another day of firsts. To be more specific, we were up at 4:30 A.M. and that was certainly a first on this trip. It was still dark, although the outlines of the mountains across the way were beginning to appear in the predawn stillness. We had a quick breakfast of coffee and some cinnamon buns we had bought at the Bunnery in town yesterday. Shortly after five, we were on the road and arrived at the Triangle X Ranch about 5:30. John Turner and sons Tote and Mark were waiting for us. We got into their carryall and were soon on our way north. About seven o'clock, we arrived at the marina on Yellowstone Lake.

Despite the early hour, a fairly strong wind was whipping across the lake, which is nestled in pine-clad hills. Lake Yellowstone is about 20 miles long, with a surface area of 136 square miles. It's a very cold lake, never going above 40 degrees Fahrenheit, and is 350 feet deep. We're told that this is a good season for cutthroat trout. This whole area was the result of an enormous volcanic explosion many, many years ago. The hugh resulting caldera became Yellowstone Lake.

Despite the wind, which kept changing direction every few minutes, and a very clear sky with bright sunlight, we practically froze the first couple of hours. Then the fish began to bite and we forgot about the coldness. Rather quickly, we caught about thirty cutthroat trout. Another dozen or so got off the hook. On the way back Ned and I prayed our Breviary for the day, with John Turner joining in approximately on the "Glory be to the Father, the Son, and the Holy Spirit" responses. When we got back to John's ranch, he said he felt pretty holy.

About 4:30 P.M. we had Mass in John's mother's house. She is a valiant lady who lives here year-round. About twenty-five people, including a young Notre Dame lawyer, who are vacationing here, attended Mass today and participated with great fervor. We had hoped when coming West that we would not only see the beauties of the land but the beauty of the people, and we are getting a good sense of that, for which we are grateful. The people on this ranch, especially the Turners, really seem to care about each other and about their guests. Also, they have a good, healthy spirituality which is very visible as they attend Mass.

There is still another first to be mentioned today. In addition to catching cutthroat trout for the first time, we had the temerity to cook them for dinner. This was such a culinary triumph that I feel compelled to recount the details. I squeezed lemon juice into the body of the fish after they were cleaned. Then I put a good slice of lemon in each fish and also green peppers to give them some flavor. Then I wrapped each whole fish in three strips of bacon held in place by toothpicks. Finally, I wrapped them in foil and put them in a 350-degree oven for half an hour. They tasted much like salmon, for they have delicate pink flesh and much more flavor than brook trout. I am not overly fond of fish and neither is Ned, but we both cleaned our plates. To add to the incongruity of the situation, I also had rustled up some baked beans with a few added ingredients.

After dinner we went out on the veranda, discussed the battle plans for tomorrow, and had black coffee and cigars before finishing our prayers for the day together. I hate to admit it, but both of us were really yawning by eight o'clock. I guess it was the wind, the lake, the sun, and all of those firsts. We watched the sun go down behind Grand Teton, the highest of all the Tetons. The setting sun etches at least a dozen other peaks, looking for all the world like the spires of distant cathedrals. It's almost ten o'clock now and the mountains are still backlighted against the western sky. The cool of the evening is upon us and I can hear the rustle of the Gros Ventre in the valley below us.

TUESDAY, JULY 7
Jackson, Wyoming

Last night, tired as I was, I nonetheless decided to finish Parkman's *Oregon Trail*. The biggest surprise of all was that he didn't really take the Oregon Trail and didn't get farther west than Pueblo. I was also surprised at how wantonly they killed buffaloes in those days (the 1840s). They'd shoot these magnificent animals just to cut off a tail for an ornament. Or they'd just leave them to die.

We went into town this morning for a whole variety of tasks that needed doing. One of our surprises on this trip is how much time needs to be spent on logistics that we took for granted or had done by someone else. We had the oil changed in the Chevy, the tank filled, and the car washed, since it was filthy dirty from driving these gravel roads and being dragged behind the Lindy. Also, I bought a book that was No. 1 on the New York *Times* best-seller list last week, Louis L'Amour's *Haunted Mesa*, which is about the Anasazi, mentioned earlier. We also dropped off some dry cleaning, picked up a half dozen items at the grocery store, and grabbed a BLT for lunch. Afterward, we visited Senator Alan Simpson's daughter Suzie, who is the assistant director at the Great American Wildlife Museum, which we had visited last Sunday. We took Suzie out for a half-hour coffee break. She is just as delightful as her mother and father, Ann and Alan.

About three o'clock, we again made the twenty-five-mile journey to the Triangle X Ranch, where we met up with a small group of people and drove down to the bank of the Snake River to take a two-and-one-half-hour rubber-raft trip. Just as we arrived at the ranch, a fellow came up to me and said, "How's my classmate?" It was Charlie Osborn, class of 1938, and his wife, Harriet. I thought that would do it for Notre Dame today, because while we were in town, Mike Cottingham, class of 1968, and his wife (a graduate of St. Mary's, Notre Dame's sister school) came up to us while we were having coffee. He had seen Ned walking down the street and spun around to say hello. Mike is running a ranch out here that sends 350 teenagers in smaller groups out into the wilderness areas throughout four or five Western states, as well as Alaska.

The trip down the Snake River was wonderful because we saw a good deal of wildlife, including moose, ospreys, and some bald eagles. Also, we got to see a different view of the Teton Range. A closing note about Yellowstone: As you enter the park you pass the Continental Divide at about 7,988 feet. The Snake River, which originates here, flows westward and, after a long and tortuous journey through many canyons, reaches the Columbia River and eventually its waters empty into the Pacific. The Yellowstone River, on the other side of the Divide, flows to the Atlantic by way of the Missouri and Mississippi. Four rivers, side by side, go to the two oceans that border our land, east and west. This really is the Continental Divide.

WEDNESDAY, JULY 8
Jackson, Wyoming

We got up early and drove straight through to Lake Lodge, a distance of exactly 100 miles. There we had lunch with the manager, Jim Fredian, a 1978 Notre Dame grad. He also invited Nancy Lauen to lunch. She's a Notre Dame premedical student living in Lyons Hall. We had a wonderful lunch with a lot of good conversation. Afterward we called ahead to the Buffalo Bill Museum to tell them we might be a little late. Along the road, we met a very big buffalo, at least twice the size of the ones we saw in the Black Hills. We are now in the Shoshone National Forest and going down through the canyon to the east entrance to the park. About two hours out of the Lake Lodge, we came to Cody, the hometown of my good friend and associate on the Select Commission on Immigration and Refugee Policy, Senator Alan Simpson.

We drove directly to the Buffalo Bill Museum and got in touch with the director, Peter Hassrick, and his development person, Larry

Means. This is a wonderful museum, probably the best in the West, for viewing Western art and ethnological data and, of course, the life of Bill Cody, better known as Buffalo Bill. We spent over two hours going through the museum looking at the pictures and the artifacts dealing with Buffalo Bill.

The exhibits were all the more interesting to me because I had earlier discovered something I never thought existed: an interesting government report. It's titled *Exploring the American West (1803–1879)*. It begins with President Jefferson and progresses to beyond President Grant. Mainly it speaks of those intrepid explorers, mountain men, artists, and photographers who opened up the West and made it romantic for the American people. (If anyone is interested in reading this publication, which is about 116 pages, it is classified as United States National Park Service, Department of Publications, F5-592 E96-1982.) It's an absolutely wonderful compilation of everything that made Americans want to go West and what they did after they got there.

After visiting the museum, we took a ten-minute walk through the town—that's all you need—then dropped in at the Hotel Erma, named by Buffalo Bill for his eldest daughter, where we had a fine beef dinner. We then walked back through town for another mile or so and turned in.

THURSDAY, JULY 9
Cody, Wyoming

Today we're on our way back into Yellowstone for a tour of the park and then to our habitat at the Biolchinis' house. It was another day of unprecedented sights. Somehow, coming from Cody through the east entrance of the park was much more beautiful than going the other way. We thought we were back in Bryce for a while because there were so many chimney rocks and weird-shaped red sandstone canyon walls dotted with pines. As we passed Buffalo Bill Lake and started up the canyon, the whole horizon looked like something right out of "The Mountain Men," a Charles Russell painting we have at Notre Dame.

Once in the park, we did the lower loop, where most of the

excitement is. Just beyond the east gate, one comes to Lake Yellowstone, where we fished the other day. Behind it, one sees the Absaroka Range, which is snowcapped and forms a wonderful backdrop for this beautiful blue lake. Birds, including some you might not expect to see, are everywhere: white pelicans, sea gulls, cormorants, a wide variety of ducks, and, of course, numerous Canada geese.

The whole area is constantly covered with great billowing white cumulus clouds and an incredibly blue sky, which seems to go on forever unless interrupted by a mountain range. Twice along the way, we were interrupted: first by 300 or 400 buffaloes that decided to cross the road, then by a line of stopped cars whose occupants were photographing a large herd of elk, some with magnificent racks of antlers.

The two best-known attractions in the park are Yellowstone Canyon and Old Faithful. The canyon is about 1,500 feet wide and 1,200 feet deep. The sides are made of decomposed rhyolite lava rock which comes out yellow, giving the park its name. The Yellowstone River and two great waterfalls with drops of 100 and 300 feet are at the bottom of the canyon.

When we arrived at Old Faithful the prediction was that it would erupt at 4:52, give or take five minutes. That gave us about a half-hour leeway, so we did the unthinkable and went to a concession stand and bought ice-cream cones. This meant we were really relaxed; Ned couldn't remember the last time he had an ice-cream cone. We then joined a throng of about 5,000 people who had formed a ring around the geyser. It shot up a couple of minutes after 4:52, but well within the five-minute leeway time. The eruption lasted about a minute. While we were waiting, we saw several smaller geysers in the area shoot skyward.

We arrived back at the Biolchinis' about seven o'clock, having left Cody this morning about nine. I decided to get fancy and turned out two chicken pot pies, which, thanks to Mrs. Stouffer, were marvelous. Another first. After dinner we sat out on the veranda with Joyce Hank's cookies, cups of steaming black coffee, and cigars. What we were watching tonight was a normal electrical show going on beyond the Tetons to the west, but moving our way.

It made all of our Fourth of July celebrations seem puny as the lightning flashed across those dark skies, outlining the mountain peaks. We knew it had arrived for us when raindrops began to fall. So we came indoors and looked out through the marvelous twenty-foot-high window front of the house and watched the pyrotechnics continue, this time to the accompaniment of thunder. This was the first heavy rain we had experienced in the four weeks we have been traveling.

I always start the Rosary when I go to bed at night, but I'm going to have to get a different system because I rarely get beyond the third Hail Mary these nights before falling into a profound sleep. Maybe it's the relaxation, maybe it's the mountain air. I don't want to claim a completely clear conscience, but the fact is, we both have been sleeping like the dead. Tomorrow will be cleanup day before we leave again and also a day to welcome the owners of this house, Bob and Fran Biolchini and three of their six children. I dropped off to sleep to the sound of heavy rain beating on the roof.

FRIDAY, JULY 10
Jackson, Wyoming

It was still raining and we were completely fogged in this morning when we arose, somewhat late, I should confess. For the first time we can't see the Tetons. After a minimal breakfast, we began the cleanup operation. It's amazing how much paper one accumulates in a few days. We also had a whole spate of phone calls to make. When I called Helen she told me that the plane on which we hope to go to Alaska had been laid up with a shattered windshield, but is now back in good operating condition, so the Alaskan trip is still on. She also gave me my plane reservations from Bellingham, Washington, to South Bend to open the Special Olympics which will be held in Notre Dame Stadium this year. I also learned that the new administration is now assembling at our summer camp in Land O'Lakes, Wisconsin, to prepare for the coming year and many more that will follow. Yesterday in Cody, Ned and I offered Mass for their success.

Fran Biolchini arrived right on schedule at 4:30 P.M. after a two-day, 1,100-mile drive from Tulsa with three of her children. Bob arrived a few hours later by air and we had a nice dinner at the country club. After dinner, we went back to the house and talked until 1:30 A.M. Shortly thereafter we all went to sleep, only to be awakened a couple of hours later by three moose who were rubbing their noses against the Biolchinis' bedroom window.

SATURDAY, JULY 11
Jackson, Wyoming

We had Mass with the Biolchinis and blessed their house, which is only a year and a half old now. The weather began to clear this morning, but it still drizzled intermittently and clouds still covered the three large Teton peaks. Fran sent us off with a terrific breakfast, which held us well after we crossed the border into Idaho. Rather than retrace the route we had taken so many times up to Yellowstone, we headed south through Jackson, then over Teton Pass at 8,431 feet, and finally north toward Glacier National Park. Nobody thought we'd make it over that pass, and, in fact, we slowed to 14 miles an hour in low gear. But eventually we made it.

After Teton Pass, we soon crossed the border into Idaho, our eighth state so far. We drove through a section of Targhee National Forest, then over rolling hills green with wheat, hay, and plants growing that famous Idaho potato. A great deal of irrigation goes on as well, but the land looked very fertile. As we proceeded north, the road became like a roller coaster, up and down between the fields. At every quadrant of the compass, we could see mountains off in the distance against that far-off big sky, now bluer than ever.

By prearrangement, we arrived at the summer home of Bob Bauchman, class of 1943, and his wife, Alice, near Macks Inn, Idaho. They live in Las Vegas and are in the communications development business, mainly construction. Recently, they participated in a Notre Dame fly-in. About seven of the Bauchman family and in-laws have Notre Dame or St. Mary's connections, so we felt right at home. After we had all the daughters, sons, and in-laws sorted out, we drove to a little log cabin down the road for dinner. We were practically the only guests, but the meal was splendiferous—shrimp and crab, rice, and a marvelous cream sauce. It was great to enjoy someone else's cooking for a change. After dinner, we went down to Macks Inn and saw how they recreate on Saturday night in the mountains. There was country music and a kind of dancing that is a few cuts above square dancing and very fast. All of the family seemed to be terrific dancers with a lot of moves and a lot of speed. Bob was the best. Bob, Alice, Ned, and I came back early, had a nightcap and a long conversation before the young people arrived and piled into the Jacuzzi. When we finally turned in, we all were asleep about two minutes after hitting the pillow.

SUNDAY, JULY 12
Macks Inn, Idaho

At nine o'clock the whole living room was full of men, women, and children who had come for Mass. It was my turn to celebrate, so I preached on love and the family. It fit fairly well with the Gospel, which was about planting the seed and having it grow or die. After breakfast, we went to the top of a Federal Aviation Agency radar station on Sawtell Mountain. From a distance, Sawtell looks like a reclining Indian. At about 11,000 feet, it's up there where the snow falls in July. From this vantage point, we were able to see about 100 miles in all directions. Fortunately, the clouds had lifted, so we had a splendid view of the Tetons from the west. North of them, we saw Yellowstone Park and behind them, the snowcapped Absaroka Range. Farther to the north was the Gallatin National Forest and Crazy Mountain beyond, also snowcapped, and to the south, we could see almost to Idaho Falls. To the west was the Bitterroot Range, which we will be seeing later.

We thought we'd get underway about 1:45 P.M., but our Chevy got tangled up in the pine trees in the driveway, so we had to undo the whole business, Chevy and Kaddy Kar, and back the RV up to get out. We finally negotiated everything and were on our way by 2 P.M. We headed north to Bozeman, Montana. When we joined Interstate 90, I took the wheel and drove to Butte. We checked into the trailer park, where we unhooked the Chevy. We did a quick tour of the city, which looked like a once prosperous mining town, now defunct. We returned to the Lindy around seven o'clock, and prepared a light supper of toasted ham and Swiss cheese sandwiches and baked beans. Believe it or not, we're still eating Joyce Hank's cookies for dessert.

Tomorrow we'll get our muffler fixed. Today coming into Butte it was making so much noise I practically had to scream while reading the Breviary so Ned could hear me.

MONDAY, JULY 13
Butte, Montana

We started the day by refilling our propane tank and visiting a muffler shop. Luckily, all the muffler needed was some minor repair. That done, we got back on Interstate 90 and headed toward Missoula. At first we saw good-sized, rolling hills that were rather barren for about half the trip. Then the valley narrowed, the hills increased in height, and thick stands of fir trees appeared on their flanks. The valley opened up just as we came into Missoula. Continuing northwest on Interstate 90 out of Missoula, we drove through a beautiful valley with hills that were slightly higher and covered with pine trees. The trees gradually disappeared from the brown hills, and soon we were confronting mountains. As we came over the final rise, there was Flathead Lake, a beautiful deep blue-water lake that stretches to the edge of Glacier Park.

We stopped in Polson to meet relatives of two Notre Dame graduates from Ned's hometown of Spartanburg, South Carolina: Rob and Carol Tiernan. Rob met us in town shortly after our arrival and conducted us around the south end of Flathead Lake, which is about twenty miles long and sixteen miles broad at its widest point. We unhitched the Chevy before starting because he said it was a difficult road and he wasn't kidding. The Tiernans' house is about 150 feet above the lake and looks down through wonderful ponderosa pines and Douglas firs. There was also a smattering of cedar, blue spruce, lodgepole pine, and larch along the shore. We sat out on the veranda having a cold beer and discussing how we might approach our visit to Glacier. Then Carol turned out a great chicken and rice casserole. Both of them are ski instructors in Aspen, he in downhill and she in cross-country. Because of 140 days of intensive work there, they are able to have a wonderfully peaceful summer by this beautiful lake and in this secluded cabin, a family heirloom.

We're going to get an early start tomorrow, so we're turning in early tonight.

TUESDAY, JULY 14
Polson, Montana

Bastille Day dawned bright and clear. We had Mass on the front porch of the cabin, a perfect setting as the sun came up behind the mountains to the east and turned the lake into pure crystal. We drove about sixty miles up the east side of the lake and then over to the Swan Range. Rob and Carol are real outdoor persons, and they knew of an old lumber road on which we could drive up to about 6,000 feet. Then, with Carol in the lead as our navigator, we hiked up the mountain for another 2,000 or 3,000 feet. It was up and up for the better part of two hours with very little rest on the way. It was painfully clear that Carol was in a lot better condition than we were. Finally, we reached Jewel Basin, a high valley dotted with beautiful blue-green lakes, and sat down to a picnic lunch of fruit, crackers, and cheese, topped off with cookies made from a chocolate substitute.

We had planned to take the Tiernans out to dinner in town tonight, but were so pooped when we arrived home that all of us just pitched in and put together a simple but tasty meal in the Tiernans' kitchen.

WEDNESDAY, JULY 15
Polson, Montana

We rearranged some things in our somewhat disheveled Lindy, thanked the Tiernans for their hospitality and, after hitching up the Chevy again, struck out northward on U.S. 93 along the west edge of Flathead Lake. At the north end of the lake the alfalfa and wheat and grazing land began to be replaced by Christmas-tree farms. The Christmas trees are beautiful Scotch pine that are trimmed into perfect cones. We are told that Flathead Lake is the largest freshwater lake west of the Mississippi. I assume that means natural lakes and not lakes created by dams.

We pulled up in front of St. Raymond's Church in Columbia Falls, where we know both the pastor, Father Bud Sullivan, and his retired assistant, Father Emmett O'Neil. Father Bud is related to Father Mike Murphy, a C.S.C. at Notre Dame. I have known Father Emmett since we studied together at the Gregorian University in Rome in 1937–40. Our paths kept crossing because we were both interested in many of the same apostolates. Father Jack Hunthausen, who is dean of the local clergy here, joined us for supper. He is the brother of Archbishop Raymond Hunthausen of Seattle, much in the news lately. The archbishop, by the way, has an advanced degree in chemistry from Notre Dame.

THURSDAY, JULY 16
Columbia Falls, Montana

Father Emmett decided to come with us to Glacier National Park, giving us both a navigator and a good companion. Glacier Park, as the name indicates, was created by glaciers that were formed a few million years ago. They finished their work here about 4,000 years ago. After the Europeans arrived and the 49th parallel was established as a boundary between the United States and Canada, the park was cut in half. The Canadian park, called Waterton Lakes, was created in 1895, and Glacier, on the American side, fifteen years later in 1910. In 1932, the two countries decreed that it would be called the Waterton-Glacier International Peace Park to symbolize the peace and friendship between the two nations.

On entering the park we cruised along the east bank of Lake McDonald, which is about sixty miles long and half a mile wide, making it the park's largest lake. At the end of the lake we beheld a veritable procession of mountain peaks of all sizes and shapes. Based on the sheer grandeur of the peaks alone, I would have to say that Glacier is the most dazzling of the parks we have seen so far. After Glacier Lake we went on a long climb over Logan Pass with its spectacular drop-offs all the way to the top. The road, called the Going to the Sun Highway, must be one of the most beautiful drives in America.

Once over the pass, we dropped down on the other side to St.

Mary's Lake, second to McDonald in size. St. Mary's is about ten miles long and a mile or so wide, with a depth of 246 feet. All the lakes here are deep and blue, and all the more beautiful when their glassy surfaces reflect the towering peaks of the surrounding mountains. From St. Mary's, we headed for the border and the Prince of Wales Hotel in the Canadian portion of the park. It's a beautiful lodge, in miniature much like Banff and the Hotel Frontenac in Quebec, although more rustic. They have only eighty-two rooms and we were fortunate to get the last two. From here, we took an invigorating walk in the woods and made several side trips in the Chevy.

FRIDAY, JULY 17
Glacier National Park, Montana

Finally, it happened. We woke up this morning to a drizzly rain and black clouds. This is the first bad travel day we've had since leaving Notre Dame on June 11, so we're not complaining. (We did have one day of partial rain in the Tetons, but we weren't traveling that day.) It was a dreary trip back to Columbia Falls, but fortunately we saw most of Glacier's spectacular scenery yesterday.

We had a wonderful dinner in the rectory tonight. Bud had invited Father Jack Hunthausen, who was here the other night, and Father Tom Fenlon, a retired priest. It was one of those special evenings that happens when priests long in the vineyard get together—filled with reminiscences, stories, theological discussions, and limericks. All in all, it was a nice way to end a rather dismal day.

SATURDAY, JULY 18
Columbia Falls, Montana

We had Mass in church for a change, then took to the road and headed northward with the Rockies looming on the right. We stopped in Eureka to see the wonderful little church, Our Lady of Mercy, where a wedding was in progress. As we continued north, the view to the right was much like the Black Hills, but higher. Then we came out into a flatter area where there was some agriculture, mostly irrigated fields for cattle. Once more we crossed the border into Canada. This time the customs officer on duty insisted on searching the RV. As I was unlocking the door to the Lindy, he asked me my name. When I told him he said, "I thought I recognized you. Would you please give me your autograph?" The search was then discontinued.

Once we passed the border, the road was much better, which doesn't say much for the United States compared with Canada. There was a good deal of irrigation along the way, mostly to grow forage crops for the stocky Charolais cattle that we saw in great numbers alongside the road. We then entered our eleventh national park, the Kootenay. As we continued northward, we had the Rockies on both sides, and we could see snow on the higher peaks. The weather continued to be cloudy with intermittent rains all along the way, nothing heavy, but persistent. After about 250 miles, we arrived at our destination for the day: Golden, British Columbia. Once we were settled in at the RV campground, we had a drink and dinner that I prepared, consisting of beefsteak, rice, and peas. Ned couldn't quite believe that I put it together by myself. After dinner, we took a walk around the camp and were amazed at the wide variety of recreational vehicles that these camps attract each night. They come in all shapes and sizes and ours is by no means the largest.

SUNDAY, JULY 19
Golden, British Columbia

Last night it grew quite cold and rained all night. We both used our sleeping bags and were grateful to have them. When we got up and saw it was still raining, we just went back to bed and slept for another hour. It was my turn to give a homily on the Gospel, which was an easy one on sowing good wheat only to have the enemy sow weeds in the wheat. Jesus says let them grow together. At the harvest, God will separate them and burn the weeds. Even the good Lord does not eradicate all evil in this world, although He could if He wanted to. When He gave us our personal freedom, he allowed us to do good freely but also evil. He lets evil exist until the end of time, when all will be made aright. Most modern reformers want to eradicate all evil before midnight. The first reading said that it is not enough merely to be just; we have to be kind at the same time. Several good lessons for the modern Church. We have to love people and be understanding of their failings if we want to help them to be better.

The rain continued, and it looked as though it was going to be a day for reading. Having read a lot of theology last night, I turned on some Mozart in our tape deck and went through about 400 Spanish vocabulary cards to get ready for Latin America, our next travel objective. Despite the intermittent rain, we took a long walk up into the hills after lunch. If it doesn't clear up tomorrow, we will skip Lake Louise and Banff. These are wonderful tourist spots in Canada. However, we've both been here before and there's no point in going into the mountains when the fog is only a few hundred feet off the ground.

MONDAY, JULY 20
Golden, British Columbia

We woke up today to more rain and low-lying clouds, so it was off to the west again on Trans-Canada No. 1, as good a highway as you're going to find. Fortunately, the skies cleared as we headed west. We went down a long valley with snow-covered mountains on both sides. As we headed up through Rogers Pass, we drove through five tunnels. The top of the pass was only about a mile high, but there was an absolutely marvelous view of the mountains on every side. This is the end of the Canadian section of the Waterton-Glacier National Park. We're now heading into the Coast Range and the Pacific time zone along the Mackenzie and Fraser rivers. At Kamloops we decided to spend the night at a campground called Cache Creek. It was quite warm by the time we arrived there, but we had done over 200 miles and it was time to stop if we hoped to get into a camp for the night. We hooked up our utilities, fixed ourselves a simple meal, and took another fairly long walk around camp to limber up our legs before turning in.

TUESDAY, JULY 21
Kamloops, British Columbia

Today, the road turned out to be much more spectacular than yesterday as we came into the Lillooet Range of the Coast Mountains. We passed down through some tremendous valleys between the mountains and up over passes which culminated in Hells Gate. This is where the chasm narrows and the Fraser River comes roaring through, much as the water does at Murchison Falls at the headwaters of the Nile in Uganda. Again, we were going through tunnels all day and, for some reason, we saw more trains than we had seen on all of the American railroad lines up to this point. Two of them were more than a hundred cars long. We enjoyed great mountain scenery all morning, then left the Coast Range behind around noon and broke for lunch at a truck stop. After lunch we continued south to Bellingham, where we checked into a hotel. Our plan is to leave the Lindy and the Chevy here while we fly back to Notre Dame for the Special Olympics. After that, we'll leave from Notre Dame for Alaska, and then fly back here to resume our RV itinerary.

The first thing we did was look around for a Ford truck dealer, since we had blown our muffler again and the Lindy sounded like a Sherman tank. But we couldn't find a place that could fix the muffler; nor could we find a parking facility where we could store the Lindy and the Chevy. We therefore decided to push on to Seattle in the morning, in the hope that we'd find what we needed there.

During dinner in the hotel here tonight, we got into a conversation with two young ladies, one our waitress and the other the maîtresse d'hôtel. They were questioning us about our work in life, and when they found out we were priests, they both admitted they were fallen-away Catholics. One thing led to another, and I think we finally talked them into reconsidering their current religious positions. As we left the restaurant, the waitress said, "I guess it's Providence at work again; the good Lord sent you around to talk to me tonight." We will remember them both at Mass tomorrow morning.

WEDNESDAY, JULY 22
Bellingham, Washington

Today could have been justifiably called our day of frustration. We left Bellingham around 9:30 in the morning and were in Seattle by early afternoon. We thought we had really lucked out when we noted that only a few blocks from the Holiday Inn was a large Ford truck service center. We pulled in, but when the service manager came out, he said simply, "We don't take care of RVs." We answered, "The RV is fine. We just want you to fix the muffler on the Ford truck chassis." He just repeated that he didn't take care of RVs and that was that. He did tell us that there was an RV repair place about twenty-five miles to the south. Since we were getting nowhere with him, we decided to go there after checking into the Holiday Inn. But when we tried to check in we were told that no rooms were available. Finally, after some heavy persuading on Ned's part, the manager told us to come back in a couple of hours, and in the meantime he'd see what he could do. In our free time, we decided to go down the road to the RV repair place. When we found it we got the answer: "We don't fix mufflers." They sent us to another place, which looked like a fly-by-night operation. It was little more than a shack, but the proprietor said if he could stretch his welding equipment far enough, he'd try to weld our muffler and exhaust pipe together, which would have solved our problem.

We pulled the RV in as close as we could and went inside the RV to fix ourselves some lunch. Finally our luck changed. When the man finished welding, we had a muffler that was as quiet as the Chevy's. And when we went back to the Holiday Inn, we had a couple of rooms. Storing the RV and the Chevy, however, was another matter. There was a storage place available, but it would have cost us an arm and a leg to leave the rig there for two weeks. What's more, security didn't appear to be too tight. At that point, it seemed to us that the better part of valor would be to push on tomorrow to the University of Portland, a Holy Cross (our order) operation where we would be among friends and could undoubtedly find a secure place to leave our two vehicles.

THURSDAY, JULY 23
Seattle, Washington

We pulled into the University of Portland about noon and went in search of friends. We soon ran into Father Dave Sherrer, the academic vice president there. He took us to lunch, where we met a number of our other Holy Cross priests and Brothers and made a few new friends. After lunch, Dave and Father Tom Oddo, the president, took us over to Father Dick Rutherford's house, which has two bedrooms. Father Dick was away for the weekend so we inherited his place.

I called the Ford agency in town and made an appointment (it's worse than getting in to see the dentist) to have the oil changed and the Lindy lubricated tomorrow at 8:30 A.M. We'd been given an ideal place to keep our rig until we get back—right outside the university maintenance garage. With these last two days of unplanned travel, we have driven 7,572 miles since leaving South Bend. We had Mass with the Community this afternoon, then a joyous dinner, where we were reunited with many old friends. Following that, Father Oddo took us on a very pleasant walking tour of the campus. I really envy them for the seventy-year-old sequoia trees they have growing here. They're about thirty feet high and are all over campus. I'm afraid, though, that they just wouldn't survive the climate at Notre Dame.

FRIDAY, JULY 24
Portland, Oregon

We were up early to get the Lindy and the Chevy to the local Ford dealer before 8:30 A.M. Luckily we got there early, for soon there was a long line of people waiting to have repairs done. When all the service work was done, we returned to the university and had Mass and lunch with the Community. After that we began packing our small duffel bags for the quick trip back to Notre Dame and the longer one to Alaska immediately following it. We're traveling light so as not to overload the small plane we'll be flying in to Alaska. We cleaned the perishables out of our refrigerator and put them in Father Rutherford's. Then we shut off the propane gas, chained the Kaddy Kar to the Lindy, and locked the doors. With all our housekeeping completed, we're now ready for a free day tomorrow. Father Terry Lalley, who used to teach psychology at Notre Dame and is now head of the Psychological Center here, is going to show us around the area.

SATURDAY, JULY 25
Portland, Oregon

Our first stop with Father Lalley was Multnomah Falls, which are very long, wispy, and of the bridal-veil variety. We then went to Chanticleer Point, where we had a great view of the Columbia River as it comes toward the ocean from the east. Next was Bonneville Dam, dedicated by Franklin D. Roosevelt in 1937. It has developed more than $3 billion worth of electricity since its dedication, and was one of the first dams used to experiment with accommodating the spawning of the salmon.

Finally, we came to Panorama Point about fifty miles from Mount Hood. Snow-covered Mount Hood almost looks like one of the Himalayas as it rises majestically from the valley floor. It simply dwarfs the other mountains around it. We were also able to see Mount St. Helens from here. We drove a very beautiful road that goes around Mount Hood and came up the back of it to Timberline Lodge. The lodge is truly majestic, with heavy wooden furniture and immense wooden beams. The room President Roosevelt had used is now a kind of museum, and you can listen to a tape recording of the speech he made here. We enjoyed another great view by taking the ski lift up to 7,000 feet. We ended our tour at a Portland restaurant that served clams by the bucket as well as crab Louis. We sampled both.

After this brief interlude in Portland, we flew directly back to campus to participate in the Special Olympics, for which I had agreed to be honorary chair.

TUESDAY, AUGUST 4
Notre Dame, Indiana

We've been back at Notre Dame for a week and a day and now are getting ready to fly to Alaska. On the day we left Portland it had been seven weeks since I'd been on an airplane, by far my longest spell without a flight in almost forty years. The most exciting event of the week, and the reason we were here, was, of course, the Special Olympics, the largest affair of this kind in the history of the world. Credit for organizing the Special Olympics, not only here but world-wide, goes to Eunice Kennedy Shriver and her husband, Sarge. It was a thrilling sight to see those 5,000 smiling handicapped men and women marching around the stadium to cheers during the opening ceremonies, perhaps feeling for the first time in their lives a sense of importance and dignity. There was the usual hoopla with celebrities in attendance. It was my small task as honorary chairman to say a minute's prayer. I prayed for peace and for the splendid example that these young people from so many conflicting nations were giving us by competing together and upholding the dignity of human beings so denigrated because of retardation or disability. If they can get together despite all of their difficulties, so can we. It was really the human spirit that we were celebrating. As somebody said so well, "Here everybody wins; there are no losers."

Everyone back here at Notre Dame was surprised that those who were not supposed to get past Gary managed to put over 8,000 miles on the Lindy and the Chevy. So far, so good. May the good Lord be with us as we continue.

It was, of course, great to be back at Notre Dame, if even for a week. Neither of us has missed the daily schedule of the past thirty-five years, but home is home, and we were both happy to see it, however briefly.

We were up at 6:15 A.M. today. Ned and I offered Mass together, then went to the airport, where we met Ollie Cunningham, his wife, Millie, and their copilot, Ted Byron. We are flying a two-engine Cessna Conquest, a prop jet that easily seats four passengers besides the pilot and the copilot, with plenty of room for luggage. By 8 A.M. we were in the air, and a few hours later, after fuel stops in Aberdeen,

South Dakota, and Great Falls, Montana, we landed in Bellingham, Washington.

WEDNESDAY, AUGUST 5
Bellingham, Washington

We were not leaving for Alaska until tomorrow, so today the four of us got a rental car and drove up to Vancouver for some leisurely sightseeing. We toured beautiful Stanley Park in the middle of the city, saw the site of the World's Fair, had lunch in the Bayside Hotel, and walked along the wharf for a while. Back in Bellingham we met Ted Byron for dinner at the Yacht Club.

THURSDAY, AUGUST 6
Bellingham, Washington

The day dawned bright and sunny as we took off in the Cessna from Bellingham, but by the time we were approaching Sitka, Alaska, we were in dense fog. When we broke into the open on our approach, we were only about 100 feet off the deck.

Sitka was opened by Alexander Baranof and the Russian American Company, a fur-trading operation. Baranof was the governor of the Russian colony here from 1799 to 1818. The local Indians, the Tlingit, who were hunters, gatherers, and especially fishermen, destroyed the colony and drove out Baranof and the Russians in 1802. Baranof and the colonists recaptured Sitka, which was then called St. Michael's, in 1804.

Baranof was a very forceful character and created here what he called "the New Archangel," a great Russian port on the Arctic Ocean. He traded widely, even selling ice to the residents of San Francisco for $25 a ton. He also built a steamship and sent the colonists' children back to St. Petersburg for their education. In the center of town, the Russians built an ornate Russian cathedral, St. Michael's. Sitka began to be called "the Paris of the Pacific" because of its beauty. In 1867, thanks to the efforts of Secretary of State William Henry Seward, the United States bought Alaska from Russia for $7.2 million. The purchase was called "Seward's Folly," even though it came to two cents per acre. Alaska became our forty-ninth state in 1959.

Sitka is framed by the snowcapped peaks of the Tongass National Forest and Mount Edgecumbe, a volcano. The Japan Current keeps temperatures fairly moderate here—50s and 60s in the summer and 20s in the winter. The town is small enough to allow one to see everything on foot. For sightseers the major attractions here are the many totem poles. The intricately carved figures on the poles often convey themes in tribal history.

FRIDAY, AUGUST 7
Sitka, Alaska

It was foggy and rainy again today, but fortified with a breakfast of English muffins and reindeer sausage, we set off to see Sitka in more detail. Sitka National Historic Park, adjacent to the city, contains the site where the Russians defeated the Tlingit Indians in 1804. There are also nineteen very fine totem poles here. After lunch we toured Sheldon Jackson College with its president, Michael Kaelka. A highlight of the tour was seeing the room where Jim Michener researched his great book *Alaska*.

The college does a lot of fish research and currently they're running a project that puts 16 million salmon back into the bay here each year. Later we visited a Russian cemetery and what's left of old Baranof Castle, where the transfer of Alaska from Russia to the United States took place. Unfortunately, the Russian Orthodox church, St. Michael's Cathedral, was closed because most of their income comes from tourists and the cruise ship had just left town.

SATURDAY, AUGUST 8
Sitka, Alaska

We went out fishing this morning at 9:30 with two friends of Ollie and Millie: Fred Reeder, who owned the boat, and Steve Brenner. We caught a ten-pound silver salmon out on the ocean and some rock cod while trolling along the coast. That was about it. We weren't disappointed, though, because we saw so much wildlife: humpback whales, some seals swimming behind the boat, several bald eagles, and a variety of other creatures. And there was also the incredible beauty of the coast itself, even more stunning after the sun finally broke through today. We were overdue in returning all the hospitality Ollie and Millie have extended to us, so we took them to the Channel Club for dinner. It's reputed to be the best restaurant in Sitka. It's the only place I've ever eaten where the halibut tasted good to me; even the crab legs were outstanding. The beefsteak was about one and a half inches thick and legendary in these parts. We shared our choices.

SUNDAY, AUGUST 9
Sitka, Alaska

After so much rain and fog we were delighted to wake to a bright and clear day. It was so clear, in fact, we could even see Mount Edgecumbe, which is almost never without clouds. The flight north to Anchorage was spellbinding. We had snow-covered mountains and long, curving glaciers practically the whole way. Even at 27,000 feet, we could see the glacier calving off icebergs. In addition, we saw Glacier Bay, cruise boats, 18,000-foot Mount St. Elias, Valdez, the end of the pipeline, and, finally, Anchorage bathed in sunshine. I began another book on the airplane, Louis L'Amour's *Sitka*.

Archbishop Frank Hurley picked us up tonight and took us to an alumni get-together at the home of Leo and Beverly Walsh and their seven children, two of whom have graduated from Notre Dame. There were about fifty people at the party. Leo went far beyond the call as host, cooking up a wonderful batch of king salmon for the occasion. One of the guests was Wally Hickel, former Secretary of the Interior and governor of Alaska, who will be fishing with us tomorrow.

MONDAY, AUGUST 10
Anchorage, Alaska

We took off from Anchorage about 9 A.M., headed west, and descended through a thick overcast sky into the small settlement of King Salmon about an hour and forty-five minutes later. There we checked in with Pat and Carl Fundeen, a family we had stayed with seven years ago on a trip up here. We were on the river shortly after eleven. Our boat, with three of us fishing, caught eight king salmon before lunch. The largest (mine) weighed in at about thirty-five pounds. In the afternoon, we managed to double that catch. The other two boats did just as well.

Most of the salmon we caught weighed between twenty-five and forty pounds. These fish are exceptional fighters, making them great sport to catch. We had a couple of broken lines to prove it. We were back at the dock again around five. After that I traveled eleven miles with Archbishop Frank Hurley to the little town of Naknek, where he had four youngsters to confirm. The church held about thirty people and almost every one of them turned up for the house party that followed the confirmation. We rejoined the fishing party back at King Salmon, packed a couple of hundred pounds of salmon into the airplane, and took off back to Anchorage.

TUESDAY, AUGUST 11
Anchorage, Alaska

This morning I had an interview with an editor on the local Anchorage newspaper. Most of the questions concerned education and values in the other states, so it was familiar ground. Afterward I joined the rest of our group and we took a tour of Elmendorf Air Force Base, just north of Anchorage. Our guide was Father Roman Kaiser, head chaplain of the base and a diocesan priest from La Crosse, Wisconsin. We had a briefing on the role of the military in Alaska. They make up about 14 percent of the population and account for about $1.3 billion of the revenues coming into the state. The role of the base itself is to provide surveillance around the borders of Alaska, which is only about forty miles from Russia.

WEDNESDAY, AUGUST 12
Anchorage, Alaska

The overcast was very thick again today. We had to make an instrument landing in Nome, as bleak and primitive a place as I've ever seen. Many of the rough, ramshackle buildings looked as though they hadn't changed much since the gold rush. And the mud created by the heavy rain did nothing to enhance the look of the place. We hired a cab to give us a tour of the city and then up the beach where the native summer population lives. There we saw fish laid out to dry and sled dogs tied to the villagers' small huts.

Nome is the terminus of the famous annual Iditarod dog race, which has a first prize of $50,000. Lately it has been won by women, most particularly Sally Butcher, from Fairbanks. The recent dominance of women in this race has given rise to the saying: "In Nome, men are men and women win the race." Back in town we had cheeseburgers at Fat Freddie's. We suspected that the burgers were made from reindeer meat. On, Dancer! On, Prancer! Everything here is expensive. A chunk of whale blubber weighing a few pounds was priced at $12.50 in one of the local grocery stores. At the Nugget Hotel it costs $100 a night for a small room with two cots and unchanged linen. I guess everything is so expensive here because it has to be either floated in or flown in.

Nome represents the westernmost part of our trip. If we were to go much farther in that direction we'd rather quickly arrive in Russia. We heard that the weather today was slightly better in Kotzebue, which is northeast of here, so we decided to fly over there and take a look. Kotzebue is thirty-eight miles north of the Arctic Circle, so it easily qualified as the northernmost leg of our trip. When we arrived, we didn't see nearly as many people as we had in Nome, but the people we did see were practically all native Alaskans. In the trading post we visited, the oddest item we saw—and ate—was a frozen Eskimo Pie in the ice-cream cooler. But that wasn't nearly as interesting as the Eskimo woman who came in with her baby strapped to her back. She bought a small package of cigars, a large carton of disposable diapers, and three bottles of mascara with the appropriate brushes.

In the local museum we asked the native curator if he knew about Onion Portage on the Kobuk River. He said he didn't know too much about it, but there was a good book on it here and I could have it for $12.50. I was fresh out of books, so I bought it. It turned out to be *Ancient Men of the Arctic* by J. Louis Giddings of Brown University. It was from this very book that some twenty years ago I learned about Onion Portage and the long series of ancient humans who camped there during the spring and fall migration of animals. It had been recommended to me some twenty-five years ago by Father Ray Murray, a Holy Cross priest who lived across the hall from me at Notre Dame. I was asking him about the history of early man in America and he handed me this book, saying that he had done research up in that area and that Giddings was the best. I couldn't believe that I had stumbled across the same book here in Kotzebue, which is only a few miles from the Kobuk River and not much farther from Onion Portage. When we took off, I reread the chapter on Giddings's great discovery site, which is the touchstone for the study of prehistoric man in America.

Our final stop on this hopscotch airplane tour was Fairbanks. It's the second-largest city in the state, the end of the Trans-Alaskan Highway, the home of the University of Alaska, and the site of the second-largest Air Force base in Alaska. Fairbanks is quite small, although with its city population of 27,000 and a borough population of 75,000, it looms fairly large as Alaskan cities go. It has only 11 inches of rain each year and 70 inches of snowfall. Temperatures average 61 degrees in summer and 12 degrees in winter, but it can get much hotter as well as much colder. The records are 96 degrees in 1969 and 66 degrees below zero in 1934.

We ate at the Pump Restaurant tonight. On the way in we ran into Charles and Heather McCollough, Notre Dame class of 1963 and now living in Seattle. On the way out we met some South Carolinians who had connections with Ned's brother.

THURSDAY, AUGUST 13
Fairbanks, Alaska

Ned and I took a walk in the morning and bought five books at the nearby supermarket. One of mine was Anne Morrow Lindbergh's *North to the Orient*, about a flight she made with her husband in pioneering the Pan Am route to Japan and China. They refueled in Nome because Kotzebue was still icebound in June. After lunch we boarded the *Discovery III*, a stern-wheeler that's 156 feet long and 34 feet wide, yet draws only three feet of water. We went down the Chena River to an Athabaskan Indian village. The Athabaskans are one of three native American groups in Alaska, the others being the Eskimos, who mainly inhabit the northern section of the state above the Arctic Circle, and the Aleuts, who primarily inhabit the long chain of Aleutian islands arching toward Japan.

The Athabaskans were originally migrant hunters who ranged all over the central and eastern part of the state. Some of them got down as far as the western shore of Hudson Bay through Alberta and British Columbia, and others, now called the Navajo and Apache, ranged as far south as New Mexico and Arizona. Navajos sent up here by the U.S. Army during World War II discovered that they could converse in their native language with the Athabaskans.

Our guide, a young woman, showed us what life in an early Athabaskan village would have been like: the huts they lived in, the kinds of furs they trapped and traded and how they tanned the hides, the way they smoked their salmon, and how they made their clothing. Some of the Athabaskans were still following the old ways. We also had the pleasure of meeting Mary Shields, the first woman to participate and complete the Iditarod race from Anchorage to Nome. Mary introduced us to her team of seven dogs, and then had them pull a sled through a path in the woods. It's easier on snow.

FRIDAY, AUGUST 14
Fairbanks, Alaska

We had a good visit this morning in the office of Pat O'Rourke, chancellor of the University of Alaska. Most of the conversation dealt with student and faculty concerns and budgets. They've had their budget cut 30 percent in the last two years because of adverse economic conditions in the state. Next we talked to Paul McCarthy, the university's librarian. He took us around to all of the various special collections. The library is about a third the size of ours, but has excellent collections on the Arctic and Alaska, and many of the librarians in the special collections have anthropological backgrounds. We had some fascinating conversations with them about the origin of the species here and the many languages and cultures. As we were leaving, they gave us a wonderful map that showed where each language was spoken.

Our next stop was the Geophysics Center, where we were greeted by Larry Sweet and Bill Seckinger, who did his undergraduate physics with Bernie Waldman at Notre Dame, then took a Ph.D. in electrical engineering from Cornell. He is now specializing in the study of ice up here and doing some very interesting work. Larry showed us a marvelous movie of the aurora borealis, or in popular terms the northern lights. We also toured the seismological laboratory.

From there, we went to the new museum, a marvelous collection of anthropological, geological, and cultural artifacts about Alaska, including the pipeline. There are two great hits in this show. One is the enormous stuffed brown bear at the entrance and the second is Blue Babe, a small bison killed by lions north of here 36,000 years ago. Right after being killed and partially eaten, the bison was covered by mud and caught up in the permafrost, where it froze solid and is beautifully preserved. We could even see the marks of the lion's claws across its back. The skin looks as though it were preserved from yesterday.

We had lunch at Pat O'Rourke's house, where we met Frank Lloyd and Jack Tegis, young Army officers who had studied at Notre Dame and were now working in the Medical department at nearby Fort Wainwright. We also met Rick Schafer, who just resigned as the University of Alaska's hockey coach to coach hockey at Notre Dame, and Don Lucia, who played hockey for Notre Dame and is replacing Rick as coach of the University of Alaska team. We wished them both well.

Dan Walsh picked us up after lunch and drove us ten miles out into the country to visit the permafrost tunnel, a research project of the university and the Army. The first thing we saw upon entering it was a 36,000-year-old bone that had been frozen into the side of the tunnel. Elsewhere we saw an ice tunnel with wonderfully sparkling crystals hanging from the ceiling. Tonight we took all our hosts to dinner at the Ranch Restaurant. Almost everyone had halibut, which, as always, was delicious. I opted for lamb chops.

SATURDAY, AUGUST 15
Fairbanks, Alaska

Fifty-two years ago today, I received the religious habit of the Congregation of Holy Cross. I thanked God for it this morning at Mass. Then it was off to Juneau. After a two-and-one-half-hour flight and a tricky instrument approach, we landed, rented a car, and checked in at the Baranof Hotel. Juneau, the capital of Alaska, sits snugly against the mountains just off the sea. To the north is the great Mendenhall Glacier. One gets a good look at it while coming into the airport. The weather is really terrible here: rain almost every day and fog and cloudiness the usual fare. However, it has a certain aura of rugged frontier about it. Frank Hurley used to be bishop here. He had to fly himself more than 1,500 hours in float planes just to get around to see his flock. It's a little easier now in Anchorage, where he now has a two-engine plane. And it's much safer.

Our main reason for coming here was to board the *Glacier Express* for a six-hour cruise to the Tracy Arm Fjord. There were icebergs all the way and, at the end of the fjord, two glaciers—Sawyer North and Sawyer South. They were about 500 yards across and about 200 feet high, with bright blue shimmering ice that continually calved off, sending new icebergs at us. Additional entertainment was provided by seals frolicking in the chill waters, oblivious to the icebergs and safe from the killer whales that stalk them in the ocean. We had a buffet dinner on the boat and arrived back at the dock about 10 P.M.

SUNDAY, AUGUST 16
Juneau, Alaska

Fifty-one years ago today, I made my first religious vows in the Congregation of Holy Cross at Rolling Prairie, Indiana, where our novitiate was then located. Ned made his on the same date, though a few years later. The father of our pilot, Ted Byron, died ten years ago today, so we offered a special Mass for him too. Then it was off to Portland, Oregon, where we had left our RV and Chevy three weeks ago. Thanks to a brisk tail wind, our average ground speed was 310 miles an hour. We made it in three hours and twenty minutes. We drove directly to the University of Portland, where Dave Sherrer graciously put us in the Villa. The Lindy and the Chevy both started up right away. We were ready for the final leg of our journey.

It's great to get back in the land of sunshine and a bit of warmth. Alaska is a fantastic place to visit, but, as the saying goes, I wouldn't want to live there. Tremendous beauty, but too much darkness, too much rain, and too much cold. But it was a wonderful trip, thanks in large measure to Ollie and Millie, who were marvelous traveling companions, as was Ted. Nor would such a tour of Alaska have been possible without the convenience of their airplane. We owe them a great debt of gratitude, a small part of which we repaid this evening by taking them to dinner.

MONDAY, AUGUST 17
Portland, Oregon

Before leaving, we computed our mileage since leaving South Bend in June. We had put 4,125 miles on the Lindy, 3,732 on the Chevy, and 6,634 on Ollie's airplane. Total: 14,491. And now we were off again, this time heading eastward via the scenic route back to Notre Dame. We crossed over the Coast Range to Tillamook, then headed south along the Pacific coast on Highway 101. For scenery we had pine forests, mountains, and a coastline that presented both sandy beaches and jagged rocks. We checked into a campground at Coos Bay, cooked up a quick dinner, took a walk, and went to bed.

TUESDAY, AUGUST 18
Coos Bay, Oregon

We decided to see Crater Lake today. But first we had a considerable amount of housekeeping to do. Job No. 1 was cleaning up the freezer. When we were back for the Olympics, one of our cheese dips—which we hadn't known was in there—had melted all over the inside of it. Next we flushed out our water tank and put in forty gallons of fresh water. Then we figured out how to light the pilot light for the stove, which, thanks to the microwave and lots of meals out, we'd rarely used. Finally, we picked up some groceries and were off across the Coast Range again. On arrival at a Kampgrounds of America (KOA), where we usually stayed, not far from Crater Lake, we whipped up a quick lunch, unhitched the Chevy, and headed northeast to the lake.

Crater Lake was born 6,840 years ago when Mount Mazama blew its top. It spread volcanic ash twelve inches deep all the way to Idaho and covered much of Montana with another six inches. The resultant crater was 4,000 feet deep and six miles wide. Gradually, over the next 700 to 1,500 years, it began to fill up with snow and rainfall. Today it is the deepest lake in America, which accounts for its marvelous blue color. The top of the crater now is slightly over 6,000 feet high, about half of what it was before the eruption. We drove the beautiful thirty-three-mile rim road, which goes all the way around the lake, dipping through pine forests and presenting spectacular views. Back at the campground we discussed what route we would take to visit Millard Sheets and his wife, Mary, in northern California. Millard did the marvelous "Christ the Teacher" granite mosaic on the front of our library almost twenty-five years ago. Ned has kept in touch with him over the years, and to a lesser extent, so have I.

WEDNESDAY, AUGUST 19
Crater Lake, Oregon

We decided this morning after Mass and breakfast that rather than go down the easy way on Interstate 5, a four-lane highway, we would cut back across the Coast Range again so that we could see the northern California coast and Redwood National Park. It meant a lot of twisting and turning, two days' travel instead of one, but the beauty we saw was well worth the extra time and effort. We saw redwoods that have existed since the time of Christ. Some of them soar to more than 300 feet. The largest topped out at 378 feet. To give some idea of their size, they would tower 100 feet above the Statue of Liberty, or more than 150 feet above the fourteen-story Notre Dame library. When you see an entire forest of them, the experience reminds you of walking through a great Gothic cathedral.

We pulled into an RV campground in Eureka, California, then

visited a grocery store, where we bought noodles, spaghetti, spaghetti sauce, mushrooms, oil, Parmesan cheese, and a bottle of California Burgundy. All told, we spent $11. Armed with these ingredients, but still mostly innocent of true cooking, I nevertheless managed to bring off a better than average Italian dinner, if I do say so myself. And we still had enough spaghetti and noodles left for several more meals.

THURSDAY, AUGUST 20
Eureka, California

We were off after ten this morning, barreling down 101, the north-south coastal highway that we have been on so many times during the past few days. We detoured through the Avenue of the Giants, a twenty-mile stretch of redwood forest paralleling the highway. We had Beethoven's Pastoral Symphony on the tape player, a perfect accompaniment to the beauty of the redwood forest.

Two hundred and some miles after leaving Eureka this morning, we arrived in Gualala, California, where we were warmly received by Millard and Mary Sheets, their son, David, and David's wife, Susan. I wish I could give some sense of this house. Perched on a high cliff, it overlooks the rocky coast and a spectacular rockbound island that always seemed to be kicking up salt spray. Millard found the location back in the 1930s. When he saw it, he knew instantly that this was where he would spend the rest of his life. He named it Barking Rocks in honor of the noisy sea lions who inhabit the island. Inside, Millard and Mary have created a vast international art gallery with exquisite works from China, Japan, Mexico, and many other countries.

Now a word about the stunning mural Millard executed on the face of our library. With a height of 125 feet and a width of 60 feet, it is probably the largest granite mural in the world. It contains granite in ninety different colors from all over the world. Skeptics said that the mural would not last for more than ten years without major repairs, but it's been there more than twice that long and we haven't had to do a thing to it. Millard and Mary took us to dinner at a place called St. Orre's, a spectacular gourmet restaurant known throughout the United States, and Europe as well.

FRIDAY, AUGUST 21
Gualala, California

Today we were privileged to visit Millard's own museum. Among other things, it contains about thirty of his watercolors. He had recently sold a large number of them to a collector. I had the impression that he was sorry to see them go.

About noontime, we found that we had to detach the Chevy and the Kaddy Kar so that we could back up the Lindy and get out of the parking place behind Millard's house. The Kaddy Kar was really ornery today. Ned wound up with a bloody finger—not his first, I might add—while wrestling with this contraption. Unfortunately, this wasn't the end of our troubles. While we were driving out, Millard's security gate shut too fast, banged into the wheel of the Kaddy Kar, and then crunched the fender into the tire and broke one of our signal lights. We pried the fender loose, then discovered that the gate was off its track. It weighed a ton, but the two of us finally managed to wrestle it back into place.

After that unpropitious start, we resumed our southward journey on the coastal highway. This proved to be the most spectacular part of it because the Coast Range comes right down to the ocean. It's more than a little hair-raising because the narrow highway snakes along the flanks of the mountains and there is nothing, not even a guardrail, between you and the ocean, 1,500 feet below. I think this makes five times in five days that we've crossed the Coast Range. I'm wondering if we qualify for an entry in *The Guinness Book of World Records*.

We rejoined Highway 101 at Santa Rosa and crossed the Richmond Bridge over the bay into Oakland at exactly 4:30 P.M., just in time for the evening rush hour. There were six exits into Livermore, where we planned to stay at a Holiday Inn. Miraculously, we picked the right one. We talked to our secretaries back at Notre Dame, Helen and Pat, today. They both sounded just great—perhaps because we're gone and for the first time in thirty-five years they haven't had to worry about getting football tickets for our special friends.

SATURDAY, AUGUST 22
Livermore, California

We had hoped to go to Los Angeles today and spend the weekend with my brother Jim and his wife, Mary, but when I called, their house sitter said they were on a retreat up north. We decided to push on. For the first time since leaving South Bend on June 11, we would be turning the RV east to begin the long trek home.

Highway 5 runs almost straight as an arrow, a nice change from yesterday's steep grades and hairpin turns. On the downside, the green, fresh-smelling pines have been replaced by rolling hills, all very brown except where brush fires had turned them black. The winds were surprisingly strong. We noticed a lot of windmills on the hilltops, where conservation-conscious Californians were generating electricity. Soon we were passing the rich agricultural lands of the San Joaquin Valley with its truck farms and orchards.

On the other side of the Tehachapi Pass, agriculture disappeared, to be replaced by cacti and sagebrush. We stopped for gas at a station near Edwards Air Force Base, where the space shuttle lands. An attendant told us that the sonic booms are so powerful that they shake the earth here, but he seemed to be proud to have this part of the space program in such close proximity. Few places are better suited for it than this flat, dry lake bed. It extends for miles in all directions and has been used to land experimental aircraft for many years. After Mojave and Barstow, it was really a moonscape all the way to Needles. One range of the low-lying mountains was called Diablo, the other the Devils Playground. Same idea, different languages. At 6:30 P.M., we rolled into the KOA camp in Needles. We drove 507 miles today, our longest day on the road. Each of us took three shifts, and we made six pit stops.

Needles is generally the hottest place in the United States, and tonight is no exception. The temperature was over 100 earlier today and I don't think it's dropped much this evening. There's not even a hint of a breeze. Tonight's dinner was a simple BLT on toast.

SUNDAY, AUGUST 23
Needles, California

While picking up some fuel in Needles, we discovered that the tread on one of the two tires on our Kaddy Kar was almost down to the lining. On examination, the other one was not that much better. Had one of those tires blown out at 65 miles per hour, there was no telling where the Chevy might have ended up, or the two of us in the RV either, for that matter. We bought new tires on the spot. An hour and a quarter later, we were on the road again and the desert was soon slipping away behind us as the Rockies loomed ahead.

Our host at the Grand Canyon was to be Father Dutch O'Connor, a member of the Holy Cross Community and a classmate of Ned's. Dutch is pastor of the local parish, El Cristo Rey. He ministers to 1,200 permanent residents here and thousands of tourists every summer. We had a great reunion with much retelling of war stories from yesteryear.

MONDAY, AUGUST 24
Grand Canyon, Arizona

This morning we concelebrated with Dutch, dedicating the Mass to his brother, who died recently. Then we set out to see the Grand Canyon, both of us for the second time. Ned had been here fifty years ago with his family. I came here in 1949 to recover from my first fall as Notre Dame's executive vice president.

The canyon was millions of years in the making, as the Kaibab Plateau rose slowly upward and the Colorado River cut downward. Though I had been here before, I was still awestruck by the grandeur and immensity of the canyon. It stretches for 250 miles. It is a mile deep and eleven miles across at its widest point. Winston Churchill on seeing it for the first time opined that it would be a great place to throw used razor blades.

From our first vantage point near the lodge, we could see a long string of mules making their way along the narrow trail 2,000 feet below us. We walked down the same trail for about half an hour, then came back up, grabbed a quick bite, and boarded a small bus for a look at several points along the South Rim.

At night we saw a movie that was shot from an airplane as it flew through the canyon. You couldn't have seen the canyon better if you'd been a bald eagle. We took Dutch to dinner at the Red Feather Lodge in Tusayan. Actually, the owners, Frank and Hannah Rotter, who came here from Germany, took us all. When we tried to pick up the tab they refused to take our money.

TUESDAY, AUGUST 25
Grand Canyon, Arizona

On our way east we stopped for another look at the canyon at Desert View, twenty miles from the town of Grand Canyon. Not too many miles later we entered the Navajo Reservation, which covers a sizable chunk of northern Arizona. The Navajo are about 200,000 strong. They account for 25 percent of all American Indians in the country, and close to half of those who live on reservations. We stopped at a Navajo-run shop in Cameron and picked up a few items made of turquoise and silver. I bought a pendant for Helen, my secretary, and a bolo tie for myself.

About one o'clock, we pulled into Tuba City and found the home of Dr. Edward Kompare, Notre Dame class of 1961 and an internist at the Indian hospital here. He had written us before we left, volunteering to spend a day showing us the Navajo way of life. We had lunch with Ed and his wife, Maria, a St. Mary's graduate, then checked into the Tuba City Motel, parking our rig in the local Catholic churchyard. We then drove to a Hopi village.

The Hopi live in close proximity to the Navajo. In fact, their reservation is entirely surrounded by the Navajo reservation. The homes in the more traditional section of the village were small and run-down for the most part. Most had no electricity, running water, or sewerage. The people we visited were old, but they were getting good medical care because of the presence of people like Ed and the other doctors and nurses at the hospital.

We then went out into the desert and saw the footprints of dinosaurs on the petrified floor of an ancient swamp. Farther on, we retraced a part of the Mormon Trail that ran between Salt Lake City and Phoenix. Along the way, we visited a Mormon trading post that dated back to the 1860s and Inscription Rock, carved with figures by the Indians who passed by here on their way to the Grand Canyon to get salt.

We had dinner tonight at the Kompare home with Ed, Maria, two of their four children, a Franciscan priest, Father Damien, Dr. Jim Grabman and his wife, Paula, Ellen Jackson, a registered nurse, and her daughter Tori, who are Navajos, and Mia Sarokas, an exchange student from Finland who was living with the Kompares. Father Damien said he had spent all of his priestly years here working with the Navajos. He also said he was still having trouble with the language, which all agreed is extremely difficult. Naturally, most of the conversation was about Navajo life, culture, language, and religion. So far, the Navajos have been able to preserve these things pretty well, although everyone at the table said that language proficiency was beginning to wane among younger Navajos.

The key person in the culture and religion departments is the medicine man. Even though modern medical treatment is available at the hospital, Navajos will pay a visit to their medicine man, which, according to Ed, often seems to give them a boost. He and his colleagues don't care who gets the credit so long as the patient gets well. Needless to say, I was very proud to see a Notre Dame man playing such a necessary humanitarian role here.

WEDNESDAY, AUGUST 26
Tuba City, Arizona

Ed picked us up and brought us back to his place, where we had Mass and blessed the house. Before beginning our morning tour we stopped at the hospital, where Ed proudly showed us the dialysis section. The eleven dialysis machines keep over thirty patients alive. Then Ed and Maria took us to the Navajo National Monument, three large and remarkable cliff dwellings. The one we visited was called Tetaken. It reminded us of one of the cliff dwellings we had seen at Mesa Verde, and they were, in fact, inhabited by the Anasazi at one time.

Next we drove east to Monument Valley, a spectacular collection of large monolithic formations. We had a tailgate lunch in the shadow of one of them, then continued our tour, which totaled about sixty miles. When we had completed our circuit, we thanked Ed and Maria for their hospitality and headed for Farmington, New Mexico. Once again we were lucky. When we checked in at the Holiday Inn we got the last two rooms.

THURSDAY, AUGUST 27
Farmington, New Mexico

We originally planned to visit Taos and Santa Fe, but since we had both visited them before, we bypassed them in order to spend more time with Tony and Martha Potenziani at their ranch near Albuquerque. Sagebrush stretched out as far as the eye could see as we left Farmington, and in the far distance we could make out buttes of various shapes and sizes. Gradually the sage was replaced with pinyon pines, then ponderosas. We put Mozart, Beethoven, and Chopin on the tape player as we sped along, the billowing cumulus clouds drifting along with us like huge balloons.

Tony and Martha Potenziani, their daughter Kathy, and their son Frank, also a Notre Dame alumnus, gave us a warm and enthusiastic welcome. We had a wonderful dinner and the conversation lasted long into the night. They're a great Notre Dame family, who have supported the university in many ways.

FRIDAY, AUGUST 28
Albuquerque, New Mexico

After a breakfast of pancakes and fruit, courtesy of Martha, we followed Tony on a tour of the ranch, where he raises Hereford cows and bulls. Homesteaders came here after the Civil War. They found life in this dry climate very hard, and it didn't get much better as the years rolled on, particularly during the dust bowl era of the 1920s and 1930s.

Irrigation is now considered a necessity. Tony has wells that go down 280 feet. After lunch he took us up in the hills and showed us a log cabin that's more than a hundred years old. He hopes to acquire and refurbish it. We had Mass at 4:30 P.M., then drove to the town of Estancia, where we had a delicious salmon dinner at a restaurant called the Olde Co-op. Tonight it was more festive than usual because the Bean Queen of the Year was being chosen as part of the annual Pinto Bean Festival.

It was very fortunate for us that we stopped here when we did. Yesterday the step we use to get in and out of the Lindy tore completely loose. I don't know where we could have had it repaired, but here we had nothing to worry about, thanks to Allen Brandon, the Potenzianis' gifted maintenance man. He had the step repaired in no time. More importantly, he also discovered a long crack in the left wheel support of the Kaddy Kar. A few bumps and it would have broken through completely and we'd have lost a wheel. If we'd been on an interstate, there surely would have been a serious accident. After welding the crack, he found that the Kaddy Kar's wheels were seriously out of alignment and that one of the tires was overinflated by twelve pounds. He took care of those problems too. Thank God for Allen Brandon.

SATURDAY, AUGUST 29
Albuquerque, New Mexico

We were up at 7 A.M., had Mass and breakfast with the family, and were on our way by nine. The whole area was shrouded in fog, but it lifted by the time we had driven the twenty miles to get on Interstate 40. This was the homestretch. We would be on interstates the rest of the way; there would be no more national parks and national forests. Just 1,400 miles between us and Notre Dame. Not that we're in a big hurry to leave this beautiful part of the planet. I have visited about 145 countries on earth and have seen most of the natural wonders of the world. But I can say in all honesty that there is no collection of natural beauty in the world that can rival the western United States, particularly the great national parks and forests.

Because our main objective now was simply to get home in the least amount of time, we made only three stops before pulling into Oklahoma City for the night. Since leaving the ranch we had driven 518 miles and changed drivers six times, which helped to keep us fresh and alert.

SUNDAY, AUGUST 30
Oklahoma City, Oklahoma

We took Interstate 44 from Oklahoma City to Tulsa, then across the rest of Oklahoma to Joplin, Missouri, then across all of Missouri to St. Louis. We had planned to stay in St. Louis, but we decided to press on to Vandalia, Illinois, about eighty miles east. Now I was beginning to understand that old cliché about horses heading for the barn. Today we made five pit stops and rolled up 583 miles, breaking our record of yesterday. The KOA campground we stopped at will be our last. We have only 300 miles to go.

MONDAY, AUGUST 31
Vandalia, Illinois

On this, our last day of the journey, we were up before the sun. We said Mass and thanked God for delivering us safely over these many miles. Then we had a breakfast of juice, coffee, and English muffins, filled the tank, and were off.

It was a perfect day with a bright blue sky. Ned took the first shift, which brought us across the Indiana border. I drove through Indianapolis to Kokomo, where we had lunch. We had only 100 miles to go and Ned took over again. I thought it only appropriate that he drive the last segment to Notre Dame, since he was at the wheel when we left the campus on that long ago day in June.

As we rolled into Notre Dame, I did some final figuring and a quick review. We had traveled 7,876 miles in the Lindy and 3,732 in the Chevy, for a total of 11,608 miles on the road. We flew 6,634 miles in Ollie Cunningham's airplane, which brought our grand total, land and air, to 18,242 miles. We had, indeed, traveled beyond Gary.

We visited seventeen national parks and twenty-nine national forests. We drove through parts of eighteen states and missed only three west of the Missouri River—North Dakota, Kansas, and Nevada. We were guests of fourteen Notre Dame families and would gladly have been guests of many more if we'd had the time. We cooked the majority of the meals we ate and managed to lose ten pounds each, a welcome fringe benefit. We had amazingly few problems with the Lindy—a tribute more to it than to us—and managed to bring it back without a scratch. And after spending forty-four years in clerical garb we never donned a collar or a black suit once.

And so ends the first segment of our sabbatical year. We will always remember with affection the Lindy and the Chevy, and all the wonderful places they enabled us to see. We saw America at its very best. We may have bored you with all the Notre Dame connections, but that is our family wherever we go. We'll always be grateful to those who made our journey possible—the benefactors who helped finance the trip, our wonderful hosts and hostesses along the way, and, certainly not least, Art Decio for furnishing our magic carpet, the incomparable Lindy.

Part II

Latin America

I had visited the countries of Latin America often, but had not made a complete swing through them since 1956. On that occasion I was traveling with Doc Kenna, who was then Provincial of the Indiana Province of Holy Cross. I knew that a great many changes had taken place since my last visit, and I wanted to share them with Ned, who had traveled relatively little in this part of the world. I wanted him to see it all: the great cities of Bogotá, Rio, Santiago, and Buenos Aires; the lost city of the Incas, Machu Picchu; the mighty Amazon, with ten tributaries that each carry more water than the Mississippi; Patagonia, with its treacherous Strait of Magellan; and as they say in the advertisements, much, much more.

I had one other reason for wanting to take this trip. My Spanish had become very rusty. This would be a marvelous opportunity to recover some fluency, as well as to have a month in Brazil, where Portuguese is spoken. Also, Ned and I both have many Holy Cross friends in Chile, where the Community has worked for the past forty years. Finally, we had many dear alumni friends in these countries.

Our brief stay back at Notre Dame passed quickly. We had to unpack and repack for a different kind of journey. The mail on our return was mountain-high and had to be answered too.

Joan Kroc, the widow of the founder of McDonald's hamburger chain, stopped by for her first Notre Dame football game, a home opener in which we beat Michigan State. She had given us $6 million for a program in international peace studies (now named after her),

83

and I took the opportunity to have her visit with our young peace students from the U.S.S.R., China, Japan, England, France, India, and many other countries. Eppie Lederer (Ann Landers) joined us for this discussion, which was followed by a meeting with faculty members of the Peace Institute and the Kellogg Institute, the latter a research organization concentrating on Latin America. Before she left, at her request we discussed a possible international studies building. She was negative at first, but called from San Diego the next day to offer another $6 million for the building, on the condition it be named after me. I protested, but she won.

It was time to leave again. We were eager and ready for the next adventure.

SUNDAY, SEPTEMBER 27
Chicago, Illinois

Our trip actually began yesterday. We watched the Notre Dame–Purdue football game, which Notre Dame won, then left immediately for Chicago and checked into the O'Hare Hilton. We were up about dawn, offered Mass together, then walked to the Mexicana counter, where we discovered that our 9:15 flight to Mexico City was an hour and a half late. We finally took off at 10:50 A.M.

The flight was uneventful, and we were greeted in the crowded Mexico City airport by Juan Cintrón, who was to be our guide in the Mexican capital, and by Patsy León and her husband, part of a Notre Dame family in Mexico City. They had their young son with them, and Patsy was very pregnant with their second child. I gave her my special blessing for pregnant women, a practice I started in the late 1940s when I was chaplain to the married students at Notre Dame.

Juan and his wife, Linda, drove us into town, where we checked into the Crown Plaza Hotel, part of the Holiday Inn chain. We did a quick washup, then rejoined Juan and Linda in the lobby to begin a tour of the city. Our first stop was the Museum of History and Anthropology, one of the great museums in the world. There we were joined by another alumnus, Bill Dellekamp, and his wife, Yolanda. For the next hour and a half we traced the cultural history of Mexico for some 2,000 years before Christ up to the time of the Conquest in 1521.

After the museum tour, we joined a Notre Dame alumni group for coffee at Sanborn's, a landmark restaurant here. Next we took a walking tour that included Madero Street, with its wonderful old houses and the Zócalo, or main square, with its magnificent cathedral and the National Palace.

It was dark by the time we finished, so we boarded a rubber-tired subway car, getting off near the century-old Café Catuba, where we had a traditional Mexican dinner. After dinner, the Dellekamps, the Cintróns, and Ned and I went to the Ballet Folklórico, an essential attraction on any visit to Mexico City. It provides great insight into Mexican culture, music, and dance.

MONDAY, SEPTEMBER 28
Mexico City, Mexico

We were up early for a breakfast meeting with some top government officials to discuss the economic situation in Mexico and in Latin America generally. We were greeted by Gerardo Turrubiate, a Notre Dame Ph.D. in economics, and four other bright, young Ph.D.s. Our conversation ranged over a wide variety of business and economic matters, but mainly focused on the enormous debt faced by countries such as Mexico, Brazil, Argentina, Chile, and Peru. These countries pay about $40 billion a year in interest alone to the richest countries in the world. So great are their interest payments, they have nothing left to pay toward the principal. The payments eat up most of the income they have from exports, which really should be plowed back into the development of the country, and the result is that their economic growth is retarded. It's Catch-22. We discussed a wide variety of possible solutions and agreed that none of them was perfect. But one has to be found if these countries are to enjoy normal economic growth and establish and maintain their financial credit.

From this meeting, we went to another one across the street where about twenty business leaders had been convened by Julio Serrano Segovia, a wealthy businessman and our new host. Among those who attended the meeting were two distinguished Notre Dame alumni, Alejandro Rodríguez, a banker, and Martín Ricoy, head of Campbell's Soup in Mexico. Again, we discussed a very wide range of subjects. Many of those that I introduced came from *The Humane Imperative*, a book I wrote about the problems that we'll carry with us into the next millennium. It was a lively discussion, and while we didn't find a lot of clear answers, we certainly raised a lot of good questions. We also put in a few good words about corporate support of education and told them a little bit about the Business-Higher Education Forum, which I chaired for two years. The forum brings business leaders and educators together to make common cause against problems they must face together.

Following this meeting we visited the Iberoamericana University. This Jesuit university hosts our students each year in Mexico City. The new campus is extremely attractive, and the new buildings, costing about $15 million, are spectacular. After lunch and a tour, we met with a group of private educators. I spoke in Spanish in deference to the Mexican participants who didn't understand English. It had been some time since I had given an impromptu speech in that language. It was not a great performance, but I got through it and they seemed to understand and enjoy the message—despite the fact that a thunderstorm struck right as I began to speak. All the while, the lights flickered on and off to the accompaniment of thunder and lightning and rain beating against the windows.

The conference ended about 6:30 P.M., but it took us another hour and a half to make our way through the storm into town. En route, we encountered a fire, an accident, and a protest demonstration. We arrived back at the Crown Plaza just in time to wash up and head for the University Club and a reception attended by 150 alumni and eight Notre Dame students who were studying in Mexico City. This is one of our best alumni clubs in Latin America. By the time we got home and went to bed, it was well past midnight. Obviously sleep is not going to be a top priority on this trip.

TUESDAY, SEPTEMBER 29
Mexico City, Mexico

We got up at 4:45 A.M., endured a hassle at the main desk over our Holiday Inn credit card, then jumped into a taxi in the middle of a rainstorm. After traveling only one block, the cab broke down.

Fortunately, another came by and we arrived at the airport just in time to catch our flight to Veracruz.

It was a spectacular flight. Our pilot flew us right past the two great peaks that dominate Mexico City, Popocatepetl (Popo for short) and Ixtacihuatl (Ixti for short). We've never flown so close to a mountain as we did to Popo's volcanic snowcapped peak, and I thought we were actually going to land on Ixti. What it took Cortez the better part of a few weeks to traverse, we did in forty-five minutes.

Though it was quite chilly when we left Mexico City, it was hot and humid here on the coast. We toured the city of Veracruz on foot, including a couple of hours at the cultural center.

This city was for a time the capital of Mexico, and has been a major port for many years. Hernando Cortez landed at Veracruz in 1521, and crossed the country to Mexico City. He managed to conquer the country with a mere 400 soldiers, plus a few friendly natives who took a dim view of the government of Montezuma in Mexico City. The American Army also landed here during the Mexican-American War. Historically, anyone who wanted to invade Mexico headed this way because to capture this port was, in a sense, to capture the vital resources of Mexico, most of which came from import taxes levied here.

We walked through the old fort, which once protected the city against pirates and other invaders. It also served as the prison for the whole country. It wasn't exactly a pleasant place to visit, but the buildings are classic in design and the fort looks like something right out of Vauban, the famous French designer of ports and fortresses.

Juan Cintrón had his car driven down here to save us the drive, so we all climbed aboard around noon and headed west along Cortez's route. Our first stop was the place where he anchored his ships on his arrival here. Then we continued on to Jalapa, a classic Mexican town, very clean and very historic. After a typical two-and-one-half-hour Mexican lunch, we visited what has to be one of the most spectacular new museums of the world, the Museo de Jalapa, designed by the famous American architect Edward Durrell Stone. It has about 30,000 items from the three classic cultures of this area—Olmeca, Totonaca, and Huasteca. These cultures originated about 2,000 years before Christ and are enormously important in the history and culture of the Americas. It is difficult to describe the beauty of this museum, the care with which all of these remarkable objects are displayed, and the finesse with which this whole collection is assembled and arranged. The curator and his assistants were awaiting us on our arrival, even though the museum had closed an hour and a half before. They treated us to a two-hour tour and then presented us with marvelous books as mementos of our visit.

Ned and I were touched again and again by the marvelous courtesy and hospitality of these old and new friends. This segment of our trip was arranged by Fernando Sepúlveda, a 1976 graduate of our MBA program.

Following the museum tour, we visited the university and then, as darkness gathered, toured the town, the restoration of which reveals much of its ancient culture and architecture.

By the time we finished, it was dark, and we had a long drive to Puebla. It was raining hard and the road was crowded with trucks. We arrived at El Mesón del Angel, the Inn of the Angel, at 11 P.M., just in time to celebrate Mass. Again, it was a long day.

WEDNESDAY, SEPTEMBER 30
Puebla, Mexico

Bill and Yolanda Dellekamp and Juan Cintrón joined us for Mass, and we all had breakfast with Dr. Sabino Lleno, Director of National Monuments in the state of Puebla, who would be our guide for the day. Once again, courtesy of the local alumni, we were getting a private tour by the ranking official.

During breakfast I visited with another group in the dining room who were celebrating an anniversary of the Puebla project of the Rockefeller Foundation. I had inspected the project several years ago as chairman of the foundation. It's one of the best agricultural projects in the history of Mexico, having greatly increased the production of corn, beans, and wheat throughout the country, but especially in the state of Puebla. The President of Mexico at that time, López Portillo, had told me that he would like to see similar projects established in all the Mexican states. However, he never did it.

Puebla is an extremely clean, bright, orderly city filled with churches. Fittingly, we began our tour by visiting the great cathedral here. Although it is a beautiful building, I was saddened to note that you can't see the altar, because the entire middle of this magnificent church is taken up by a choir. This kind of layout symbolizes the attitude of the time the cathedral was built, which held that the Church was primarily the bishop and the clergy. The laity were almost incidental. The massive front door of the church was only used when the bishop went in or was carried out in death. Others had to enter by the side doors.

Now, of course, all of that has changed. The Church is seen as the People of God, not just as the special domain of bishops and priests. The monarchical model has given way to the familial. The result is a much better Church. But I cannot lay the blame for the church's architecture on the Mexicans; one sees the same architectural monstrosities in all of the great cathedrals of Spain.

We saw several other churches and learned a good deal about a rather remarkable bishop here by the name of Juan de Palafox de Mendoza. He arrived here on July 22, 1640, riding on a mule and carrying secret orders from the king of Spain to pass judgment on the viceroy of Mexico. Shortly after arriving, he went to Mexico, fired the viceroy, and appointed himself viceroy. Next he appointed himself bishop not only of Puebla but of all Mexico. Immediately he moved to curb the enormous power of the religious orders—Jesuits, Franciscans, and Dominicans. He made himself head of the armed forces and generally revamped the country from top to bottom. Some wags say that his power resembled that of the extemely powerful Mexican Presidents of modern times.

After Palafox finished his work in Mexico City, he returned to Puebla, where he built this cathedral and established an enormous seminary. We visited his library. It contains 40,000 books, many of which I would love to see in our library at Notre Dame. It's a fantastic collection.

Our next stop was the nearby town of Cholula and its huge pyramid. Actually, it's two pyramids, because the last one was built upon the first one and greatly enlarged. The pyramid was dedicated to the Aztec god Quetzalcoatl. Next, the Spaniards came along and, in an attempt to obliterate the indigenous culture, buried the pyramid under 125 meters of soil. Then they built a large church on top. Thanks to long tunnels carved by archaeologists, we were able to explore far into the interior of the original pyramid, which contained mosaics that were created centuries before the time of Christ.

After the pyramid tour and a quick look at Cholula, we had a long Mexican lunch with the chief archaeologist, who plugged some of the gaps in our knowledge of Cortez. It was a marvelous chronicle and made me determined to reread Bernal Díaz's chronicle of the Conquest, *Historia Verdadera de la Conquista de la Neuva España.*

This evening we drove to Cuernavaca and checked into Las Manzanitas, a beautiful inn known for its exceptional food and lodgings, as well as for the brightly plumed peacocks that strut across its spacious grounds.

THURSDAY, OCTOBER 1
Cuernavaca, Mexico

Juan and Linda picked us up at ten o'clock in the morning and we drove through the hills to a wonderful series of temples called Xochicalco. They're almost as large as Monte Albán outside of Oaxaca. The temples stretched over an area larger than the campus of Notre Dame. Among the many ruins was a ball court where it mattered a lot how you played the game; if you lost, you were killed.

It was obvious from the carvings outside some of the temples that the Mayas once held sway here. This particular development began around 300 A.D. and continued almost up to the time of the Conquest.

Our next stop was Taxco, which is the site of one of the largest silver mines in the world. It's been worked for 400 years and is still producing. The town perches on the side of a mountain. Its whitewashed buildings with their red tile roofs give it the appearance of a seaside town on the Mediterranean. We visited the cathedral built in 1748 by José de la Borda, owner of the silver mine. It reflects the ornate churrigueresque style, which is Mexican rococo. We toured the city, bought a few items at several of the silver shops, and had lunch at a wonderful restaurant on the hill opposite the town. It was called Ventana de Taxco, or Window on Taxco. True to its name, it provided us with a great view of the city. Then it was back to Cuernavaca and Las Manzanitas, which, by the way, means Happy Tomorrow or Happy Birthday.

FRIDAY, OCTOBER 2
Cuernavaca, Mexico

Mass this morning was at Marymount High School, run by a Sister Audrey from Los Angeles. All of the students and some of the parents assembled on a large patio. Ned and I concelebrated with Father Watner, a former Divine Word Provincial who has taught here for the past fifteen years or so. After Mass I gave a talk to the students, all young women, about the role of women in the modern world. We then sat down to a sumptuous breakfast, which was attended by a number of prominent residents of Cuernavaca. Both Ned and I gave talks. Each of us stressed the necessity of community support for the school.

The way the school came to exist in the first place is something of a miracle. Sister Audrey and another sister were sent down from New York to scout a location for a school. They stayed with a family whose next-door neighbor was a man named Colonel Stewart. Their host introduced them to Stewart, who was so impressed by the nuns and their plans for a school that he sold them his estate for a fraction of its true value— $250,000, payable at the rate of $25,000 a year for ten years, with no interest. Each year's payment went to one of his ten grandchildren. It's a marvelous place. The artwork alone, formerly from the collection of William Randolph Hearst, is probably worth ten times the purchase price.

After breakfast, we were off to Mexico City again for a quick visit to Our Lady of Guadalupe and then to the home of Nicholas and Mari Carmen Mariscal. Nicholas and Mari Carmen had assembled religious leaders from all over Mexico and we had a fine lunch with them, followed by a very complicated discussion about religion in Latin America, and especially in Mexico. That evening we checked in at the home of Bill and Yolanda Dellekamp, who had invited about forty Notre Dame alumni and their spouses to a dinner party in our honor. We played videotapes of Tim Brown's two touchdown runbacks against Michigan State. Ned and I both gave talks, mostly just to thank everyone for the wonderful week that the alumni had organized and conducted.

SATURDAY, OCTOBER 3
Mexico City, Mexico

It's never easy to get out of bed at 5 A.M., and after the big party the night before, it was even more difficult. Fernando Sepúlveda left the party more than an hour after we did, but he was waiting for us in the lobby, to take us to the airport. We were on our way to our second Latin American country: Guatemala.

The flight to Guatemala was short and uneventful, and once again we were met at the airport by alumni—Luis and Renée Beltranena and Adolfo and Margaret Cordón. After a cup of coffee, we drove out to Antigua, the old capital of Guatemala. Antigua has managed to retain its charming old Spanish character, despite its considerable growth since I was here last, about a decade ago. While touring the original university here, Luis brought us up to date on new university developments in Guatemala City. They have added several private universities to the local state university, San Carlos de Guatemala, which now has 50,000 students. The Catholic leaders here were upset by the Marxist tendencies of the university, so in 1962 they built a university of their own and named it after Rafael Landiver. The new university is really a Jesuit university, but a lot of Catholic laymen helped them to get it started. It now has about 8,000 students.

Another university was founded in 1972 when many of the local priests here began to display revolutionary tendencies. It was named after Francisco Marroquín, the first bishop. It has about 3,500 students and seems to be doing well. Our host, Luis Beltranena, has been dean of the faculty of law at both universities for a total of almost twenty years. He is also on the law faculty at San Carlos, the original university here, one of the oldest in the New World. It was founded in 1568, sixty-eight years before Harvard was established.

While in Antigua, we also toured the old cathedral, which was destroyed by earthquakes in the eighteenth century. It was begun in 1525, a scant five years after Cortez landed in Veracruz. The ruins indicated how immense it was. A corner of it is still being used as a chapel.

Leaving Antigua behind, we continued up the road to one of my favorite towns—Panajachel. It's on the shore of Lake Atitlán, a large and very deep lake (12,000 feet) which fills an ancient crater and is surrounded by wonderful cone-shaped volcanoes, all named for saints. The Beltranenas have a summer house on the lake, and this is where we are to stay the night.

SUNDAY, OCTOBER 4
Panajachel, Guatemala

About four o'clock this morning, the fireworks started going off. The explosions gave us a bit of a fright, because as we drove along the mountain road on our way up here yesterday, Luis had shown us the various points where the guerrillas attacked passersby on the highway. Until two years ago, this was a hotbed of guerrilla activity. When the fireworks started at 4 A.M., I thought the guerrillas must be laying siege to Lake Atitlán. Then I remembered that today is the Feast of St. Francis and that the Spanish name for this town is San Francisco de Panajachel. Once we had this figured out, we promptly went back to sleep.

After breakfast, we launched a boat into the lake and explored many of the little villages along the shore. At one point we disembarked to tour a coffee plantation. Later on we went over the side for a swim. Volcanic activity under the lake causes streams of hot water to rise to the surface along the shore, in sharp contrast to the very cold water elsewhere.

Back in town, we walked around for an hour and enjoyed the fiesta in honor of St. Francis. I even met one of my former students, Stewart Prentice, in the crowd. There were demonstrations of horsemanship, a soccer game, and more fireworks. The Indians, who make up most of the population in this area, wore their native costumes. If you were familiar with the various distinctive designs, you could tell at a glance the village or the area that each person was from.

About three o'clock in the afternoon, we had lunch on Luis's veranda. It was so good that Luis and Father Ned promptly conked out. With no one to talk to, I just sat back and enjoyed the view—the whitecapped lake and the volcano of Santiago on the other side. The whitecaps are whipped up by a wind called the *chocomil*. It comes across the lake from two directions and meets itself in the middle, causing the waves. It also brings a very fresh breeze which is welcome on this sunny, warm day in October. Peace is the name of this scene. I think we needed such a day after our whirlwind trip around Mexico.

This evening Luis drove us back to Guatemala City. As we drove, we talked about the possibility of a federation of all the Central American states. It's an old political debate. Proponents contend that none of the countries of Central America is large enough to be viable as a modern state in today's world. The notion is easier to understand when you consider how few people most of these nations have: Guatemala, 8.5 million; Honduras, 4.5 million; El Salvador, 5.5 million; Nicaragua, 3.2 million; Costa Rica, 2.5 million; and Panama, 1.5 million.

As members of a federation, these small nations would have much more clout than they could ever dream of having as independent states. In addition, they wouldn't have to maintain duplicate versions of such things as ambassadorial services, armed forces, and central banks. We didn't reach any hard-and-fast conclusions, but Ned and I both learned a lot from Luis, who had done his doctoral thesis at Notre Dame on the notion of federation in Latin America. When we arrived in the city, we drove to the beautiful new home of Adolfo and Margaret Cordón and checked into the guesthouse.

MONDAY, OCTOBER 5
Guatemala City, Guatemala

Luis Beltranena picked us up after breakfast and took us to the philosophical and theological faculty of Francisco Marroquín University. These faculties are quartered in the Salesian House, which teaches not only the Salesian seminarians but seminarians from other orders as well. Members of other orders are also on the faculty. Our host for this tour was Father Félix Serrano, a Salesian priest from northern Spain.

We then went to the university, where the main building is built on the edge of a deep ravine, descending about seven stories in spectacular fashion. We also visited with the vice rector, Rigoberto Juárez-Paz, a graduate of Indiana University and the University of Minnesota.

Lunch was at the Industrialists Club with Luis and several of his colleagues on the law faculty. Later on, Adolfo took us to visit some private elementary and high schools he had helped to establish. The idea for the schools was born out of the dissatisfaction of parents with the public schools. About seventy of them banded together and founded seven independent schools, financing them primarily through private donations and some bank loans at 22 percent interest.

I found the schools bright, clean, and delightful compared with others I have visited in Latin America. They are also very Catholic, with daily Mass and occasional retreats. I never thought I would see private Catholic schools like these in Latin America. But here they were.

In all of the conversations we have been having so far with our Guatemalan hosts, there seemed to be considerable disagreement with the government here, as was true in Mexico. The main strain of these conversations was conservative, and I imagine we would have heard a different story had we been talking with the foreign missionaries here. However, these are all very good people, and it's important for them to work together to find a new vision for Central America, one that will bring them all together, both left and right, liberal and conservative. No one, I am sure, wants to repeat the bloodshed, violence, and military dictatorships of the past forty or fifty years.

Around six o'clock in the evening, we left for a local museum where we were having a meeting of our Notre Dame alumni and, conjointly, a meeting of many members of the board of trustees of Marroquín University. The trustees made me an honorary professor of the university. With help from Luis, I made my acceptance speech in Spanish. My Spanish is getting better every day because I'm hearing it all day long and having to use it a great deal. I hope the progress continues. Though Ned is hearing the language for the first time, he's beginning to understand more too. Incidentally, Ned was reunited with a first cousin. She lives here with her Guatemalan husband.

TUESDAY, OCTOBER 6
Guatemala City, Guatemala

We were up on schedule at 5:15 A.M. and off to the airport, before the sun was up, to fly to Honduras. There we had a meeting with the Honduran President, José Azcona Hoyo. Alumnus Mike Facusse had provided his plane and two pilots for the trip. Adolfo Cordón and Luis Beltranena decided to come along too, in order to have a few words with the president on Guatemala's new tax laws. We landed at

Tegucigalpa in just under an hour, and Mike was at the airport to meet us, together with the president of the university, the head of protocol and foreign affairs, and about ten functionaries.

The presidential palace is an ornate building, and the soldiers standing guard there are even more ornate in seventeenth-century uniforms and ancient rifles. Others carried Uzis. We were taken immediately to Azcona Hoyo's office, where he was awaiting us with his wife, Miriam. They seemed glad to see us, Señora Azcona Hoyo in particular, because she had accompanied her daughter to Notre Dame only two or three months earlier to begin her sophomore year. She also has a nephew at Notre Dame.

We had a pleasant conversation, mostly about national affairs, which is the main topic of conversation in all Latin countries. We knew that Luis and Adolfo wanted to get a word in on the new tax legislation, so I made an opening for them with a casual remark that there was going to be a complete walkout in Guatemala tomorrow. They made their presentation. Afterward, Mike said, "Well, you got the commercial in," and "It sounds like the oligarchs don't want to pay taxes." No point in getting into the local controversy here, but the fact is, the oligarchs in these countries don't pay the taxes they should. Perhaps President Cerezo Arévalo, of Guatemala, went a bit overboard in this latest legislation, but something needs to be done so that all persons pay their just share. (I remember one year when the Italian government said, "This year we'll pay taxes on the honor system," and nobody paid any taxes at all. Most Latins just don't like taxes—or government, either.) After photographs and goodbyes, we went across town to the American Embassy. We were met there by Mike O'Brien, a former Bolivian Peace Corps volunteer who's now with the embassy here. It was like getting into Alcatraz, since just about every door had a guard and a lock and required a special combination to enter. Marine guards are in evidence everywhere. Most embassies in Central America look very much like Fort Apache.

The ambassador, Ted Briggs, an old friend of mine from the time of the election survey in El Salvador, was away on leave, so Mike took us to meet the chargé d'affaires, John Penfold. He gave us an extensive explanation of the problems caused by the refugee camps along the border with El Salvador. He said that for all practical purposes, they were refuges from the Salvadoran guerrillas.

John and the cultural affairs officer, Donna Roginski, accompanied us to the National Autonomous University of Honduras. On our arrival at the university, we were welcomed by Humberto Cosenza, a Notre Dame Ph.D. who studied microbiology under Morris Pollard. We then went to the rector's office, where we met all of the members of the university council and all of the deans. It was only then that I found out that they were conferring upon me their highest decoration, which was named after their founder, a priest by the name of José Trinidad Reyes. He established the university in 1847, just five years after Father Edward Sorin founded Notre Dame.

After the ceremony, during which I had to give an impromptu speech in Spanish, we went to the University Club for lunch, then raced to the airport, where we jumped into Mike Facusse's plane again and flew to Palmerola, the large American air base in Honduras. After a briefing on the military situation by Colonel Charlie Carlton, the base commander, we toured the base and enjoyed a short chat with the chaplain, a Benedictine priest from Wisconsin, Father Anderson.

With a few alumni and Mike Facusse, we flew into Tela, another 150 miles or so to the coast, where Ned's father worked for the United Fruit Company. Ned was born here, but left at the age of one month when the company evacuated its employees during World War I. Ned had not seen Tela since then. As soon as the plane came to rest on the nearly deserted airstrip, he knelt and kissed the ground.

Most of Honduras's bananas are exported from Tela, and today two large white ships were being loaded with the fruit. We watched for a while, then checked into a rambling hotel complex. It had been converted from residences that formerly belonged to the United Fruit Company. The hotel is right on the beach, and Tela is everything that a tropical port town should be.

For dinner tonight we went up to a restaurant in the mountains behind the town. As usual, the conversation centers on the political, social, and economic situation in Central America with special reference to Honduras. It's a tortured, twisted story with no easy answers.

WEDNESDAY, OCTOBER 7
Tela, Honduras

We all had a good night's sleep, due in large measure to the steady roar of the sea coming through the open windows. After breakfast we went out to look at Lancetilla, a forest preserve near Tela. It specializes mainly in tropical trees, and was put together by Wilson Poponoe, who worked for the United Fruit Company. He took this preserve of about 4,000 acres and planted more than 700 varieties of tropical trees from all over the globe.

This is a unique facility in all of the Americas; in fact, in all the world. One finds all kinds of fruit-bearing trees, as well as a number of trees that produce things as various as bay rum, strychnine, oils used in perfumes, cardamom, and cinnamon. There is also a wide variety of other trees that produce culinary and medicinal extracts.

We were joined this morning by John Sprang, who runs the PX at the air base, and by Frederico Lang, Notre Dame class of 1974, who is working with the Standard Fruit Company southwest of here in San Pedro Sula. With them we toured the old town, which is across the river from where we are staying. We then went up the beach for a wonderful lunch of conch soup and lobster. The beach here extends for many miles and is one of the most beautiful tropical beaches I have ever seen.

After lunch, we flew down to La Ceiba, which is the headquarters of the Standard Fruit Company and the third-largest city in Honduras. We had planned to fly out to the Bay Islands, home port of the pirates who attacked the Spanish galleons north of here. Unfortunately, a hurricane hit the islands, and we had to return directly to Tela.

We had Mass with about seven Notre Dame alumni, followed by cocktails and dinner. During our cocktail hour, we had a fantastic seminar on the economic and social situation here in Honduras, plus the concept of a Central American federation and several other subjects. Consul Mike O'Brien joined us from the American Embassy and delivered a very good summary of everything that was discussed. It also emerged from our discussion tonight that one of the problems here is the fact that 80 percent of the population is born out of wedlock. Some of these children are the products of common-law marriages, but many simply don't have a father. That is hardly the way to build a nation.

Another problem that disturbs me is that after 450 years of Christianity this country is not able to produce enough priests to take care of the people. The majority of the priests here are from other countries. The same might be said of most of Latin America.

THURSDAY, OCTOBER 8
Tela, Honduras

After breakfast, we inspected a banana boat belonging to the United Fruit Company, now called United Brands. The ship, with Chiquita on its side, was one of those large white ships that hold 240,000 boxes of bananas, each weighing 40 pounds and selling for $18. They were putting the final boxes aboard as we made our inspection. The bananas go in green and are refrigerated so that they stay green all the way across the ocean to Europe. As long as they are kept refrigerated after landing, they stay green, and just enough are removed each day to satisfy demand. After inspecting the ship, we took a long drive along the coast and marveled at the wonderful beach houses there. Then to lunch and more superb conch soup and lobster.

After lunch we boarded the plane again and flew to El Salvador, where we were met by President José Napoleón Duarte himself. I should mention that he was a student of mine when I was teaching a social justice class at Notre Dame. Ever since then I have called him by his more familiar name of Nappo. The mayor gave us the key to the city and a large proclamation of welcome, handsomely engraved on parchment. The usual photographs were taken, but thank God, we didn't have to make any speeches.

There was a large cocktail party and dinner at the presidential palace, where we are staying. We met many old alumni friends. I should note that the palace is decorated with about two or three dozen of Nappo's oil paintings, not a few of which are very good. Nappo looked quite tired to me, and I could understand why. He had just spent two days negotiating with the leftist guerrillas.

During the course of the negotiations, he surprised them by putting two points for discussion on the table: an amnesty or pardon for everyone in the country, including them, and nonviolence for the future, specifically a laying down of arms. He was somewhat discouraged when they told him he wanted to talk ethics and they wanted to talk politics—namely, sharing the power. He told them that the accepted way of achieving power in a true democracy is by running for office and getting elected. He told me that he had left the door open for more conversations.

We also discussed the idea of a Central American federation. He is the first one I've talked to down here who said he thought it was a great idea. I continue to have the impression—one I have held since Nappo first sat in my classroom—that he is fundamentally a good man, striving for peace and justice against overwhelming odds.

FRIDAY, OCTOBER 9
San Salvador, El Salvador

First on our agenda today were visits to two private universities— José Matías Delgado, which is only ten years old, but quite well developed, and the University of Central America, a Jesuit institution. At José Matías Delgado we were met by Guillermo Drigueros, the rector and a distinguished practicing lawyer. He gathered all of his deans together and they told us about the various programs that are taken by the 3,000 students.

The largest facility seems to be in economics, which also includes business administration and computers. Most of the courses here prepare people for employment in areas like communications, banking, applied arts, agriculture, languages, and executive secretary work. Tuition ranges from $20 to $40 per month. We found one curious twist here: in addition to the regular curriculum, the school requires its students to take courses in such things as respect for religion, knowledge of El Salvador, knowledge of the flora and fauna of the country, personal defense without arms, first-aid courses (which came in handy when the earthquake hit a year ago), leadership, Salvadoran nonviolence, and, believe it or not, social graces. These required small courses take about ten hours each and are spread over four years.

Though the school is professedly private and nonconfessional, it is dedicated to Our Lady of Fatima. Before we left, Ned and I blessed the shrine behind the school and said a few words to the students.

At the University of Central America we were greeted by Father Ignatius Martin Baro, the vice rector, who told us that although the university is Jesuit, it is not designated as Catholic. The twenty-two-year-old university is beautifully located on a hillside and has a wonderful physical plant, which seemed to escape much of the violence that was visited on the state university here, where the Army destroyed whole libraries and laboratories. The university received its initial funding of $12 million from the Inter-American Development Bank some twenty years ago. Father Ignatius told us that the university is dedicated to excellence in teaching, but also sees itself as a social force.

There are three main disciplines—humanities, economic and social sciences, and engineering. In addition, the school has an MBA program and a theological faculty. They have about 100 full-time faculty and 250 part-time to take care of 6,500 students. There are twelve Jesuits attached to the university, nine of them full-time teachers. After discussing the university at great length, we got into the local situation of the Church and the influence of religion in social change here. It was a very lively discussion, because some of the local people think the Jesuits are too politically involved, especially with the guerrillas. We also discussed possible interaction between this university and Notre Dame's Kellogg Institute. (Father Baro was one of the six Jesuits murdered by the military a few months later.)

Tonight we were guests at a large cocktail party given by Nappo. We expected a good-sized gathering of alumni and friends, but when we arrived, there were many others too. The papal nuncio was there, the American ambassador, and the rectors of all the universities in El Salvador. I suspected something was up when I saw television cameras, and I knew it for sure when I was led up to the front of the room. Nappo said some very nice things about me, then presented me with the country's highest decoration, the Medal of José Matías Delgado. Delgado was the George Washington of El Salvador, and the medal is spectacular. As Nappo pinned it on me, he said that he was making me a citizen of El Salvador.

With the television cameras still grinding, I had to make up an acceptance speech in Spanish. Thanks to the Holy Spirit, it came out all right, although I admit to getting a lot of mileage out of a little knowledge. Then there was a long reception line and a lot of good cheer for the next two hours. It's impossible to describe the warmth, affection, and dedication of these alumni, so far from Notre Dame and yet so loyal.

SATURDAY, OCTOBER 10
San Salvador, El Salvador

This morning we went with Nappo by helicopter to the dedication of a new housing development. He gave a great talk, mentioning his connection with me and thanking the Italians for the gift of over $100 million to build the first 1,000 houses of a planned total of 40,000. They will be occupied by the people who were rendered homeless by last year's earthquake. I signed and blessed an ornate scroll, a kind of cornerstone, and together we buried it in concrete.

Next we helicoptered to Tikal, a new city where 1,000 apartments are being built by the Guatemalan government and another 50 by the Germans. Nappo spoke with great gusto, then made me get up and take a bow as the professor who got him started in social development.

The most poignant moment came when the first woman to sign up for one of the new houses turned out to have the name Amelia. That was Nappo's mother's name, a determined, self-sacrificing woman who spent her life sewing so that her children could get a good education in America. Another brief note: The guerrillas who inhabit the mountain just behind the first housing development cut all of the electric lines last night, undoubtedly to embarrass Nappo when he started speaking into the microphone. Fortunately, they were repaired before he began to speak.

We concluded our stay in San Salvador by having a festive lunch with about thirty alumni. They sang the Notre Dame fight song for Ned and me and presented both of us with books on El Salvador that they had all signed. Finally, it was time to leave for Costa Rica. On the way to the airport we passed the spot where the American Maryknoll nuns were raped and murdered several years ago. We both experienced the sadness of that atrocity all over again.

We landed at San José, Costa Rica, in a rainstorm and were met at the airport by Sandra Rucavado, the PR representative for Coca-Cola here, and Pancho López, the father of Frank López, an outstanding student in Notre Dame's College of Business Administration. Costa Rica is the oldest democracy in Central America, with a fine constitution that goes back to 1948. It prohibits them from having an army, which makes them unique in all of Latin America. They do have a kind of civil guard—5,000 to 6,000 strong—to keep order in the country.

I would guess that the biggest problem that Costa Rica has is a debt of $3.5 billion, which if worked out per capita would be enormous, even by Latin American standards. As is well known, their President, Oscar Arias Sánchez, has presented a Central American peace plan which will be tested in the months ahead. Most people in Central America are somewhat suspicious of it, not because of the plan, which is a move toward peace, but because of the Nicaraguan agreement with the plan. People take a skeptical view of this, because the Communists, once in power, rarely give it up. (Nicaragua did hold elections, the Sandinistas lost, and President Arias received the Nobel Peace Prize.)

We checked in at the Hotel Cariari, then went to dinner with the López family as their guests, and finally back to the hotel and to bed. It had been a long, eventful day.

SUNDAY, OCTOBER 11
San José, Costa Rica

Sandra, our Coca-Cola hostess, picked us up and took us on a driving tour. We inspected the wonderful classical theater just off the Plaza Mayor, then headed west over the mountains. The peaks are dominated by the Irazú volcano. It erupted a few years ago, covering San José with ashes.

We said a prayer at the Shrine of Our Lady, Nuestra Señora de los Angeles, at Cartago. The shrine commemorates the appearance of Our Lady to a peasant girl on August 2, 1625. There is still a spring where the apparition took place and, as at Lourdes, many people come to fill bottles of water and to pray. We have just enough time left to take a quick tour of the Coca-Cola plant and then catch our flight for Bogotá.

When we arrived at the airport we were told that our plane was going to be half an hour late. It had a flat tire of all things! The half hour became an hour, causing us to miss our connection with Avianca in Barranquilla, Colombia. We had no choice but spend the night in Barranquilla and take the first flight out to Bogotá at 6:20 the next morning.

MONDAY, OCTOBER 12
Barranquilla, Colombia

We made our flight in the darkness before dawn, arrived safely in Bogotá, and were immediately whisked to the Hilton, where we were taken to the thirty-ninth-floor suite of alumnus Ramón De La Torre, head of Exxon here and our host during our stay in Bogotá. We spent a few minutes enjoying the view, then met José, Ramón's chauffeur, who gave us a quick tour of the city. It's amazing how much it has grown. I would guess there are at least a million new apartment dwellings to the north and east of Bogotá. All of this has happened in the last twenty years.

Next, José drove us to Ramón's finca, the Spanish word for ranch. We set up for Mass as soon as we arrived. Ramón was there, of course, along with his wife, María Cristina, plus all the people who work at the finca and their children. After Mass we had a drink on the back lawn with a great view of the fields, the pastures, and, in the distance, the mountains. I was here just a year ago last August, meeting with the local alumni. We had a picnic on this same lawn. Today, however, it rained, so we had our lunch inside.

There was much good conversation about Latin America and Notre Dame, but Ned and I were both pretty wiped out after the travel hassles of the previous day, so we went back to the hotel in the early afternoon, skipped dinner, and turned in early.

TUESDAY, OCTOBER 13
Bogotá, Colombia

Today was the funeral of the murdered president of Unión Patriótica, the Communist Party in Colombia. Things have been fairly touchy here in the violence department, so the government was quite nervous. They declared the next two days to be under what they call *ley seca*, or the dry law, which means all of the bars are closed. You can't even get a drink in the hotel. All transport was called off for the day, and practically everybody in town dismissed their employees as soon as they arrived for work.

Today we had appointments with the Archbishop of Bogotá, two presidential advisers, two university rectors, and a couple of other people. Because of the potentially explosive situation in the city, however, most of these appointments were canceled. Two events that did survive were a luncheon with the officers of the Banco de Bogotá, where Ramón is a board member, and a cocktail party with the Notre Dame alumni back at Ramón's home. Because of the unrest in town, only about half of the alumni showed up for the cocktail party. There were security guards everywhere.

The funeral went quite peacefully in the afternoon. The exception was inside the church. So many people piled in and made so much noise that the celebrants had to skip most of the funeral service in order to get through the Mass. Violence seems almost endemic in this part of the world, with the military and the oligarchies on one side and the leftist guerrillas and drug dealers (called *narcotraficantes* here) on the other. The violence is bad enough in itself, but it has also retarded social and economic growth and destabilized governments. Of great concern right now is the business relationship between the guerrilla groups and the drug cartels. The latter make billions of dollars raising cocaine and selling it in the United States.

Tonight at the party, there were at least five or six armed guards around the house, even though it is deep within a secure residential area, protected by high fences and other guards. When we returned to the hotel, the city seemed almost deserted. Most people were staying indoors and hoping for the best tomorrow. And so it goes.

WEDNESDAY, OCTOBER 14
Bogotá, Colombia

This morning the city looked a lot more normal, at least from our thirty-ninth-floor window. We reached the airport without incident or delay. Our destination: Quito, Ecuador.

Once again, we were met by the Coca-Cola people, led by Omar Besoain, who runs the operation here. Ecuador has 9 million people; 1.2 million of them live here in the capital of Quito. Sixty percent of the population are Indian and 65 percent are illiterate. Ecuador's principal products are oil and shrimp.

The country was founded in 1534 by the Pizarros. To put

everything in perspective, you have to remember that Cortez landed in Mexico in 1521 and conquered the Aztecs and the Mayans. Thirteen years later his officers, the Pizarros, advanced south to what is now Ecuador and Peru, where they conquered the Incas.

After checking in at the Hotel Colón we planned the day's sightseeing. The two greatest attractions here are the Compañía Jesuit Church and San Francisco Church. The Compañía was founded in 1605. It is perhaps the most ornate church in all of Latin America. From the front door to the apse, it is completely gold-leafed. San Francisco, however, is the older of the two, having been built in 1553.

We walked through the markets for a while, then went out to the Muchacho Trabajador, where Father John Halligan has for twenty-five years been running an educational and social upgrading program for the children of slum dwellers. He ministers to about 800 youngsters here, and even more at a second center he has established. It's a unique operation. The youngsters have a full program, from a day-care center on through high school and vocational training. They also get decent meals and full medical and dental care at no cost. But they have to meet certain requirements, such as taking a hot shower every day and starting a savings account at age six. They all have part-time jobs, and the program includes a job placement service. Many of those who have graduated from here return to work for the good of other youngsters.

From Father John's place we went to the university, where we had a fine discussion with Father Julio Teran Dutari, S. J. It's amazing how much this university has grown since I was here fifteen years ago. It now has over 10,000 students and seven different faculties. Tuition is about $200 a semester, remarkably low considering the physical plant and curriculum.

This evening we attended a diplomatic reception. I had a long talk with the American ambassador, as well as with Ernesto Iturralde, a distinguished architect who has designed over twenty-five of the most modern buildings in Quito. He graduated from Notre Dame in 1963, and was the first of three students who initiated our Rome program. He and his wife, Carmen, later joined Father Ned and me for dinner back at the Hotel Colón.

THURSDAY, OCTOBER 15
Quito, Ecuador

Only two alumni were on hand when we began Mass this morning, but by the time we were finished we had a pretty good-sized crowd, a few of whom saw us off when we boarded our plane for Lima, Peru, our next destination. We arrived in Lima about an hour and forty minutes later, having seen some wonderful snowcapped volcanoes en route. Jaime Pinto of Coca-Cola met us and drove us to the Sheraton, then took us for a tour of Lima.

Ned and I seem to have a genius for arriving in cities when crises are happening. Here the banks had just been nationalized. There was no sign of unrest, however, especially not at the old (1565) Franciscan monastery that we visited on the edge of the city. They are down to twenty-five monks, and I gather they must have had ten times that many in their heyday. The place is very large and filled with wonderful religious paintings from the famous schools of Cuzco and Quito. The paintings in that monastery would have been sufficient to set up at least ten art dealers in business.

We then went to the Museo de Oro, the gold museum, which has one of the most spectacular displays of pre-Columbian gold art objects in the world. Parts of this museum have toured the world. One could cover a wall with the itinerary of this traveling show (one-hundredth of what we saw today). It seemed to be booked everywhere between Japan and Paris.

Peru has a population of about 20 million people, roughly half of whom are Indian. Six million people live in Lima. As in most other cities, there are enormous extremes of wealth and poverty here. Many of Lima's residents are Indians who have arrived here penniless from the countryside. With no place to go and no money, they've built shacks from anything they've been able to find—tin, tar paper, mismatched boards, you name it. The city is totally surrounded by these barrios of poor souls. This is the curse of urbanization that one sees in all of the large cities in Latin America. It's simply not possible to assimilate several thousand new arrivals every day, much less provide them with adequate housing, health, sanitation, and education. Alan García, the new President from the Aprista Party, had a reputation as a problem solver when he was elected, but his move to nationalize the banks appears to be a decision taken in desperation. On the bright side, there has been a lot of new construction and road improvements in Lima since my last visit some years ago.

FRIDAY, OCTOBER 16
Lima, Peru

Today was our day for education. First, we went out to the Catholic University. About a decade ago, the Ford Foundation gave a half million dollars to the Catholic University so that they could collaborate with Notre Dame's development group to learn how to raise money for their new campus. We also took a number of their best professors to Notre Dame and had them study for doctorates at a time when there was not a single Ph.D. in chemistry here in Peru. Both projects worked out very well, and it was the realization of an old dream today to walk on that campus and see the many fine buildings and the 10,000 students who are getting a good education. The campus resembles a huge garden. Everywhere one looks, there are beautiful trees and flowers. We had a fine visit and tour with the rector, Pepé Tola, a mathematician. He has now been on the job about ten years and remembers well the university's former associations with Notre Dame.

The state university, which we visited next, was, by contrast, an absolute mess: graffiti all over the place, no grass or flowers. In fact, no students. They were on one of their frequent strikes. If one had to find the perfect example of a fine institution (and it used to be one) politicized to the point of insanity, this would be it.

Our next stop was the Immaculata, a Jesuit boys' school with a mountain backdrop, lots of new buildings, and 2,300 students from first grade through high school. My old friend Felipe MacGregor is rector here. We had a wonderful reunion and exchanged war stories from the days when we were building the International Federation of Catholic Universities and the Ecumenical Institute in Jerusalem.

Over lunch Felipe and I discovered that we share a common interest in world peace. Felipe has organized and presides over an organization called APEP (the Peruvian Peace Research Association). He has also been working in the same area with the United Nations

University in Japan and the United Nations Peace University, just created in Costa Rica. We discussed the possibility of his coming to Notre Dame to bring our Peace Institute people up to date on all that is going on down here.

On the way home, we detoured to the Pacific coast and then back through Miraflores, one of Lima's nicer residential areas. Back in the hotel, we packed our bags for Cuzco and Machu Picchu. We're taking one small bag apiece and leaving the rest here in storage. Tonight we had dinner with several alumni. Reveille tomorrow morning is at 4:15.

SATURDAY, OCTOBER 17
Lima, Peru

Even though the sun was not yet up, the airport was crowded. Fog delayed our departure by an hour, and held us up again for a while when we began descending into Cuzco, a city of 300,000 population over 11,000 feet above sea level. It stretches out along a valley, and parts of it climb up the hillsides.

Our hotel is the Picoaga, formerly an old colonial house. As soon as we checked in, they gave us some special tea which is supposed to protect us from *soroche*, the high-altitude sickness here. The Coca-Cola people arrived with some books about the place and tote bags. I didn't think we needed any more bags, but that was before Ned went shopping. Among other things, he bought one of those beautiful multicolored blankets that the Incas weave. Because it was still fairly early in the morning, we conked out for an hour and a half, the first daytime nap we've had since leaving South Bend.

Cuzco was the capital of the old Inca empire, which extended from Ecuador through Peru and Bolivia and into northern Chile and Argentina. It was a true socialist society; everything belonged to the emperor, the Inca. There were thousands of miles of road through these tortuous mountains, with terraces for growing food and passes higher than Pikes Peak. The potato was born here, and some think corn was too.

This huge empire was taken over by a few hundred Spaniards under Pizarro. The Inca empire numbered about 4 million people at the time. Eighty thousand of them lived here in Cuzco. That made it the largest city on this continent. Fortunately for the Spaniards, the empire was past its prime and ripe for the picking.

There were two Incas or leaders at the time the Spanish arrived. They met the first one, Atahualpa, in the northern part of Peru and imprisoned him in Cajamarca. They told him to reach up as high as he could in a room about 100 feet square and to fill the room that high with gold, plus two others with silver. They told him that if he did this, they would spare his life.

After he did it, of course, they killed him. But not before offering to baptize him, which they said would get him to heaven. "Are you fellows planning on going to heaven?" he was reported to have asked them. When they said they were, he supposedly said, "Then let's skip the baptism."

Before killing him, they asked him where the silver and gold came from. Because he had been having trouble with his half brother, Huáscar, who was the legitimate son of his father (Atahualpa was born of a concubine), he pointed the Spaniards in the direction of Cuzco, and even gave them two guides to help them get there. The Spaniards marched across the mountain passes and over suspension bridges. When they arrived in Cuzco, they were received peacefully. They stayed for two years, grabbing all the gold and silver in sight.

After lunch, we went to the Temple of the Sun, an ancient Inca temple reminiscent of those in Egypt. Its windows and doors are shaped like trapezoids, wide at the bottom and narrow at the top. The Dominicans built their Church of Santo Domingo on these ruins, using the solid walls of the temple as a foundation. When the earthquakes came, the Inca walls stood firm, while the colonial walls all fell. Ned did some research on the cathedral and discovered that it has a bell called María Angola. It was cast in 1659, which was about a hundred years after the Conquest. It's the largest bell in South America, and its ringing can be heard twenty-four miles away.

We visited the Coriacacha Temple and admired the wonderful masonry work of the Incas. Without metal instruments, they were able to carve stones to fit together so tightly they could withstand the earthquakes. And they didn't use mortar either.

We then drove up the mountainside to visit Saqsaywaman, the great fortress that lies at 13,000 feet, above the city of Cuzco. Cuzco itself is at about 11,600 feet. Here they fitted massive stones together, again so closely that a knife cannot be put between the stones, and some stones had as many as fourteen or fifteen joints with other massive stones. In addition, they had to bring these stones from eighteen miles away without wheels or other moving equipment.

We spent most of the afternoon up in the high hills, seeing various fortresses and temples built by the Incas and marveling at their engineering feats. They even had an irrigation system throughout this whole valley. How they did it without modern surveying instruments is a wonder in itself. This is my third visit here, but I never cease to be awed by the accomplishments of this ancient civilization. Tomorrow's reveille is 5 A.M. We're taking the train to Machu Picchu.

SUNDAY, OCTOBER 18
Cuzco, Peru

With a lot of help from the early morning church bells, we had no trouble getting up before five. Even at that hour, the railroad station was very crowded. We boarded a four-car diesel train and began climbing through the switchbacks from the valley to the 12,000-foot plain. We rumbled along the plateau for a while, then descended 6,000 feet down to the Urubamba Valley and the river of the same name, both sacred to the Incas. The valley is narrow at first, then broadens out. Judging from the fields and the terraces clinging to the mountainsides, I would say that a lot of food is produced here.

Practically everyone here speaks Quechua, the ancient language of the Incas. They have no written language, but in the old days kept their records on knotted cords, called quipus. The placing of the knots and the color of the cords recorded what they wanted to remember.

The river became more and more turbulent and muddy as we continued along it. Curiously, there were cacti growing along the banks, as well as yellow broom flowers. As we neared Machu Picchu, the hillside turned from brown to deep green. The Indians call this part of the world the Eyebrows of the Jungle. When we arrived at Machu Picchu, we had been traveling for a little over three hours since leaving Cuzco. Then we had to wait, as there were only three buses making the twelve-kilometer trip up the mountain to the place

people come from all over the world to see: the Lost City of the Incas.
Whenever someone tells me that they are traveling to Latin America,
I tell them that if they only have time to see one place, make it
Machu Picchu.

We finally worked our way up to one of the buses and started the
hair-raising climb to the top of the mountain. I would judge it to be
somewhere between 8,000 and 9,000 feet high. The most impressive
sight here is a monumental sundial called IntiWatana, which in
Quechua means "to tie up the sun." From there, we climbed up to
the guardhouse, which commands a view of the agricultural terraces,
the city, and the adjoining mountain. Though we were rather tired
and sweaty by the time we had reached this altitude, we continued up
the mountain and around a bend. The trail was very narrow and
rocky, with 3,000- to 4,000-foot drop-offs on our right. Ned and I
smiled when we saw a sign indicating that we should pass carefully. If
you're not careful in a place like this, you're a goner very quickly.

Across this path on the other side of the mountain we saw a
suspension bridge of the type that the Incas had strung across the
chasm long ago. It was swaying back and forth in the wind, with only
a few jungle vines holding it together. The Spaniards used to go across
on all fours, and I can't say that I blame them.

This has been our shortest day in a long time. We were back at
the hotel soaking wet and worn out about four o'clock in the
afternoon. We're staying here tonight and heading back to Cuzco
tomorrow afternoon.

MONDAY, OCTOBER 19
Machu Picchu, Peru

It rained fairly heavily all night and continued on into the morning.
We were glad we had seen most of Machu Picchu yesterday, because
the weather was clearly against us today. We walked through the
ancient city one last time, then boarded a bus for the trip back to
Cuzco. The ride down was even more hair-raising, if that's possible,
than the ride up had been, because the road was now muddy and
slippery. The bus slid around a lot, and out our window, just beyond

the wheels, we could see the precipices dropping off a couple of thousand feet. There wasn't a guardrail to be found anywhere.

How that bus made it down safely, we'll never know, but we were very glad to see the train station. When we went inside, however, we were told that the train would not be going all the way to Cuzco, because of the heavy tourist traffic. Instead, they took us to Urubamba and bused us into Cuzco from there. This was not all bad, because we saw some new scenery, including several snowcapped mountains that rose to 19,000 or 20,000 feet. The only disconcerting part of the trip was the bumpy road. We were sitting in the rear of the bus, where it was bumpier than ever, and I was afraid my back wouldn't be able to withstand the beating it was taking (Ned's either).

When we came up over the top of the last mountain it was night and the city of Cuzco lay beneath us, its lights twinkling in the darkness. It was a beautiful sight. I have been reading Hiram Bingham's *The Lost City of the Incas* and have just about finished it. I read it once before, but reading it again here has given it new meaning for me. Bingham, a Yale professor, found this city early in this century.

TUESDAY, OCTOBER 20
Cuzco, Peru

It would be hard to describe how crowded the airport was this morning. A real zoo, with everybody milling around and nowhere to sit down. As it continued to rain and the clouds rolled down from the mountains, it was obvious that the incoming flights from Lima, where all the flights originated and where we were headed, were going to have a hard time getting through the pass. To no one's surprise, every flight was eventually canceled. The only good thing about the wait was that it gave us plenty of time to browse through the airport shops. I bought two nice watercolors of Cuzco, a bronze llama as a souvenir of the trip, and a small owl figurine for Eppie Lederer, a collector of owl art and an old friend of mine.

With no hope of getting out of Cuzco today, we returned to the hotel, got our rooms back, and invited the cleaning women to join us for Mass. One of them stayed after Mass to get some advice on a troubled marriage. After lunch, we took naps for the second time since leaving

South Bend, then went for a walk around the town in the continuing drizzle. First, we bought some rubber sandals, which will be very useful on the boat that we're scheduled to board tomorrow for our trip down the Amazon. Then we got haircuts. No one can complain about prices here. We paid three dollars a pair for the sandals, a dollar each for haircuts. The barber taught me how to say thank you in Quechua: *dios solpika*. You're never too old to learn. He also told me that there are two universities in Cuzco, a public one, which is large and not all that great, and a better, private one, which is Catholic.

Tonight was a classic example of bringing victory out of the jaws of defeat. We had a marvelous evening with Jorge Gómez Salhuana, who is No. 2 at Coca-Cola here in Cuzco, and engineer José Vásquez Cáceres, who is the head of the bottling plants for four major cities. They took us to a wonderful restaurant called "The Hole" in Spanish, where we not only had a good meal but also enjoyed wonderful performances of Inca music. They do marvels with the flute. The mixing of the two cultures, Spanish and Indian, has produced a spectacular musical blend.

WEDNESDAY, OCTOBER 21
Cuzco, Peru

The day dawned fairly clear, and by 9:30 A.M. we were in Lima, where we were met once again by Jaime Pinto. The problem was that our bags were stored downtown separate from the bags of our fellow travelers. We jumped into the car with Jaime and hurried down to the Sheraton Hotel, only to find out that Lima Tours had picked up our bags with the others and taken them to the airport. So it was back to the airport again in time to check our bags and take the flight north to Iquitos, the embarkation point for our trip down the Amazon on the *Society Explorer*.

We landed at Iquitos at 2:30 in the afternoon. What a change from Cuzco, where it was high and cold. Here it was low and hot and humid. After a quick turn around town, which is really sleazy in the extreme, we drove to the riverfront and had a quick lunch. The riverbank here is lined with shacks on stilts. One of the streets is called Buzzard Street because of all the birds that alight here to feast on the garbage.

I can't describe how good it felt to board the Society Explorer, so sleek and red and holding the promise of adventure as it rocked gently at its moorings on the river's edge. We were also glad to unpack our bags and put things in closets for the first time in four weeks. Then we both took showers because we were soaked with perspiration from the humidity.

After dinner we were introduced to the crew, several of whom delivered lectures about the ship and our itinerary. Then we went to bed. I don't know about Ned, but I was asleep before I got through the first decade of the Rosary.

THURSDAY, OCTOBER 22
Iquitos, Peru

We were up at 6:45 A.M., just as the ship was leaving Iquitos. The river looked to be about a quarter of a mile wide here, and the water, of course, was very muddy and flowing at about six knots. The temperature here today was just under 90 degrees and quite humid. One of the first things we did was to figure out how to offer Mass in the tight confines of our small, two-bunk cabin. Our next challenge will be to avoid eating large breakfasts. As you know if you've taken a cruise, there are a lot of temptations at mealtimes. We will have that problem for the next twenty-six days.

As always on the first day aboard ship, we had the fire drill and learned how to put on the latest kinds of life preservers. We have two kinds. We'll wear the lighter ones when riding in the zodiacs, rubber boats propelled by 40-horsepower engines. They hold about sixteen people apiece, including the driver and crew. We spent another hour or so rearranging our luggage and storing it in every nook and cranny.

At 11 A.M., Dr. Ian Prance, of the New York Botanical Gardens and a graduate of Oxford, gave us a fine lecture on the Indians and the flora of the Amazon jungle. Apparently most of the Indians live along the upper Amazon, through which we will proceed over the next few days. They speak over 300 tongues belonging to several language families. Every few miles there is a new dialect.

The Indians used to be a lot more numerous than they are today; about ninety tribes have become extinct in this century. Even today, while they look healthy, their average life span is only about thirty-five to forty years.

After lunch, we all piled into seven zodiac boats to go up the Ampiyacu River for several miles. First, we came to the Bora Indian village, where we walked around and saw the various artifacts that were for sale. We stayed for about half an hour, then took a path through the jungle to visit the Huitoto tribe. They put on a series of dances for us, then showed off their wares. One craft they have mastered is the making of paper by pounding on the bark of fig trees. They make dyes from fruit juices. I bought a nice hummingbird. It was about a foot square and made of this local bark paper. I bought it because it reminded me of the many hummingbirds that spend the summer at Land O'Lakes, Wisconsin, Notre Dame's ecological center, and then fly down here to the Brazilian jungle for the winter. (It's now hanging in our lodge there in Wisconsin.)

About an hour and a half before sundown, we came back down the river with Ian Prance and his wife and a dozen or so other people. If there were any birdwatchers in the group they must have been in ecstasy. All along the way we saw toucans, parrots, and orioles flitting around in the flowering trees that lined both banks of the river.

The sun was setting as we approached the ship. The sky was absolutely filled with pastel colors. A porpoise surfaced alongside of us, and the tropical forest came alive with the sounds of the many nocturnal creatures who make it their home. Tonight was the captain's dinner, so everyone got gussied up.

FRIDAY, OCTOBER 23
On the Amazon

We woke up to a very rainy and foggy morning. The fog was actually low-lying rain clouds, dark and heavy with moisture. This was a three-stop day, the first being at Alegría, Peru. Right next door on the river is Leticia, where we checked in and out of Colombia. Lastly, down the river a little farther was Tabatinga, where we checked into Brazil, the country we'll be traveling in for the next twenty days or so.

We went ashore at Leticia, which used to be the center of the cocaine trade. Most of it came here to be refined and was then shipped out, mainly to the United States. We took a boat in to shore before breakfast and had hardly left the ship when we were pelted by a very heavy rain. We were soaking wet before the zodiac touched the shore, a muddy hillside littered with every kind of garbage. With the rain pelting down, it became very slippery and several people fell while attempting to make their way up the hillside. I made it to the top without a fall, but slipped and fell to my knees when I reached the muddy main street.

There wasn't much to see or buy, except in the markets that lined the shore. Once the day's marketing is over, the vendors simply walk away and let the vultures come in to pick up the litter. The vultures are all perched on trees across the small tributary stream where we landed. Without a doubt, this is one of the sleaziest towns anywhere in the world, but we made the best of it. I changed my Peruvian intis into Brazilian cruzeiros and Ned bought a bright red poncho. Judging from the weather we've had up to now, he's going to need it. I've lugged my trusty plastic raincoat this far, so I'm sticking with it. I was so wet and cold when we got back from visiting Leticia (curiously, both Alegría and Leticia mean joy) that I took another hot shower.

Further evidence of the drug trade along the river included float planes and speedboats with 140-horsepower engines. The Army is in evidence, but there doesn't appear to be much law enforcement here. People are out in broad daylight exchanging wads of bills three inches thick. It's not a place where anyone would want to live, but it will flourish as long as Americans and others are dumb enough to buy cocaine.

At 2:30 P.M., we had another lecture by Ian Prance, this one on the vegetation of the Amazon. Fifty percent of this land is upland rain forest. Just to give you an indication of the variety of flora, there are 175 different species of trees in and around Manaus alone. They range from the ironwood to the kapok, from which life preservers are made. In the Amazon as a whole, there are 30,000 species of plants.

Along the side of the river, there is a special area called *várzea*.

The river often overflows its banks here, depositing nutrient-rich silt that makes this a very fertile agricultural area.

For two hours after the lecture, we sailed down the Amazon through wonderfully thick forests on both sides. The river here is about a half mile wide, full of small craft plying their way between the villages. Finally, as the sun was setting, we came into Belém de Solamões. And by the time we were on our way up the tributary in the zodiacs it was dark. When we arrived at our destination, another Indian village, we couldn't believe our eyes. The streets were illuminated with electric lights.

This particular village was home to about 3,000 members of the Tacuna tribe, making it the largest of all the Indian villages. Ned distinguished himself by buying about three necklaces, one made out of crocodile teeth, and a very large basket. Others in our party also bought baskets—plus face masks, paddles, hammocks, and bows and arrows. Everything appeared to be of good quality, and the village was very clean, much better in that respect than the cities we've seen so far on this trip.

SATURDAY, OCTOBER 24
On the Amazon

Today we visited another Tacuna village. This is one of thirty such villages with about 2,000 people in each. They are very neat and well kept. The houses are built on stilts, and everyone sleeps in hammocks. Each of these villages has a primitive school. The youngsters get a couple of hours a day in Tacuna and Portuguese for about three years.

A council of chiefs makes political decisions for the 50,000 Tacunas they represent. What the Indians really want is land tenure, since technically they are squatters in their various villages along the river, never mind that they were here long before the Brazilians arrived.

There was the usual bartering for baskets of all sorts, and the masks that the Tacunas use in puberty rites. Carvings from a beautiful red hardwood were also very popular. With the exception of the heat—temperatures have been above 100 degrees—the weather has taken a definite turn for the better, with blue skies and bright sun.

It's hard to believe that we are playing southern California back home at Notre Dame today. It will probably be a long time before we find out who won. So far we've had no luck in getting the Armed Forces Network on the shortwave radio we brought along.

A word about the Amazon. It begins as a small stream in the Peruvian Andes, not too far from Machu Picchu. The name of the river changes several times as it is joined by other tributaries. As it flows through Peru, Colombia, and the western part of Brazil, it is called the Rio Solimões. But from Manaus, where it joins the Rio Negro, to the Atlantic, a distance of nearly 1,000 miles, it goes by its more familiar name of Rio Amazonas, or simply the Amazon. It is the longest navigable river in the world. Oceangoing steamers like our own can ascend it for more than 2,300 miles.

The river has a water flow five times that of the Congo and twelve times that of the Mississippi. It accounts for one-fifth of all of the fresh water discharged into the world's oceans. The river flows along at about 1.5 miles per hour. That doesn't seem so fast until you consider that it drops only 210 feet from the time it leaves the Peruvian frontier until it empties into the Atlantic at Belém, a distance of more than 1,900 miles. The water level varies greatly. During the rainy season, it can rise anywhere from 30 to 60 feet.

David Campbell, one of our specialists, gave a talk this afternoon on the fishes of the Amazon. He pointed out that because the Amazon is so long and has so many tributaries, it is home to a vast number of local fishes. One is a prehistoric-looking catfish. We went fishing right after Campbell's talk, and I caught three of them.

SUNDAY, OCTOBER 25
On the Amazon

We had about thirty people show up for Mass this morning, including a majority of our Protestant friends aboard and practically all of the old gang who were at Cuzco with us last Sunday.

We took the zodiac boats in to shore again for a walk through the forest. It was fairly difficult because we had to clamber up a steep bank first and then cut our way through the thick vegetation with machetes. We saw a buttress tree with large flangelike buttresses coming out for roots. This botanical adaptation is necessary because the tree is under water during the rainy season. We also saw some interesting hanging vines. Our guide showed us how to cut them open to get a drink of water.

Our lecture back aboard ship this afternoon was on forest-dwelling birds. I was surprised to hear that there are 1,132 different species of birds here on the Amazon, the largest variety of any place on earth.

MONDAY, OCTOBER 26
On the Amazon

This morning we took a boat to the sleepy little town of Foz de Jutaí, which is about one and a half miles up the river. We toured the town in about 115-degree heat and high humidity. It was amazingly clean and orderly compared to what we had seen upriver.

We're really in the tropics now. Every time we come in, we're soaking wet through every layer of clothing. There's usually a breeze as we move downriver, however, and that helps.

We learned some more about the Amazon today. It has over 200 tributaries flowing into it, two of them more than 1,000 miles long. The river is 200 miles wide at its mouth and discharges three billion gallons of water into the Atlantic Ocean every minute. That's why you'll find fresh water many miles out into the Atlantic.

This afternoon Ian Prance gave us the first of two lectures on the deforestation of the Amazon. There are several reasons for it. Some of them, in the beginning at least, were the result of good intentions. For example, in 1970 President Médici embarked on a plan to improve life for the people who were struggling to survive in Brazil's arid northeast. To do this, he encouraged them to move to the Amazon. The plan called for highways into the region, and along the highways, villages every 50 kilometers, towns every 150 kilometers, and cities every 500 kilometers.

Millions of people moved here and received 250 acres in return for clearing their land for farming. The trouble was, the soil here is very thin and it wore out very quickly. The crops failed and the people who had moved in were soon as bad off as they had been before. The government tried to blame it on the small farms, and they opened up the area to large farming operations. Tracts as big as 100,000 acres were made available to commercial farmers from Germany (Volkswagen), America (Armour), and the Japanese. Ten percent of them were successful in cattle ranching, but most of the others failed.

To give you some idea of the magnitude of this deforestation, it amounts to 50 acres a minute or an area the size of West Virginia every year. Today, only 3 percent of the rain-forest land is left in northeastern Brazil. There is also considerable devastation of animal life here. Turtles are becoming largely extinct, and so are manatees and jaguars.

About 5 P.M., we arrived at the Costa do Jacaré, where we went "alligator hunting." What we actually did was to go fifteen miles up a small tributary and back down again, playing searchlights on the shore. The alligators' red eyes were supposed to reflect the light and make it easy for us to find and catch them. There were five boatloads of us. For our efforts, we succeeded in bagging exactly one alligator. It was about one foot long.

TUESDAY, OCTOBER 27
On the Amazon

We spent most of the day twisting and turning our way from Uara downriver to Cuxin Mini. All the turns made me curious, so I went to the bridge today to look at the chart. In an area that would have taken maybe two miles to cross, the river headed north, then east, west, and south again, probably amounting to more like twenty-five miles.

The river appeared to be close to a mile wide here, yet the fathometer showed that we had about sixty feet of water under the keel. There are islands all along the way; in fact, we're almost never without an island in sight.

We listened to a lecture by Ian Prance this morning entitled "Rebuilding the Rain Forest: Alternatives to Deforestation." Ian's fundamental theory is that we ought to be interested in conservation versus utilization, especially when utilization destroys the rain forest. Rather than introduce cows, we ought to use animals that are accustomed to this kind of climate and ecology, water buffaloes and tapirs, for example. He said that corn and manioc grow very well here, as do some commercial crops, such as jute, introduced by the Japanese in 1949, and rubber trees. He also said that bananas, pineapples, and Brazil nuts grow well in the rain forest. While all of these are possible solutions, it seems to me that we need a larger solution that would affect many more people.

Later on, Ian's wife, Ann, delivered a lecture on the Caboclos: "People Who Live Along the River." We have been observing these people ever since we left the Indian villages to the west slightly beyond Iquitos. They live in small clearings, each with five to fifteen houses. The houses sit on the high ground just above where the floods come, although at times the floods get that high too, so they are all on stilts. After the rainy season begins in November, they'll be able to park their canoes at their front doors. Now they are about thirty feet up the bank.

All of these people along both shores of the river are called Caboclos and they are today's true Amazonians. They've descended from three genetic sources—Indian, European, and, as one gets closer to the Atlantic Ocean, African. Caboclo is a Guarani Indian word meaning "wild savage," but they are anything but that. We've found them genial and welcoming whenever we've met them in their villages or passed them in their boats. At one time, millions of Indians lived along the banks of the Amazon. Due in large measure to deforestation, however, their numbers are considerably fewer today.

The Spaniards, Portuguese, and Dutch who came this way were either soldiers or traders, the Spaniards coming from the west and the Dutch and the Portuguese from the east. They had no women with them, so they mixed with the native tribes. That was the beginning of the Caboclos.

The Indians fought and died for their lands. Some of them went inland, where eventually the greater number of tribes perished. The Africans were introduced by the Dutch, who brought them in to work the sugar plantations along the Atlantic end of the Amazon. The year 1888 saw the end of slavery here, so many of the free blacks moved up toward the Amazon and again intermingled with the local population, which was mixed European and Indian.

The Caboclos are the mestizos of Brazil. There is a small

intermixture of Japanese as well, but the Indian strain is certainly the strongest.

The Caboclos followed the Indian agricultural method of slash and burn, and raised the same crops that the Indians had survived on here—cassava, rice, corn, and beans. They also used Indian methods for fishing, although the Europeans introduced nets for fishing and guns for hunting. They traveled in canoes more than other kinds of boats. Occasionally a canoe will have an outboard motor on it. They all sleep in hammocks, again an Indian custom.

The influence of religion was strong here. The Jesuits arrived in 1549, only eight years after the first traverse of the river. The Franciscans soon followed. The Jesuits collected people in reservations, and this really destroyed Indian culture, because they came from many different tribes and languages and had to work out a lingua franca so they could talk to each other. This language was ill adapted to handle the abstract notions of religious belief. The early missionaries tried to connect Christian beliefs with what the Indians did understand, their own native religion. This gave birth to a kind of syncretism which, while fervently Catholic, hedges the bet with the old Indian religion.

Catholicism suffered a good deal when the Jesuits were expelled in 1759. The African tribes brought in a religion called macumba, which is really a kind of devil worship. It's still practiced in the Amazon, and especially around Bahia on the Atlantic. Today one also sees a lot of evangelicals, who seem to be well supported and so are making inroads into the Catholic majority.

The culture and life of the Caboclos are influenced most of all by the river, which is their highway and the source of much of their food. The negative part of living along the river is the annual flooding. Between floods, the Cabaclos have to both sow and harvest their crops. The floods also disperse the fish population, and bring in rats and snakes that are seeking higher ground. The floods have mandated stilt houses as well as floating houses, which are simply mounted on large logs that rise and fall with the river.

In one of our lectures we learned that family life among the Caboclos is very close-knit. They demonstrate great love and caring toward both their youngsters and the elders. The extended family, including relatives in need, is also very much a reality here. Most of the families have eight to ten children. Young women are married at a very early age, thirteen or fourteen. Life expectancy is about forty-five years, and there is a good deal of infant mortality. Schooling is, of course, poor because the youngsters are spread over thousands of miles along the river in small settlements. Most of the schools operate in three shifts—morning, afternoon, and evening—and students of all ages attend, though for only three or four years.

Some of the villages now have electric generators and TV, although most of the programs they receive are poor-quality reruns from the United States. There is little crime along the river because people respect each other's property.

In summary, one would have to say that the Caboclos are survivors, and have been for several centuries. As their popular song goes, it's not just enough to live, but one must live happily. From what we have seen along the shore, I'd say they are doing just that.

As a kind of follow-up to our lecture, we landed at the little village of Cuxin Mini this afternoon. All the youngsters were lining the shore as we arrived in our zodiac and clambered up a muddy bank. The youngsters accompanied us into the village, where we met Dona Elena, a blithe spirit of indeterminate age and the mother of about ten children. When we arrived she was studying mathematics. She introduced us to several members of her family and then took us on a tour of the village, which was made up of fourteen families, each with about twelve members.

In the middle of the village, they had a schoolroom, very well kept, although primitive, and a chapel dedicated to St. Francis of Assisi. They had had a big celebration in honor of St. Francis. Everybody came from up and down the river and apparently they had several hundred people here for the event. Dona Elena's home was way down at the end of the row with cattle, pigs, and chickens in the yard, but also a very nice flower garden with exotic tropical blooms. Along the way, she explained that this was a cashew nut tree and this was a fruit tree, and she would knock the fruits down so that we could examine them close up. It rained intermittently as we toured the village and we were always ducking in and out of one house or another to avoid getting soaked. But we were always welcomed, and the occupants let us look around and ask questions. Because none of us spoke the Indian dialect, we had to ask our questions in Portuguese, which, of course, is the language of Brazil and is understood by many Indians. In general, I understand 90 percent of what is being said here in Portuguese.

As we were about to leave, Dona Elena looked at me somewhat longingly and said "We haven't had a priest here for years, and while we have a beautiful chapel, we never have Mass. Could you say Mass for us?" I said, "We're leaving at midnight, but if you round up the villagers, I'll go back to the ship and pick up my Mass kit."

I scrambled down the hill and jumped into the zodiac, and asked the boatman to take me back to the ship. I picked up my Mass kit and a few school materials to give them—pencils, crayons, notebooks, etc.—and then boated back to the village. It was just beginning to get dark, but with the help of a flashlight we got up the hill again, then over to the chapel. Meanwhile the villagers had managed to find some gasoline and had the generator running. So besides all the candles burning in the chapel, we also had lights.

Ann Prance, wife of Ian Prance, had come back with me, so we were able to put on a credible Mass, thanks to her Portuguese and my Spanish. Between the two of us, I'm sure they understood most of what we had said, and I even gave a little homily. Also, because they had been without a priest for so long, I had them all say an act of contrition and gave them a general absolution so that they could receive Communion. They insisted on taking a picture in front of the altar (fortunately our zodiac driver had a Polaroid with him), so we left them with a few memories of the Mass and then, with the help of our flashlight, worked our way back down the jungle paths to the riverbank and down the hill to the zodiac.

I showered off the mud and the insect repellent just in time to join a farewell party that was already in progress for our genial French guide, Nicole Preveaux, whom we had dubbed "Mère Supérieure." She is leaving us in Manaus. There was much good cheer, and somebody even provided champagne. After a few short speeches, we adjourned to the Explorers Lounge, which also serves as a bar.

WEDNESDAY, OCTOBER 28
On the Amazon

We began the day by touring Coari, the hometown of Moe, our resident Caboclo. It's quite a large town with a good mile of harbor along the river. The harbor was crowded with the small Amazonian craft that serve as river buses between settlements. They are ungainly-looking and potbellied, but they serve the purpose. People bring their pigs and chickens aboard, sling up their hammocks, and off they go. We visited the market and saw all of the fish we had been catching for the past few days, plus a few larger ones. We then went to the Redemptorist church and school, which recently became a public school for lack of funds. We met two American priests here, Father Tony Judge of St. Louis and Father Andy Thompson of Chicago, both Redemptorists. It's a tough mission here because their people are scattered in so many small villages. To minister to them, the priests must constantly travel up and down the river in their own boats.

Coari is nice enough as Amazonian towns go, but I wouldn't want to live there for long. The heat and humidity are depressing in themselves, and as in all tropical towns, the buildings tend to take on a very shopworn look about two years after they are completed. Everything looks like something out of a Graham Greene novel.

We returned to the ship about 10:30 A.M. and offered Mass for the priests and their mission and for the people of these poor villages.

Today is the last day aboard for those getting off in Manaus. We lose about thirty of our seventy-five passengers, mainly a large group from the University of Washington. At 3:30 P.M., the zodiacs lined up again and we went fishing at Badajós. We caught about fifty piranhas, plus another very large fish which did something you hear about only in fish stories: it jumped into the boat.

THURSDAY, OCTOBER 29
On the Amazon

We were up at 6:30 A.M. to see the mingling of the black waters of the Rio Negro and the brown waters of the Rio Solimões, on which we have been sailing. Just as our shipboard experts had predicted, you could easily tell them apart, even though they were now part of the same river. The water on the left side of the river was black; the water on the right side of the river was the color of chocolate. Most of us went back to bed for another hour while the ship continued on, eventually docking at Manaus.

Manaus has had a checkered history. During the rubber boom in the Amazon, it was the capital where the rubber barons lived. The boom came to an end after the British smuggled the rubber seed out to England and eventually to Indonesia, where the rubber trees grew better. The rubber barons built a big opera house here in 1880. It's the first one I've ever seen with wicker seats. I guess in this climate any breeze is welcome, from whatever direction.

We then went to the museum, which is run by the Salesian Sisters. They get most of the artifacts from their missions, and I noticed that the collection had vastly improved since the last time I was here. I asked one of the Sisters if there were any native Indian priests. She said the only priests were Brazilian. There are, of course, a lot of foreign priests in the country from Europe and the United States as well. When I asked her about native Indian Sisters, she told me there were three in the novitiate and four in the postulate, but that the native Indian women did not persevere very well.

Next we visited two hotels where I had stayed on previous trips here: the Tropical, where we had lunch, and the Hotel Amazonas, which is surrounded by the sprawling free market. At least 1,000 vendors sell a wide variety of imported, duty-free goods. People come here from all over Brazil, attracted by the $600 duty-free exemption and the variety of goods available. I bought a watch strap to replace the one I had. It was rotting away in the tropical heat and humidity and threatening to separate me from the watch that Notre Dame's Business Administration Advisory Council had given me last year. The strap would have cost me between $12 and $15 in New York. Here I paid less than $2.00. Ned and I both bought some Brazilian cigars after scouring practically the whole market to find a place that sold them. Most Brazilian cigars seem to come from Bahia on the east coast, where we'll be stopping.

Checking a marine chart today, I found that the Rio Negro shortly before reaching Manaus is over twelve miles wide. It then narrows for a short distance and is 350 feet deep at that point. Its normal depth is about 150 feet. Since it is a black acidic river, there is nowhere near the fish life that one finds in the so-called white or chocolate-colored rivers, which are full of silt. It's a good thing there is plenty of water around, because the heat can be stifling. In Manaus during the dry season, which coincides with our summer, the temperature ranges between 95 and 118.

Manaus is the halfway point in our journey down the Amazon. We've traveled about 1,100 of the 2,200 miles from Iquitos to Belém.

FRIDAY, OCTOBER 30
On the Amazon

We made good time during the night and arrived at Carauacu at about 9 A.M. Instead of going ashore for the tour, we stayed on the ship and read a week-old copy of *Newsweek* that we picked up yesterday. At 4 P.M. we came to Boca de Valeria, so named because it is at the mouth of the Valeria River. We lowered the zodiacs to visit a nearby Caboclo village. As we made for shore, we found out what the dry season can do to the water level. For the better part of an hour we were in the water pushing or pulling the boats through the shallow spots.

The village was built on the site of a prehistoric Indian community that had existed here before Columbus discovered America. The archaeologists who had studied the site and the artifacts it contained concluded that it must have been a fairly large settlement. It commanded a hill overlooking the river and would have been relatively easy to defend against any enemies attempting to climb up and attack it. Before we left we presented the villagers with several boxes of medicine, bought with funds raised at an auction a few nights earlier aboard ship.

I had hoped we might be able to offer Mass in the village, but we had only fifteen minutes ashore, owing to our late arrival. By the time we returned to the ship, it was dark and they were shining the searchlight to guide us back.

Tonight the captain held a welcome party for the new group that came aboard in Manaus. They had flown in from Miami the night before and numbered about the same as the group that had just left.

SATURDAY, OCTOBER 31
On the Amazon

Some hardy souls who survived the party last night were up at 4:30 A.M. to see the dawn at Lago Grande. Ned and I were not among them. At lunchtime, the ship turned into the Tapajós River, a blue clear-water river in contrast to the muddy Amazon. The town of Santarém is east of the juncture of the Tapajós and the Amazon. Our Holy Cross Brothers have a school there called Don Amando. I visited the school many years ago. Ned and I would love to have visited the school today, but the ship didn't stop there. Instead, we continued up the river to Altar do Chão, which means "Altar of the Earth." The town was a bit more prosperous than the others we've been seeing. That's a sure sign that we're getting closer to the Atlantic coast, where the standard of living is much higher than in other parts of Brazil.

We dropped anchor just off the large and beautiful sandy beach at Altar do Chão, and several of us took a swim. Afterward, we changed into dry clothes and tried to find out the score of the Notre Dame–Navy game on the Armed Forces Network, which the ship was picking up and playing over the PA system. The announcer said he would read all the scores right after the end of the half, but as the half ended, the broadcast suddenly ceased. A member of the crew must have turned off either the radio or the PA system, because there was dead silence. About five minutes later the broadcast resumed, but the scores had already been given and we were left in ignorance. As Ned said, "There is hardly any way we can lose this one." Later we found out we had won it.

In the late afternoon we went back to the beach for a cookout. Normally this lovely strip of white sand would have been covered by water, but the dry season had turned it into a beautiful, Caribbean-style beach. The menu included barbecued ribs, steak, sausage, salad, and many other delectable foods, plus a concoction made of lime juice, sugarcane, and some kind of liquor. It was very good and, I suspect, quite potent. As the stars came out, we took the zodiacs back to the ship.

SUNDAY, NOVEMBER 1
On the Amazon

We had a fine group at Mass this morning, almost a full house in the Penguin Lounge, where we have all of our academic lectures. It was the Feast of All Saints, and Ned gave a fine homily on that theme. I would guess that not more than half a dozen of those in attendance were Catholic, but they all seemed pleased to have this religious service on Sunday morning.

Today was relatively uneventful. For the first time, "nap time" is listed on our schedule. Ned and I used the time to read.

About four o'clock in the afternoon, we launched about five zodiacs and went up a tributary to a settler's cabin in the woods. When we arrived, the only one home who could communicate with us was a little girl. She told us her name was Maria Socorro. She was watching her little sister, who was lying semicomatose in a hammock. The little sister didn't say a word, and we concluded that she was probably mentally retarded.

There were only two rooms in the house, one serving as a combination kitchen and bedroom. Most of the actual cooking, however, was done outside on a platform behind the house. The main room had a lot of hooks for putting up hammocks. Compared with the huts we visited farther upriver, this one was quite well equipped. We saw a sewing machine, another machine for grinding sugar, a lot of pots and pans, and a religious picture on the wall. We asked the little girl if she had been to church for All Saints' Day, and she said she had. She also told us that during the week she paddles upstream for twenty minutes every morning to go to school.

The sunset today was spectacular—massive clouds and a riot of color. It's been a wonderful Sunday and we were reminded that it was exactly five weeks ago that we headed south to Mexico City from Chicago. The weeks have passed quickly. Tomorrow is the beginning of the end of our Amazon trip. We arrive in Belém Tuesday morning.

MONDAY, NOVEMBER 2
On the Amazon

We arrived at Rio Pucurui at exactly 5 A.M. and dropped the hook. A few minutes later, there was general reveille. Just about everybody answered the call this morning, even though it was still dark. They knew it was our last morning in the jungle, and they wanted to make the most of it. Piling into five or six zodiacs, we made the half-mile run from the *Society Explorer* to the mouth of the Pucurui River and started upstream.

It was still pitch-dark. The people in the zodiacs fore and aft of us were sweeping the shoreline with handheld searchlights, looking for crocodiles, but no luck. After another mile or so we shut down our engines and just sat and listened to the sounds of the jungle in the predawn darkness. The initial sounds we heard were not quite what we expected. The first was the crow of a barnyard rooster. The second was Brazilian rock and roll from Belém. The music suddenly blared from a cabin on the shore, where moments before the only sign of life was a candle burning in the window.

Though the exotic night sounds we had anticipated didn't materialize, the trip was far from a total loss. The stars were brilliant in the black velvet sky, and the jungle trees etched eerie silhouettes along both riverbanks. As dawn arrived, the clouds became rose-tipped and the sun, already hot and red, appeared in the east. We were told that the unusual redness of the sun was due not to normal atmospheric conditions but to burning. At the end of the dry season, everyone sets fire to the dead vegetation on his land and the resultant smoke and particulate matter create a filter between the earth and the sun. Why do they do it? Probably because their fathers did.

Once it was light, we began a mile-and-a-half walk along a trail blazed by a rubber collector. These poor fellows have to cut these trails through the thickest jungles to get to the wild rubber trees, the only ones that flourish here. When you put them on a plantation with thousands of other rubber trees, as Henry Ford tried to do at Fordlandia on the upper reaches of the Tapajós, they become infected with a leaf disease. Curiously, when rubber trees are transplanted to plantations in Indonesia, they don't get the disease. In any event, the only usable rubber trees today in Brazil are those spread in pepper-and-salt fashion throughout this thick jungle.

David Campbell, our jungle guide, went ahead of us on the trail, cutting vines to make the trail more passable. We saw a good number of rubber trees with the chevrons cut into them herringbone fashion. This allows the rubber to drip into a little can that's attached just below the cut. Every so often the rubber cruiser comes along and collects the drippings.

We also saw army ants. Millions of them were traveling together in a long line, carrying food to and from their bivouac, which they create anew each day along the trail. But the best part of the hike was simply the last, close-up look it gave us of the deep *várzea* rain forest. As a bonus, it was reasonably cool at this hour of the morning, quite unlike the last jungle walk, which was as hot and humid as a sauna.

We arrived back at the ship about nine o'clock, just in time to have some breakfast. As we ate, the crew weighed anchor and headed the ship toward the narrows on the south side of the river. At 11:30, Ned and I offered our three Masses together for the poor souls and all of our deceased family, as well as the Holy Cross and Notre Dame family members. Only on Christmas and All Souls' Day, November 2, is provision made for three Masses.

Since early morning, we have been going through the middle of the island of Marajó. It's larger than Switzerland and honeycombed with streams. The movie this evening is *China Seas*, starring Clark Gable and Jean Harlow. Ned says he's looking forward to it. The movies they show aboard ship range from oldies to fairly recent releases. One of the reasons for the improvement I've noticed in shipboard movies is that they can now get them in video form.

TUESDAY, NOVEMBER 3
Belém, Brazil

We made good time during the night and arrived in Belém, which is Portuguese for Bethlehem, early this morning. The city is about ninety miles from the Atlantic Ocean, but it's the traditional port of entry to the Amazon from the Atlantic. The first thing we did this morning was to visit the fort. The Portuguese built it in the middle of the harbor to protect both the city and the entrance to the Amazon from encroachment by the Dutch and the British.

The most interesting sight in Belém is undoubtedly the chapel of Our Lady of Nazareth. It takes its name from a statue that was brought here from Nazaré in Portugal over 250 years ago. It was discarded on the bank of the river, but discovered by a peasant in 1700. From then on, the site was a place of devotion and miracles. The church, a minor basilica, was begun in 1909 and finished in 1923. It's a miniature copy of St. Paul's Outside the Walls in Rome. Each year on the second Sunday of October, over a million people (Belém itself has about 1.1 million inhabitants) turn out to carry a replica of the original statue from this church down to the cathedral and back. The old statue never leaves the church, but for fifteen days after the procession it's brought down from the high altar to be closer to the people.

The original forest has been preserved here, so there are 200-foot-high trees smack in the middle of town. At the zoo, we had our first look at a manatee, a kind of sea cow. Unfortunately, the boa constrictors and the anacondas were out to lunch.

We had lunch with Micheline Place, our cruise director, and Ann Prance at Em Casa, a popular restaurant whose name means "In Your Own House." We had some special fish dishes, although, curiously, my grilled fish had been smoked and dried earlier, so it wasn't all that great. The crab, and the special Belém ice cream, *aici*, made up for it.

A few more people got off in Belém. As a result, Ned and I have separate cabins now, which will give us a little more room and flexibility. After lunch today, I took a long walk through the main street in town, Presidente Vargas, and then along the open market, which is very colorful but stinks to high heaven, especially where the fish are sold. I'm sure the Brazilian cigars I bought today also stink to high heaven, in the opinion of some. I can go to the top deck and position myself downwind when I smoke them.

As we come to the end of our trip down the Amazon, I should mention that when we left Iquitos, we had two pilots, who guided us through the various difficult channels, which change from year to year as the river changes course. After Manaus, we picked up two more pilots, who brought us to Belém. Now we have another pilot, who will take us to the Atlantic. From then on, the captain and the crew will do the navigating.

At night we decided to break out some red wine that was given us by some of our Coca-Cola friends. We shared with some of the Machu Picchu group who were at dinner, and we'll share the rest of it with the others tomorrow night. Two of our traveling companions, the Harrises, a nice couple from Flint, Michigan, bought Ned and me a gift. We had met them in town this afternoon and they were both wearing very neat-looking hats made of bark. They are high in the crown and wide in the brim like a Western hat, only different. I think we probably envied them their hats too much, because they presented each of us with one.

As we neared the mouth of the Amazon, the ship began to pitch and roll. It really feels like we're in the ocean, even though we're still a good forty miles away.

WEDNESDAY, NOVEMBER 4
At Sea

We had a very pitching-and-rolling night once we reached the ocean. I guess sailors would call this a moderate sea, but after so long on the placid waters of the Amazon, it doesn't seem so to us. Everybody has to learn how to walk again. It requires some acrobatic ability just to brush your teeth or take a shower.

I was up on the top deck after breakfast plowing through Massie's *Peter the Great*. After an hour I had to quit, because we changed course a bit and the wind was whipping the spray over the deck and dousing us every few minutes. At breakfast and lunch, it was apparent that about half of the passengers were ill, including Ned. He did, however, manage to get through Mass just before lunch. It's amazing how many different gadgets and medicines people are using to avoid seasickness. Some have wristbands, some have tape behind the ears, Dramamine is available to everyone on the counter of the Command Center, and all along the corridor handrails are seasickness bags. So far, I'm depending on my Irish luck.

Peter Harrison gave us a talk this afternoon entitled "Ocean Nomads," which was really about the albatross. Peter is a born teacher and a very eloquent lecturer. I now know more about the albatross than I thought I'd ever want to know, and I've certainly proved that it's never too late to learn. Too bad Peter didn't have another lecture prepared for the evening. It could have replaced the movie, an abomination called *The Tall Blond Man with One Black Shoe*. If the rest of the movies are anything like this one, I'll finish *Peter the Great*, a very thick book, in record time.

THURSDAY, NOVEMBER 5
At Sea

The sea is again running high and we're rolling just about as much as we were yesterday morning. We had a few more people for breakfast, but there are still a good many coping with their seasickness, mainly by staying in bed.

Peter Harrison gave us a lecture this morning, "The Totorore Expedition." This is an expedition that he and two other ornithologists made in a 36-foot sailing vessel. They landed on many of the islands that surround the Cape of Good Hope, favorite nesting grounds of many seabirds, including penguins. Peter had a couple of close calls on this expedition, once by falling off a 125-foot cliff when he lost his grip, another time by getting caught three miles off Tierra del Fuego in a hurricane. Peter not only writes about birds but also paints them. I plan to get one of his books and have him autograph it for our collection at Notre Dame.

Ann Prance gave a good talk this afternoon entitled "Victoria Amazonica." This is a large water lily that I've seen in several places in the lakes alongside the river. The lily pad is about five feet across and it has a wonderful white flower that opens at sundown. It then closes slightly, so that the beetles that enter it scrape off some of the pollen they are carrying from previously visited lilies. The next day the pollinated lily opens again, turns completely red, and dies. Nine months later, the pollinated seeds, which have traveled down the stem, give birth to another such flower.

This afternoon a skua flew alongside the ship on its annual migration from Newfoundland to Antarctica. This bird has the best of both worlds, spending the spring and summer in Alaska or northern

Canada and then flying 18,000 miles to spend spring and summer in Antarctica, where the seasons are reversed. I saw a number of them around McMurdo Sound on Ross Island when I was down there for the National Science Foundation in 1963.

Tonight I finished Massie's *Peter the Great*. It's a wonderful book, but 855 pages is a bit long, especially when they're in small print and you're bouncing around on choppy water.

FRIDAY, NOVEMBER 6
At Sea

The sea was heavy all night, but flattened out some today, and almost everyone seems to be back on their feet again. Peter Harrison gave another fascinating lecture on seabirds. He can really make them interesting.

After lunch today, Ned got me involved in a bridge game with the Harrises. I hadn't played bridge in sustained fashion since 1969, when Doc Kenna, one of my oldest and very best Holy Cross priest friends, and I were on a ship from Los Angeles to Sydney for twenty-two days. Ned and I had good cards and won easily.

After a lecture by Ann Prance on the history of Fernando de Noronha, a group of islands we'll be visiting tomorrow, Peter Harrison began hawking raffle tickets for three of his bird paintings to help finance his next trip with the Totorore Expedition. For that reason, and because the paintings were very good, Ned and I both bought tickets. We didn't win!

This night we stayed up past midnight playing bridge again with the Harrises. Once more the cards fell our way. There was an ancient movie on while all this was happening. It starred Gloria Swanson and William Powell, if you can remember back that far. I can't even recall the title.

SATURDAY, NOVEMBER 7
Fernando de Noronha, Brazil

Around seven o'clock this morning we dropped anchor at Fernando de Noronha, the group of islands that Ann Prance had told us about in her lecture yesterday. The islands rose from the sea as volcanic lava some 12 million years ago. The first recorded mention of them was in 1500 by an anonymous navigator named Juan. He called them Cuaresma, which is the Spanish word for Lent. Three years later, Amerigo Vespucci put into port here en route to Bahia. The islands had abundant water and large trees at that time, both of which they lack today. The Portuguese built eleven forts on the islands, the main one being Our Lady of Remedies. In more recent times the islands have served as a penal colony, a U.S. Army base, and a tracking station for the NASA space program.

A number of distinguished scientists have done research here, among them Charles Darwin, Sir Charles Thompson, and a Dr. Ridley of the Royal Society, who wrote a botanical history of the islands.

We sailed in zodiacs down the shore of the main island to a protected cove where the dolphins breed and cavort. With the help of the Harrises, I chalked up another first: I went snorkeling. It was great fun. I would judge we were in about fifty feet of water, but the bottom was clearly visible, as were a number of fish, both large and small. But the most exciting part of the experience was an underwater encounter I had with a couple of dolphins; one of them came within about fifteen feet of me. Fortunately, there were no sharks.

We went back to the ship to get into dry clothes, then lowered the zodiacs again for a trip into town. The water became very shallow as we neared shore, so we were forced to make what is called a "wet" landing. That simply means that you get out of the boat before you reach the shore and slosh the rest of the way through the water, à la General MacArthur. As luck would have it, I had just cleaned and waxed my brown walking shoes.

The town is all one would expect of a speck in the ocean with a population of only 1,000. To put it as kindly as possible, there wasn't much to see. The most prominent feature of the island is a 1,000-foot volcanic peak with an airplane beacon at its top. The church on the island was built in 1722. Though in good repair, it hadn't seen a priest in a long, long time. If we'd known that earlier, Ned and I could have had Mass there today.

SUNDAY, NOVEMBER 8
En Route to Recife, Brazil

Another beautiful Sunday morning. When I looked out the porthole, I saw a tanker in the far distance going in the same direction as we were, but we were traveling faster. The next time I looked it was gone. We had Mass at nine o'clock and another fairly full congregation, 98 percent of whom were not Catholic. It was my turn to preach. I talked on death and immortality, resurrection and hope. Also, about not being afraid to die, but looking forward to death with great anticipation and wonderment. I also talked about being ready to greet the Lord when He comes again, as He surely will come to all of us at the hour of death.

We docked in Recife about 12:30 P.M., just as we sat down to lunch. Recife is a port on the bulge of Brazil and the first Latin American city I ever visited. The last time, in 1956, I flew in from Dakar in Africa. It has a population of 1.5 million people, with another 1.5 million in the environs. The city was founded in 1535 by the Portuguese, and is often called the Brazilian Venice because of its three islands, four rivers, and thirty-four bridges. It's a very, very pretty tropical city, and we all enjoyed the bus tour provided for us.

Our next stop was Olinda, a lovely city built on low hills six kilometers to the north of Recife. Olinda was founded by the Portuguese in 1535, has seven churches, including a Benedictine monastery, and is home to the first university in Brazil. Because of its outstanding architecture, it's been designated by UNESCO as a cultural center to be preserved. We took a walking tour through the town. I had visited it once before, but I was impressed all over again by the way the colonial character of the town had been preserved. Besides the colonial houses and architecture, Olinda is festooned with all kinds of flamboyant trees, which come in pink, red, yellow, and a few other colors.

It was over 90 degrees and very humid here today, so after walking up and down the hills in Olinda, we went out to a beachside restaurant for a tropical drink. We then returned to the city and visited the cultural center, a former jail that has been converted to a complex of shops that sell local handicrafts. Dinner was at a well-known seafood restaurant on the beach. It's been six weeks since we left Chicago.

MONDAY, NOVEMBER 9
At Sea

Just a few words about Salvador, which we will be visiting tomorrow. It used to be called São Salvador de Bahia de Todos-os-Santos, which means the Holy Savior of Bahia of All the Saints. Bahia is the Brazilian state in which Salvador is located. Brazil was discovered by the navigator Cabral in 1500. A Portuguese gentleman named Thomé de Sousa founded Salvador in 1549. It is just below the shoulder of Brazil, about a day and a half's sail from Recife.

Sugarcane was first introduced to this region in 1530. It's a labor-intensive undertaking, and Indian slaves performed most of the labor. The Portuguese raided villages in the interior and brought the Indians back by force, an estimated 7,000 of them. The Indians turned out to be poor workers, however, at least in the opinion of the Portuguese, and as a result they were replaced by Africans in 1538. By 1585, one-fourth of all the inhabitants of Salvador were black slaves, numbering about 14,000. Over the next 300 years, some 3 to 5 million blacks were brought from Africa.

Salvador, like Recife, was attacked by the Dutch, who occupied it from 1625 to 1654. The Dutch were finally expelled. They went to the Antilles in the Caribbean and took a good part of the sugar-growing expertise with them. Salvador fell to second place in the production of sugar for Europe. It continued to prosper, however, because it was on a beautiful bay and had a deep-water port and rich soil.

In 1822, independence came to Brazil. The most powerful leader at that time was Dom Pedro II, who bore the title of emperor. When precious metals were found in the interior, in Minas Gerais, many of the slaves were moved there to work the mines. Slavery was abolished in 1888, but the blacks remained and they now constitute about half the population. Over the years they have exerted considerable influence on the language and customs of the country, but their most noticeable legacy is in religion, where they have combined the spiritism of their native Africa with the Catholicism that was forced upon them when they arrived as slaves. The resultant amalgam is called macumba or urbamba. Some of the blacks practice Catholicism, but still attend macumba services where they invoke good and bad spirits and practice certain black arts. But the fastest-growing religion here is the Protestant charismatic church, which requires its adherents to renounce macumba.

We didn't see the coast at all today, as we were too far out to sea. But the sea was reasonably calm, and we should arrive in Salvador sometime tomorrow morning. Ann Prance found me the latest possible *Time* magazine at the airport yesterday, so I read it today and am now only a week behind in the news. Though it is late Monday, we still don't know who won the Boston College game at Notre Dame on Saturday. We are really out of touch.

TUESDAY, NOVEMBER 10
Salvador, Brazil

When we arrived in Salvador we were met by a bus for a kind of once-over-lightly tour to give us the lay of the land. We then struck out on foot, first visiting the cathedral and some other nearby churches. There are 170 churches in Salvador, which is really something when you consider that the population here is 2 million. Most of the churches were built by religious orders—the Franciscans, the Carmelites, and the Jesuits. The Jesuits built the cathedral.

Many of the old streets here are cobblestone and lined with sidewalks of wavy black-and-white patterns strongly reminiscent of those in Lisbon and along the Avenida Atlântica in Rio. Ned and I bought some more cigars today. As I mentioned earlier, the state of Bahia is a great cigar-making area and the price is right.

Around midnight I heard the seamen pulling in the ropes and getting ready to take off for Rio, the last lap of our trip on the *Society Explorer*. We've had some wonderful experiences on this ship, and I know that Ned and I will both miss it after we get off, not to mention the many friends we've made aboard.

WEDNESDAY, NOVEMBER 11
At Sea

This morning right after breakfast, we saw the oceanography segment of David Attenborough's *Planet Earth* series. It presented the latest scientific data on the interdependence of oceans, atmosphere, and weather throughout the world. A little later we went back to the Penguin Lounge for Ann Prance's story of how she managed to live in Amazonia with two small children while her husband was away on field trips most of the time. Making the transition from New York to a one-room apartment in Manaus was a real challenge.

Ned and I had Mass before lunch. Our little book of daily Masses has run out, so we're picking our own Epistles and Gospels from a small New Testament we carry with us. Peter Harrison gave a marvelously crafted talk this afternoon on penguins. After dinner we were entertained by the crew, who performed songs and skits of various kinds. There were also some traditional Filipino dances by the largely Filipino crew.

THURSDAY, NOVEMBER 12
At Sea

The sea turned rough about midnight last night, about the same time that the crew's show ended and most of the passengers were preparing to turn in. The heavy rolling continued throughout the day, and most of the passengers stayed in their cabins.

We called Jorge Giganti, our Coca-Cola contact in Rio, on the ship's radiotelephone. We told him we'd be arriving around 7 A.M. tomorrow morning and disembarking shortly before nine. He said he'd have a car and driver waiting. We spent our final night on the ship saying our goodbyes at Captain Torsten Olbrich's farewell cocktail party and dinner.

FRIDAY, NOVEMBER 13
Rio de Janeiro, Brazil

We had a wake-up call at 5:30 this morning for those who wanted to see the Rio harbor from afar. I got up for it, but it was too foggy and I took one look and went back to bed. We landed here about 7:30 and were finally off the ship at nine o'clock. Gustavo de Sá, a fine young fellow who's Coca-Cola's public relations man in Rio, smoothed our way through customs and delivered us to the Othon Hotel on Copacabana beach. Our rooms, one atop the other on the eighth and ninth floors, have a magnificent panoramic view—Corcovado, the mountain with the famous statue of Christ the Savior on its top, plus the whole bay and the beach.

Our main activity today was nailing down all the reservations we're going to need between now and December 6, the day we return to the United States. It was no easy task, even though we knew, generally, where we wanted to be and when. Because of a strike, all the computers at the airport were down. Fortunately, the travel department at Coca-Cola came through for us—as they have done several times before.

Once we had the nitty gritty travel details out of the way, I went out to buy a topaz for my ever-faithful secretary, Helen Hosinski, who will have to type all of these notes. Again, thanks to Coca-Cola, I not only found a fine stone at a third of the price it would cost in the states, but at a 25 percent discount as well. As you probably know, Brazil leads the world in the production of semiprecious gemstones.

Rio looks a lot better than it did when I was here several years ago with the Chase Manhattan Bank board. Yet the country is in terrible financial shape and the most familiar gripe is about the economy. Somehow, though, most people on the street appear to be happy. It probably has something to do with the customary upbeat attitude of the people who live in Rio. They call themselves Cariocas, which means people who put happiness and good times ahead of work and worry.

We were warned repeatedly not to walk alone on the beach or to take along anything of value that could be easily snatched. The explanation was that there is so much poverty here that those who are accustomed to living by their wits are using them a little too broadly these days.

Tonight we had dinner at the home of Roberto Marinho, often described as the most important person in Brazil. He's the editor of *O Globo*, one of the two main newspapers in the country. In addition, he owns about sixty radio and television stations and, more important, has donated airtime to the teaching of reading and writing to illiterates. Roberto is also a member of our International Advisory Council for the Kellogg Institute of International Studies at Notre Dame. I met him for the first time a few years ago when he and I received honorary degrees from the University of Brasília.

Our young Coca-Cola friend, Gustavo, and his girlfriend, Cristiana, who works in Marinho Enterprises, were also invited to Roberto's house for dinner. The other invitees were Father Laercio Dias de Moura, a Jesuit who is rector of the Catholic University here, and Walter Poyares and his wife, Maria Lucia. He is a professor of communications and a top adviser to Roberto.

The Marinho home is almost impossible to describe. First of all, it's high on a hill with a wonderful view of the statue of Christ the Savior. At night the view is even more spectacular, because the statue is lighted. The house is set in the middle of a primitive jungle forest with a stream running through it. Inside, the walls are hung with one of the best art collections in Brazil.

Roberto is in his eighties, but looks much younger. When we arrived, he said "Tonight we speak French." His younger wife, Ruth, prepared a very tasty dinner to go along with the conversation, which included a discussion of our Kellogg Institute at Notre Dame. During the course of the conversation I tried to persuade Roberto to come to our next meeting. By the way, Ned and I dressed up in black tonight, the first time we've done this in the last six weeks.

SATURDAY, NOVEMBER 14
Rio de Janiero, Brazil

It was a kind of lazy day in which Ned really saw Rio for the first time. We went out to the Catholic University to visit with the rector. The university had grown like Topsy since I first visited it in 1956. At the Jesuit Retreat House we visited with Father Alonso, who was rector when I first came here. He is now eighty-six years old and still working and writing about education.

We lunched alfresco with our driver at an Italian restaurant, then drove to the top of Corcovado—the word means "hunchback"—and climbed the hundred or so steps up to the base of the statue of Christ the Savior. While I had been here three times before, I was still dazzled by the view—the most spectacular in Rio.

Our next stop was Pão de Açúcar, better known to English-speaking visitors as Sugarloaf. It also provides a great view of the city, but not from so lofty an altitude as Corcovado. There is a large funicular that goes up in two stages, swinging out over a 1,000-foot drop. It's a memorable ride if you're not bothered by heights.

Finally, we went over to see the new cathedral, which is like an enormous rounded pyramid about 250 feet high. When I was here last, about eight years ago, they were still working on this building. But it now appears to be about a hundred years old because the concrete exterior has taken on that dirty black look that buildings quickly acquire in the tropics. They need to be whitewashed every year, otherwise all new buildings soon look moldy. Inside, it's quite attractive, with its long stained-glass windows and circular seating area. On a scale of 1 to 10, I would give this architect a 1 for the outside and possibly a 7 for the inside. Too bad, because most people see this church only from the outside.

Tomorrow we're going to Petrópolis, the summer watering hole of Brazil's former royalty.

SUNDAY, NOVEMBER 15
Petrópolis, Brazil

We were up early and on our way to Petrópolis with Gustavo and Cristiana. The road there is an experience in itself, climbing from sea level at Rio to 3,500 feet at Petrópolis, which is in the mountains. We visited the Imperial Museum, formerly the residence of the emperors—Pedro I, Pedro II, and Isabel, the daughter of Pedro II. We also saw the Crystal Palace and a wonderful old hotel that used to be the gambling center when gambling was legal here.

We looked in at Mass at the cathedral, but didn't stay, because we had Mass right afterward at the home of Cristiana's grandparents. They live in a wonderful wooded valley where every tree had been planted by Cristiana's grandfather. We had Mass for them, plus several other relatives, the cook, and the housekeeper. Gustavo and Cristiana did the three readings in Portuguese. Following Mass, we blessed all the houses in the family compound. Then we had a real Brazilian lunch, black beans and rice, among other Brazilian specialties.

We arrived back at the hotel around seven o'clock in the evening, but skipped dinner. So far, no word on the Alabama game yesterday. We really have a news blackout here, despite the fact that the Othon Hotel is full of Americans.

MONDAY, NOVEMBER 16
Rio de Janiero, Brazil

Shortly after 5:30 A.M. we celebrated our last Mass in Rio. We arrived at the airport around seven and after an hour's delay were in Brasília by 9:30. As usual, we were met by someone from Coca-Cola, a driver named Jonas, who spoke only Portuguese, but understood my Spanish perfectly. I told him that this was Ned's first visit to Brasília, and I think Jonas tried extra hard to make sure that Ned saw everything.

First we went up in the TV tower in the middle of town so that Ned could get a look at the whole government setup, which runs on north-south and east-west axes. Once we had grasped the layout, we did a quick drive-by tour of all the main buildings. These included the cathedral, the Senate, the House of Deputies, all sixteen ministries, the Supreme Court, the Presidential Palace, and, later on, the president's residence.

The city has grown a great deal since I was last here. It now has about 1.2 million inhabitants. That makes it much smaller than either Rio or São Paulo, but it must be remembered that Brasília was carved out of the jungle from scratch. When I was here the first time more than twenty years ago, it was just a barren plain and everything was full of red dust. Today, there are lawns and flowers and greenery everywhere. Because the city was planned, it has much better buildings, housing, roads, and general organization than either Rio or São Paulo. The buildings were designed by Oscar Niemeyer, perhaps the most famous architect in Brazil.

For lunch we had *currasco*, a first experience for Ned. This typical Brazilian dish is a combination of pork, lamb, chicken, beef, and sausages, all barbecued. It's served with rice and farina, a coarse flour concoction, and, of course, cold beer. I remembered the restaurant from my last visit. It had a reputation then for the best *currasco* in town, and it was apparent to both of us that the quality had not diminished. Ned was hooked immediately.

After lunch, we made quick stops at the Coca-Cola office, the university, where we spent a few minutes with the rector, Dr. Cristovan, and the American Embassy, where we stayed just long enough to find out from the Marine guard that Notre Dame had beaten Alabama last Saturday. Then it was on to the airport for our flight to São Paulo, where we will stay just long enough to have a chat with Chris Lund, a Notre Dame alumnus from the States.

Chris and his daughter Carmen, a Notre Dame student, met us at the São Paulo airport and took us to the family home on the outskirts of town. We had a long talk, mainly about the scholarship that he is setting up for Latin American students, especially those here in Brazil. After that, it was off to bed in the guesthouse.

TUESDAY, NOVEMBER 17
São Paulo, Brazil

This was our final day in Brazil. We were up at 6:30 A.M. for Mass with the family and household staff. After a continental breakfast, we dropped Chris off at the Brazilian Chamber of Commerce office, where he is president for São Paulo, the largest council in Brazil. Then it was on to the airport. The horrendous traffic doubled our travel time compared with the day before. Once there, we found a Miami paper and learned that we really clobbered Alabama last Saturday. This news was especially welcomed by Ned, who looked after Notre Dame athletics for all those thirty-five years he was executive vice president, and for whom the lean years of the early 1980s were still a fresh memory.

Our flight to Santiago, Chile, took about four hours in a 737. At the airport, waiting to welcome us, were our good friends Father George Canepa, a Chilean Holy Cross priest, and Father Charlie Delaney, a classmate of Ned's. Ned stayed with Charlie, who is in charge of seminarian formation here, and I moved in with George. When I arrived at the Casa Santa María, my billet for the stay here, I called Helen back at the office to catch up with the news. I also asked her to arrange for overcoats for Ned and me in New York, where we'll be arriving in about three weeks with nothing but summer clothes.

Tonight, Ned and I had dinner with Alejandro Foxley and his wife, Giselle, at their home. Father Ernie Bartell, director of the Kellogg Institute, also joined us, so there was a lot of shop talk, as might be imagined. Mostly, we discussed the new Hesburgh International Building at Notre Dame, which will house our Kroc Institute for International Peace Studies as well as the Kellogg Institute for International Studies. Both these institutes are doing very important work, and in the years ahead I will be devoting a great deal of time to them, as chairman of their International Advisory Boards.

WEDNESDAY, NOVEMBER 18
Santiago, Chile

There are five of us living here in the Casa. I've taken over George's room, which is crammed with books. Across the hall is Father Bob Simon, the new rector of the school that the Holy Cross priests operate in the slums here. Next to him is Father Frank Provenzano, an old friend from my seminary days and an engineer who teaches math, physics, and computers at St. George's, the high school that our Holy Cross priests run here. Father George Canepa is across the hall from him next to me. Then there is Father Joe Dorsey, who has been here forever. He is the fellow who really keeps things going in this house.

George told me they bought this place years ago for $120. It's only one story high, but has a nice living-dining room, plus a glassed-in porch with a wild eagle in the backyard and a lot of flowers and plants. After seven weeks of hotels and the boat, it's good to be staying in a place that feels so much like home.

This morning I took time to read, pray, and take a walk. Then my colleagues took me on a tour of one of the nearby slums. It was a place that the Holy Cross priests plan to work in. Next we went to St. George's High School, or Colegio as it's called here. The military had expropriated it for about a dozen years, during which time it went to the dogs academically. We have it back now, but it's still in the academic recovery process.

Ned, George, Ernie, and I took Ignacio ("Nacho") and Marta Lozano to lunch at an exceptional seafood restaurant today. They're from Los Angeles, where Nacho, a Notre Dame Trustee, publishes *La Opinión*, the largest Spanish-language newspaper in the United States. Nacho is here for the Inter-American Press Conference. He will be elected president of that large association tonight.

After lunch, I visited CIEPLAN, which is Alejandro Foxley's economic research institute. Alejandro is on our faculty at Notre Dame, but spends half of his time here in Chile at the institute which he directs. (Under the new President, Patricio Aylwin, he has become minister of finance for Chile.) Many of his best researchers and students come to Notre Dame for a year or so for research and teaching. We had a kind of informal seminar with some of them.

Father Ernie Bartell is also here doing research, as is another Holy Cross priest, Father Tim Scully, who is doing doctoral studies at Berkeley on Latin American political questions.

George Canepa picked me up around six. We went back to the house to finish our prayers and then left for San Roque, a parish in the slums. Ned and I concelebrated there with Father Fermín Donoso. Fermín asked me to give a little talk in Spanish after the Mass, which I did. Then we went to the training center, where Ned is staying, for pizza and beer.

Each year about sixty Notre Dame students volunteer at graduation time to work in Holy Cross schools and parishes around the world. We call them Holy Cross Associates. This kind of volunteer work is very good life experience for the students. We've found that it stays with them for the rest of their lives. There are usually about four to six Holy Cross Associates here in Santiago. I spent a good deal of time with them last year and was happy to meet many of the same graduates again tonight and discuss what they have been doing for the past year. They all said that while it was difficult, they would do it over again if given the opportunity. Some of them are even staying on for an extra year. Fortunately, they are given three months of Spanish instruction in Cuernavaca, Mexico. After they arrive in Santiago, they receive two weeks of orientation on the history and culture of Chile and the Church here. Then they engage in educational and social work.

During a free hour today, we went to the Vicariate for Solidarity, an archdiocesan department that helps people who are in trouble with the government. In addition to those who have been killed, there are thousands of others who were kidnapped and tortured, but survived. One of them, Romero Olivares, a medical doctor whose crime was that he treated a man wounded by the military, is being put on trial next week. I promised to send a letter to the Chief Justice of the Supreme Court, voicing concern from the States about the trial. I remember being told about this same case when I visited the Vicariate last year. On returning to the States, I persuaded the Human Rights Committee of the National Academy of Sciences to make their voice heard. Seven Nobel laureates sent strong letters in behalf of Olivares, who could spend the next ten years in jail, as he has the last one and a half years. My letter may not do very much good, but it's worth a try. We were told at the Vicariate that these people tend to act more responsibly when they know that the outside world is watching. Incidentally, the Vicariate has just won the second Jimmy Carter Award for social justice work from Emory University. (P.S. Dr. Olivares was released after the trial.)

THURSDAY, NOVEMBER 19
Santiago, Chile

I spent most of the morning reading. Then we went to see the wonderful American ambassador, Harry Barnes. We discussed the situation here in Chile and the big rally that the opposition had in the park today. Actually it wasn't as big a rally as some had hoped, drawing somewhere between 60,000 and 80,000 people. I am less and less impressed by the leadership of the Chilean Christian Democratic Party, the only strong opposition to Pinochet. If they could unite the rest of the opposition they could be much more effective, but no one wants to compromise. As a result, the opposition is splintered into a dozen minor, ineffectual parties. (They later did unite and won the election.)

I brought my letter in behalf of Dr. Olivares to the ambassador so that he might deliver it to the Chief Justice of the Supreme Court. He seemed to like it, and said he would see that it was delivered.

Tonight, all the Holy Cross priests who weren't otherwise engaged got together to welcome Father Dick Warner, our provincial, who arrived this morning, and to say goodbye to Ned and me. Dick brought videos of the Notre Dame football games, so we were able to see last week's game against Alabama, only the second Notre Dame game we've seen this fall. As a going-away present, they gave us a beautiful copper cross set with Chilean stones. It was a heartwarming evening, enriched by many old and dear friends.

FRIDAY, NOVEMBER 20
Santiago, Chile

This morning we ran some errands in town. There was a luncheon meeting at the Casa for most of the Holy Cross priests engaged in education here. I suppose I could have gone, but it was a delightful feeling to be in a situation where I didn't have to go to a meeting when everyone else did. Anyway, we had to pack for our flight to Punta Arenas, far to the south. Two of our Holy Cross friends are going with us, Father George Canepa of the Santiago contingent and Father Ernie Bartell, who, as I mentioned before, is down here doing research in connection with his job as director of Notre Dame's Kellogg Institute.

Santiago looked its beautiful best today in the bright spring sunshine. The snow-clad Cordillera loomed in the distance, their peaks rising up 16,000 feet and more beyond Aconcagua, the highest peak of them all.

We left the house around the middle of the afternoon to go to Pudahuel, where we took a Landeco flight to Puerto Montt, at the end of the central valley of Chile, and then down to Punta Arenas (Sandy Point), which is the southernmost city in the world, far below Cape Town or New Zealand and Australia.

The Santiago–Puerto Montt leg of our flight provided scenery that kept us glued to the windows all the way. There was one snowcapped volcano after another, with deep valleys in between them and the Cordillera Blanca in the distance. In many ways, the scene below us resembled Antarctica: mountains buried up to their peaks in snow; avalanches and glaciers flowing down their sides; great snow-fields, serried as the snow begins to get warm and drift downward in the springtime; deep fjords slicing into the land from the sea. Ned thought it was the most spectacular sight he had ever seen. One such view would be spectacular, but to see it repeated mile after mile for an hour and fifty minutes is something else again.

It was close to 90 degrees when we left Santiago, but when we got off the plan in Punta Arenas, there was a slight drizzle and the wind was so strong it practically blew us back into the plane. We were glad we brought windbreakers along.

As we drove from the airport to the city, we could look out to the right and see the famous Strait of Magellan, which is about eleven kilometers across. The city counts about 125,000 people, many engaged in oil production. Others herd sheep and run the free port. We're staying at a small hotel with an interesting name, Los Navi-gantes, the navigators. It was still light when we drove into the city at 10:30 P.M. Dawn comes at five o'clock here, because we're a long way south now, and moving into spring.

SATURDAY, NOVEMBER 21
Punta Arenas, Chile

The four of us had Mass together at about eight o'clock this morning. After breakfast, we went over to the travel agency and arranged for a car and driver. First, we headed north out of Punta Arena along the Strait of Magellan. There were thousands of sheep along the route, also nandus, the only American ostriches. After about fifty kilometers we reached the beach, where we parked the car and started walking. There were shorebirds galore and two groups of penguins with about thirty in each group. One group was marching single file across the rocks along the shore. The other group was lazing on a small spit of land out in the water. We got within about thirty or forty feet of the first group. Then, as if on signal, they all dove into the water and swam off. Some of them came back after a while, and we took pictures of them.

After lunch, we headed south to Bulnes Fort, founded in 1840, two years before Father Sorin established Notre Dame. The Spanish built it to control the Strait of Magellan. It was restored in 1940.

On our way back to Punta Arenas, we stopped at Puerto Hambre, which means the Port of Hunger. The Spanish dropped off some 400 settlers here in 1584 in an attempt to consolidate their position along the strait. By the time the next ship returned, all of them had died, presumably of hunger. Monuments scattered around the site tell the story in detail.

We were back at the hotel around 8:30 and had a quick game of bridge. Toward the end of the game, someone wondered aloud how the Notre Dame football team was doing against Penn State. We found out that for two dollars we could call the States for one minute, so we put in a call to my secretary, Helen Hosinski. She didn't answer, so we called Ned's secretary, Pat Roth. For our trouble we found out that Notre Dame had lost the game, 21–20. So much for curiosity.

SUNDAY, NOVEMBER 22
Punta Arenas, Chile

Again, we were blessed with a sunny day, which is unusual in these parts. Today we boarded a tour bus for a look at the territory to the north of us. It was a rough ride. The roads were in poor repair in many places, and sometimes the surface was entirely gravel. At Puerto Natales we're going to take an oceangoing ferry.

As we headed north, we paralleled the Strait of Magellan until we came to the border of Chile and Argentina. There we turned west, following the Argentinian border all the way into Puerto Natales. The countryside resembled that of Montana and Wyoming, with low rolling hills to start, then mountains. In the distance the mountains were capped with snow and streaked with glaciers.

At Puerto Natales we left the bus and picked up a van with a driver. Lunch was *curanto*, an appetizing mixture of chicken, pork ribs, clams, potatoes, wieners, and dumplings, all mixed together in a pan like bouillabaisse. After downing all of that with much gusto, we climbed into the van and headed northeast to Torres del Paine, the most beautiful part of southern Chile. Along the way, we stopped to visit Cueva del Milodon, the Cave of the Milodon. The skeleton of a prehistoric bearlike animal that stood about twelve to fifteen feet tall was found in this cave some years ago. Also found were human remains dating back about 11,000 years.

After about 200 kilometers, we came to a lovely deep green lake called Lago Sarmiento. There were rock towers in the distance, and after much winding and turning we arrived at another lovely lake, Pehoe. There we checked into the Hostel Pehoe, one of the best-kept secrets in the world. It has only about eighty rooms, but it makes up for its small size by its setting. Close by are the blue-gray waters of Pehoe Lake. Behind it, a massif much like the Tetons whose top is covered with glaciers and enormous blankets of snow 100-feet thick. It's as pretty a site as any I've seen in the world.

Today was a long day. We traveled over 300 miles on bad roads. But the beauty we found here was worth it.

MONDAY, NOVEMBER 23
Torres del Paine, Chile

We awoke to another beautiful day with hardly a cloud in the light blue sky. If we seem to be extolling the weather too much, our guide told us that he had been up here eight times before and had enjoyed only one good day. So we feel very fortunate.

Early this morning I went up to the lookout point above the hotel and prayed my Breviary. With a clear view of the awesome massif, I couldn't have picked a better place to pray.

After a continental breakfast, we drove along the Pehoe River, then the Grey River, which flows into the Lago de Toro, the largest lake in this region. This brought us to the national park. We followed the Grey River up to its source in Grey Lake, the head of which is an active glacier. It took us about forty-five minutes to drive to the end of the road, a distance of about ten miles. When we got there, our driver parked the van and we walked through a forest and then across a moraine that was sand and gravel for about four miles. We saw large icebergs floating down the river from the glacier head at Grey Lake.

As they tumbled and bobbed down the river, they were sculpted into all kinds of marvelous shapes.

We also saw a lot of wildlife: more nandus, the American ostriches I mentioned earlier, guanacos or American camels, lots of rabbits, several kinds of hawks and other birds of prey, and the large south American geese, more striking in a way than our Canada geese, and about as large. We also saw some black-necked swans and pink flamingos on Lago Amargo, a salt lake in the middle of the national park, and four large condors wheeling over the mountaintops. This is about a third as many condors as are left in all of North America.

We came back to the hotel for lunch before leaving—great roast lamb and salad—then we started back through the park about 3 P.M. and bumped our way along the gravel road for another couple of hundred kilometers. We went around the backside of the massif, where you can clearly see the three towers. Some Japanese climbers were going almost straight up the rock face of the middle one.

The glacier is part of a whole series of glaciers that stretch out 350 kilometers long and 60 kilometers wide, creating the third-largest ice field in the world. The only ones that are bigger are in the Arctic and the Antarctic.

We arrived in Puerto Natales shortly after 6 P.M., but were told that we couldn't get aboard ship until nine. We are taking this ship to see from the ocean some of the wonderful fjords we saw on our flight down here. We stashed our luggage in a hotel and went shopping for supplies. While we were having dinner, some character walked in with a king penguin, which naturally received a lot of attention. When you see one of these big birds up close for the first time they are very striking.

The stateroom Ned and I were assigned is much larger than the one we had on the *Society Explorer*. We also have two fine top decks for viewing the scenery along the way, and a recreation room for playing bridge. You can't ask for more. George, Ernie, Ned, and I are looking forward to this leg of our trip with great anticipation. There are only seven other people aboard, three couples and a single woman. This ship, about 300 feet long, full of boxed and live cargo (cattle and horses), is called the *Evangelista*.

TUESDAY, NOVEMBER 24
At Sea

The sun was peeping in and out of the clouds when we got up this morning, and we could see a rainbow on the shoreline. We have two fairly large windows, or portholes, if you wish. After breakfast, we each did some reading, writing, and praying. The top deck was windy, but provided a great view of the snowcapped mountains on the shore to eastward.

At lunch we met the seven people we're traveling with and found all of them to be pleasant and engaging. After lunch, we read some more, then played three rubbers of bridge in a little room on the top deck, where we have a beautiful view of the shore. George and I have a running game with Ned and Ernie. Today, though, we had a terrible run of cards and they beat us handily. It was a cold, blustery day, but the scenery made up for it. We even saw a bit of Somerset Maugham's *The Razor's Edge* after supper.

WEDNESDAY, NOVEMBER 25
Port of Eden, Chile

We pulled into our one stop, the Port of Eden, about eight o'clock this morning, where some of the passengers haggled with the local Indians and fishermen for fish and clams. During the bargaining session over the fish and clams, one of the Indian ladies on the ship reached into her bosom and pulled out a calculator. She almost stopped the show. The fish specialty here is *cholgas*, the giant clam. We had them for lunch today, raw and mixed with onions.

The weather has been rather cloudy and occasionally rainy today. It reminds me a good deal of the inland passage to Alaska. The scenery is similar too, except that the trees are higher in Alaska than they are here.

The captain stopped by our lunchroom to tell us that we would be going into the Golfo del Penas, the Gulf of Sorrows, at about six o'clock tonight and would be in rough water for eleven hours. How rough would depend on the wind. He told us all to take a Dramamine pill about three o'clock. I hadn't intended to, but I decided to defer to the captain, who was seen taking Dramamine himself.

We had a good bridge game for a few hours this afternoon and then entered the gulf right on schedule. The ship was soon pitching and rolling with great intensity and regularity. Several people soon turned pale, and almost everyone went to bed early.

THURSDAY, NOVEMBER 26
At Sea

Today is Thanksgiving and we're back in calm waters. The bad news is that it's foggy and rainy again, and we can barely see the tops of the mountains on either side of us. We changed directions many times as we wound our way through what seemed like 10,000 islands. A lot of seabirds were following us, apparently waiting for the garbage to be dumped from the galley.

We passed the opening to Puerto Aysén in the early afternoon, but the sunshine that the captain had promised never materialized. So it was back to the bridge tables, where Ned and Ernie continued their run from yesterday. In three consecutive hands I had a total of six points. Finally our luck changed and George made a grand slam on the final hand.

Every day they showed about three videos. Unfortunately, the quality is terrible. In spare moments here and there, I read Jim Michener's *Poland*.

FRIDAY, NOVEMBER 27
At Sea

Another cloudy day, but we had a change of current and a following wind last night, so we had high hopes of arriving in Puerto Montt early. We have become very friendly with our seven fellow passengers, although I am sure it is the first time any of them have traveled with four priests in such intimacy. We eat in a tiny dining room at two tables. The recreation room is equally tiny. With so little space, it's a good thing everyone is getting along so well.

Our channel widened out a bit as we cruised along the island of Chiloé. I visited our Peace Corps project here in the early 1960s. It was, and still is, the southernmost Peace Corps project in the world.

We had our final Mass aboard the ship at ten this morning in our cabin. Jaby, our genial room steward and meal steward combined, joined us. George offered the Mass in Spanish. He also offered it for all those aboard the ship who helped make it a pleasant voyage. Tomorrow we would return to Santiago.

We came into Puerto Montt about 2 P.M. It took us another half hour or so to clear the ship. We got a cab and made a mad dash to the airport, which is about twenty miles away, arriving there around three, the time of our scheduled departure for Santiago. Fortunately, the plane was late or we probably would have missed it.

We had three people waiting for us at the Santiago airport, one of whom was Fred Hagerty, a Maryknoller I had met twenty-seven years ago in Chol-Chol, an Indian village down south where he and three of our Notre Dame Peace Corps volunteers were stationed at the time. We made a quick stop at the Casa, then continued on to the Maryknoll house, where we had pisco sours, ham and cheese sandwiches, and another two and a half hours of bridge with Father Joe English, another Maryknoller and a classmate of Ned's at Notre Dame.

I was back at the Casa around midnight. George was showing the video that he had made of our trip south. It amazes me how you can just pop the cassette into a VCR and enjoy instant replay.

George also showed me some videos of the involvement of the Church here in human rights and the ongoing social revolution. The Church has really come out of the sacristy here. It is probably the only organized force to stand up against Pinochet's regime and to speak out loud and clear for justice—even though it has cost many people their lives.

SATURDAY, NOVEMBER 28
Santiago, Chile

I did my laundry, then hung it out to dry, and caught up on my prayers. George went across the street to the tennis club to see if they'd be bringing in the Notre Dame–Miami game with their satellite dish. When he found out that they would be, Ned was in seventh heaven, and I suspect a few others were too. Naturally, we all went to see the game. It seemed funny sitting on the top floor of a tennis club in Santiago, Chile, with the Andes just outside the window, watching a live broadcast of the Notre Dame football team.

After the game, which Notre Dame lost, we took our six Holy Cross companions and Father Joe English out to dinner at a typical Chilean restaurant. The food was very good and the prices were low.

SUNDAY, NOVEMBER 29
Santiago, Chile

George and I drove out early to offer Mass in a little chapel in Penalolan, one of the poor sections in town. The chapel was full and the worshippers enthusiastic—men, women, and children all singing lustily and reciting all of the responses right on cue. George gave a good sermon for the first Sunday in Advent and asked me to say a few words in Spanish after the Communion. They listened intently and then gave me a big hand. Then the lay leader said, "He's come a long way. Let's give him another big hand." So they clapped again.

I noticed that the collection was mostly full of loose change, but there was a lot of it. I sweetened the pot a bit so they could buy some Bibles for the poorest families in the parish. They only cost a dollar apiece here.

After Mass I made my traditional Chilean pilgrimage to the Shrine of Our Lady of the Hill at San Cristóbal. It's the highest point in town and surmounted by a forty- or fifty-foot white statue of the Virgin, which was crafted in France, like our Statue of Liberty. When I first came here to set up the Peace Corps, I promised that if our first-year project was successful, I would put a votive marble plaque of thanks up there and carry it up the mountain as well. The first year was more successful than I could ever have imagined, so I climbed the mountain to deliver the plaque with Ann O'Grady and Mike Curtin, Peace Corps people from Notre Dame who wanted to have me bless their engagement at the shrine. I did, and also married them a year later at Notre Dame. Incidentally, they named their only son Ted.

The stone plaque simply said, "Gracias, USPC" (Thanks, United States Peace Corps).

We returned to the Casa Santa María, packed our bags, and drove to the airport. Destination: Asunción, Paraguay. When we landed we were met by Alberto López Bustillo, a Peruvian who is Coca-Cola's general manager here, and Peter Logan, an Argentinian associate. They showed us a bit of the town en route from the airport and dropped us at the Hotel Excelsior. Later, they picked us up and took us to dinner at the Yacht and Golf Club located a short distance out of town along the Paraná River. We had a wonderful dinner, with fresh fish right out of the river.

Though I've spent a lot of time in Latin America, this was my first trip to Asunción, the capital. Paraguay used to encompass the whole middle of Latin America, but after a difficult war with Bolivia, Brazil, and Argentina, all at once, it was chopped down to its present somewhat restricted size of about 175,000 square miles. It has a population of about 3.5 million, 1 million of whom live here in Asunción and environs.

MONDAY, NOVEMBER 30
Asunción, Paraguay

First on our itinerary today was a meeting with the American ambassador, an impressive young man named Clyde Taylor. Previously he had been in Panama City, San Salvador, and Tehran, so we had some mutual friends. We spent over an hour discussing the political situation here, which at the time was probably the worst in all of Latin America. General Alfredo Stroessner was the military dictator, plain and simple. He had been elected seven times and was going for number eight before finally being turned out of office. Seventy percent of the people here in Paraguay were born during his time in office. Under his reign, democracy was simply nonexistent. Clyde was about the only official in town who wasn't invited to Stroessner's birthday party; nor did Stroessner bother to show up when Clyde awarded diplomas to the American Peace Corps volunteers.

From the ambassador's office, we went to the Peace Corps headquarters down the street. The director there, Don Peterson, is a Notre Dame civil engineer, class of 1964. We also met several volunteers who were Notre Dame graduates. We seem well represented here.

About 12:30 P.M., Alberto and Peter came by and took us and all of our Notre Dame friends out to lunch at a nearby lake about a half hour from here. It was a wonderful lunch, and a great treat for the Peace Corps volunteers, who seldom get to eat in a restaurant this good.

After lunch, Don and one of the volunteers, David Clark, and Ned and I visited one of the Peace Corps cooperative operations. Campesinos were raising the ingredients for one of the favorite food items here, the *chipa*. They were able to borrow money from the co-op to buy the raw materials—manioc flour, pig grease, anisette, and eggs. If you were to see a *chipa*, you might mistake it for a bagel.

The cooperative operates as a kind of savings and loan. Unfortunately, there's not much money to be saved, with inflation at 40 to 50 percent a year. The interest on their loans is 26 percent, but most are short-term loans of fifteen days. That's really living from hand to mouth.

While out this way, we also saw the national shrine the Pope visited later, in the spring of 1988. The shrine, the Virgen de Caacupé, like many of the other shrines that the Pope has visited down here previously, is being fixed up before his arrival. They are actually putting copper roofing on the great dome above the basilica.

Dinner was with the Coca-Cola people at a restaurant called Tallyrand. The food was excellent; I had a hard time resisting the temptation to overindulge. But I survived by skipping the first and second courses, picking at the third, and recruiting one of my tablemates to share the other crepes suzettes.

TUESDAY, DECEMBER 1
Asunción, Paraguay

This morning we went to the Catholic University for a visit with the rector, Father Juan Oscar Usher. The university is housed in a very small building, although they are moving out to the edge of town where they have some land and will join the major seminary in the Theological Institute there. The university was founded by the bishops twenty-seven years ago and has four satellite schools around the country for educating teachers. Unlike most of the other Catholic universities in Latin America, it does not have a pontifical charter.

Ned and I had a long talk with Oscar on education and the political situation here in Paraguay. With its satellites, the university educates about 10,500 students. The cost is about $400 a year for everything. The university gets no government support; nor, thanks to Stroessner, may it accept any aid from the United States or Canada either.

Walking around Asunción, one is immediately struck by the almost total absence of Indian faces, or even mestizos, those who have mixed European and Indian blood. The same is true of most of Chile, Argentina, and Uruguay. The majority of people in these countries are clearly descended from European stock, very unlike countries such as Mexico and Peru, where Indians and mestizos make up 70 to 80 percent of the population.

WEDNESDAY, DECEMBER 2
Asunción, Paraguay

This was our three-country day. We left Paraguay, flew for forty minutes, and landed in Iguaçú, in Brazil. We quickly checked into our hotel, dumped our bags, and got back in the car. Soon we were driving over the Iguaçú River on a very high and wide bridge into Argentina.

The falls, which straddle the border between Brazil and Argentina, are absolutely spectacular. There are actually 250 distinctive falls, stretching more than two miles wide. They plunge 225 feet, 75 feet more than Niagara Falls.

It was very hot today, over 100 degrees. When we returned to the hotel we were soaked with perspiration. We had a good dinner in the hotel with a bottle of excellent Brazilian wine that cost only five dollars. Incidentally, the name of the hotel is the Bourbon. It is one of only two five-star hotels out of the eighty-five in this area.

WEDNESDAY, DECEMBER 2
Iguaçú, Brazil

We were up at 6:45 this morning to see what will probably be the largest man-made power generator in the world, the Itaipu Dam. It's just below the confluence of the Iguaçú and Paraná rivers. The total cost was to be $10 billion, but it is expected to run closer to $15 billion when it is finished. The largest dam in the world now generates about 8 billion watts of electricity. This one will generate 12.6 billion watts when all of its eighteen turbines are going. The dam, jointly owned by Brazil and Paraguay, will supply most of the electricity for São Paulo, Rio de Janeiro, and all of the surrounding states.

We took a hair-raising helicopter ride over the Brazilian side of the falls, followed by a walk down to the very edge of the river to view the falls from below. Once again today it was over 100 degrees. When we returned from the falls, we showered quickly at the hotel, checked out, and drove to the airport for our flight to Buenos Aires.

At the airport in Buenos Aires we were met by John Dunn, a travel agent. All the other Coca-Cola people were far away in Bariloche, Argentina, for an annual meeting. As we passed through immigration, they suddenly informed us that we had no visas to enter Argentina. In all of the fourteen countries we had visited so far, we needed visas only for Brazil and Colombia. Our travel agency in South Bend had said nothing about our needing visas to visit Argentina. Apparently, the requirement was fairly new, a reprisal for U.S. support of Britain during the war in the Falklands.

We were ushered into a holding area and were told that we would have to leave the country within an hour on the flight back to Iguaçú. Naturally, we tried for a reprieve, but everyone we called passed the buck to someone else. We finally got to the office of the National Director of Immigration. He said he would let us stay if he had a note from the American Embassy.

We then called the American Embassy, and once again the buck-passing started. The first gentleman said he could do nothing about it because it was up to us to get our own visas before we came here. He asked me to talk to someone else in the embassy. This one told me I was a citizen like everyone else and they were not in the business of saying who could or could not enter a foreign country. That was the foreign country's business. I suggested that maybe I ought to talk to George Shultz or President Reagan, but that had little effect. Or maybe it did.

The next time I called, after being shunted around and cut off a few times, I finally got through to Tom Holliday, the consul general here. He told me the problem was with reciprocity. If they asked the Argentinian National Director of Immigration to let us in with a note from the American Embassy, then the next time an Argentinian got off a plane in Miami without a visa to the United States, they would expect the same thing. He said they did not want to play that game. I suggested that he talk to the National Director himself to see what kind of a note he wanted. Within a half hour, if we were not allowed to stay, Varig, the Brazilian flag carrier, was under orders to put us on their flight to New York. Meanwhile, the local Coca-Cola lawyer was weighing in from the sidelines. Finally I had Holliday check with the ambassador, who turned out to be an old friend of mine.

Because there was a good chance we'd be on a long flight to New York in thirty minutes, we went into an empty office and offered Mass. They were holding the flight, ready to put us on it at six o'clock sharp if they did not have word from the local immigration chief at the airport, who in turn was waiting for word from the National Director downtown.

At one minute to six, the local chief told us that he had heard from the National Director and that we could stay. The ambassador had weighed in. Needless to say, we both heaved a huge sigh of relief. The only condition was that they would have to hold our passports overnight and we would have to show up at the national office in the morning to retrieve them. Finally, we got a lecture about applying for visas whenever required and a blunt suggestion to get a new travel agency.

It was about 7 P.M. when we checked in at the Sheraton. We first had a celebratory drink and went out to one of those restaurants on the riverfront for some Argentinian beef. It was a long day. A mere sixty seconds had made the difference between our being here and winging our way to New York.

THURSDAY, DECEMBER 3
Buenos Aires, Argentina

Buenos Aires is a lot more formal than the other countries we've been visiting, so we're back into clericals again, which I guess is good preparation for our return to the United States this weekend. Our driver, furnished by Coca-Cola, took us over to Avenida Florida, the great walking and shopping street in Buenos Aires, and then on a quick tour of the city's primary attractions. We saw the downtown section with its great avenues, ten lanes wide; the Casa Rosada, the equivalent of our White House, only red; the cathedral with the tomb of San Martín, the George Washington of this country; the great port, which stretches on for miles and has an adjacent area throbbing with nightclubs; the splendid parks, with their statues and monuments and greenery; and the graceful nineteenth-century buildings, very much in the French style and beautiful to behold. All in all, this has to be the most cultured and civilized city in Latin America.

We returned to the hotel to wash up before paying a visit to the American ambassador, Ted Gildred. He founded a research institute on Latin America at the University of California, San Diego. It's much like our Kellogg Institute at Notre Dame. Ted was seeking a new director for the institute, ideally an ex-ambassador to one of the Latin American countries. We discussed several possible candidates with him, then went back to the hotel to finish our prayers and get ready for dinner.

Our dinner companions tonight were Emilio Mignone, the great civil rights lawyer, and his wife. I couldn't help noticing the haunted look she had in her eye, and I wondered about it. Then they told me. During the time of the troubles here a few years ago, the soldiers came to their home and snatched their beautiful young daughter, whose greatest crime was helping the poor. Despite all of their efforts, they never saw her again. All they know is that she was tortured, raped, killed, and thrown into the Rio de la Plata somewhere as shark bait. Emilio spent so much time battling the bureaucracy for answers that he became one of the best civil rights lawyers in Buenos Aires. He is absolutely fearless in his pursuit of justice here.

Unfortunately, the Church here has not been as strong and as organized as the Church in Chile. The Church in Argentina could be throwing its weight behind some of the small human rights organizations here, but it hasn't done so. One reason is the bishops. Somewhere along the line, a politician came up with the idea that the government should pay the bishops' salaries. And that's about all it took to destroy their independence. Now most of them just flow along with the tide, even when the tide stinks. One bishop did buck the tide. He was murdered. Thank God for martyrs. The military regime went down after the debacle of the Falklands war.

FRIDAY, DECEMBER 4
Buenos, Aires, Argentina

We were up reasonably early this morning, so our driver could whisk us out of the city and into the countryside. The city itself has 4 million people and about 5 million more in the surrounding suburbs. The land outside the metropolitan area is notable for its large eucalyptus trees, along with the great shade tree here, the ombu. There is also much flat pastureland, ideal for grazing cattle and sheep and for raising wheat. The topsoil here is about 70 feet deep, but there isn't that much agricultural development or growth in agricultural productivity. In the university, only about 2 percent of the students study agriculture. Most want to be lawyers, and lawyers make up 70 percent of the students in the professional schools. Few have any desire to practice law. The degree is primarily a ticket to a career in politics.

Our trip north and west was to the great shrine of Our Lady of Luján, the patroness of this country. According to legend a fellow with a great ranch north of here in Córdoba decided he wanted to build a chapel. He sent to northern Brazil for two statues of Our Lady, and they were delivered in March 1630 to the port of Buenos Aires. They were then put on a caravan for the trip north to Córdoba.

The caravan stopped at the river Luján to spend the night. The next morning, when they were preparing to resume the journey, they found that one of the wagons refused to budge, even though they had a team of oxen pulling it. Thinking it was overloaded, they took everything out of it and it moved easily. But when the two boxes with the statues of Our Lady were put aboard, it refused to budge once again. They then drew the obvious conclusion that Our Lady wanted to stay at Luján, so she was ensconced in a little niche in the chapel of a small ranch there. Subsequently, they tried to move her across the river to another location, but the statue was found back in the estancia the next morning.

After that happened several times, they got the message and built a great church here in the thirteenth-century French Gothic style. It makes quite a sight as it rises suddenly out of the flatlands that surround Luján. The esplanade in front of it will hold over a million people, and there were that many here when the Pope made his two visits. The church was declared a basilica in 1930 and is now the national shrine of this country. About 800,000 young people annually walk the seventy kilometers from Buenos Aires on pilgrimage.

Back at the hotel I washed up, changed clothes, and went to visit Monsignor Guillermo Blanco, who is rector of the largest Catholic university here, Santa María de Buenos Aires. He didn't know a word of English, but by now I'm operating all day long in Spanish. He wanted to know all about Catholic higher education in America, and I wanted to know all about Catholic higher education at his university, so we spent the better part of an hour swapping information with each other. They have neither campus nor residences, and are located in the middle of town, which is no great asset here.

Ned, meanwhile, strolled up Avenida Florida, but didn't buy anything. We had cocktails with Dr. Iribarne, the lawyer who had helped us with our immigration problems, and had dinner in the hotel, followed by a long walk up the Florida. There were a lot of street entertainers out tonight, singing and playing various instruments for the appreciative groups of people who gathered around them, mostly locals.

SATURDAY, DECEMBER 5
Buenos Aires, Argentina

I worked, with Ned's help, on the talk I'm giving at the Heisman Trophy dinner when we get back to New York. The rest of the time we spent making some preliminary preparations for the trip home— lining up the luggage and throwing out papers that are no longer needed. Then we went off with our driver to see Tigre, just north of the city, where five rivers flow together to join the Río de la Plata. It's a kind of Venice of Argentina, with a lot of tour boats and rowboats running up and down the canals between the rivers.

Tonight we had dinner with Gustavo, the Coca-Cola lawyer here, and his wife, Monica. We went to the most famous restaurant in Buenos Aires, the Cabaña. It claims the best beef in the world and I am not about to argue with them. The steaks cost between seven and nine dollars and no one but a football lineman has a chance of finishing one of them at a single sitting.

We discussed some of the human rights problems of this country at dinner. The attitude here seems to be "I didn't know anything about it" or "I didn't know what was happening." I wonder how that answer would go over with the mothers of the 6,000 young people who "disappeared." Most of them were tortured and killed simply for marching in the streets. The Church should have taken a stronger stand, as they did in Chile. Ned thought I could have been a bit more diplomatic.

SUNDAY, DECEMBER 6
Buenos Aires, Argentina

This is our last day in Latin America. We gave thanks at Mass on this, the second Sunday of Advent, for so many blessings on this trip—good weather, good health, good friends all along the way, the wonders we saw, and, of course, for daily Mass wherever we were. We had an *asado*, an Argentinian cookout, with John Dunn, who had met us at the airport, and his family just before we left to make our flight. At the airport we had a glass of wine with Mr. Piacenti of Varig, who was so helpful to us when we had our visa problems. We'll be in New York in fourteen hours, including an hour-and-a-half stop in Rio.

MONDAY, DECEMBER 7
New York, New York

We landed in New York on schedule at 6:30 A.M. As we were claiming our luggage, a baggage handler told us that Notre Dame's Tim Brown had won the Heisman Trophy. That made a nice way to end the trip. And it would give me something else to talk about when I give my speech at the award dinner. Once we arrived in the city, we were caught up in the Heisman festivities, culminating with the awards dinner on Thursday night, December 10. All six of Notre Dame's former Heisman Trophy winners were present at the trophy dinner. It was a gala affair, and Tim Brown acquitted himself very well in making his acceptance speech.

Ned was off at dawn and back to school Friday morning. I had to stay in town to meet with some Russians and Americans who are setting up a Foundation for the Survival and Development of Humanity, which will be based in Moscow, Washington, and Stockholm. This was a meeting at the Carnegie Corporation preparatory to a constitution-forming meeting in Moscow on January 17. I agreed to be a founding Trustee, even though Ned and I will be on our way around the world instead of in Moscow. I'll contribute what I can at this meeting and then, thank God, fly back to Notre Dame late Friday night.

It will be good to be home again. Travel is wonderful, but there comes a point when home is more desirable than hotels and airports. I think we've reached that point in this second segment of our year's sabbatical.

Part III

ON THE CARIBBEAN ABOARD THE QE2

This segment of our sabbatical year took place in two parts—a warm-up drill and a main event. Both were on the *Queen Elizabeth 2*, one of the largest and most luxurious ocean liners in the world. (There are now some new ones—larger and just as luxurious.) The warm-up was a three-week cruise on the Caribbean. The main event was a three-month cruise across the world. I say "across" rather than "around" because we skipped South Africa and the east coast of South America. Instead, we called on the South Island of New Zealand, Australia, and Mombasa in East Africa. We then sailed back across the Pacific to China, Korea, and Japan. On the homeward leg we crossed the Pacific once again, this time calling at Hawaii en route to Los Angeles. From Los Angeles we sailed southward along the Pacific coast, passed through the Panama Canal for the second time, went up through the Caribbean again, and disembarked in Fort Lauderdale, Florida. We were gone more than 100 days and covered over 30,000 nautical miles. The whole trip was between latitudes 45 degrees south and 45 degrees north—the fat half of our globe.

The Caribbean cruise did not begin auspiciously, to say the least. We flew from South Bend to Chicago on Saturday, December 19, 1987, then from Chicago to New York, where the QE2 was waiting. The flights were predictable enough; the baggage handling wasn't. Somehow our luggage never made it onto the flight from South Bend to Chicago. Where it did go is anybody's guess. Our bags still hadn't caught up with us when we eased out of New York Harbor, headed for

Port Everglades in Fort Lauderdale. They did, thank the Lord, make it to Fort Lauderdale just a few hours before we headed out to sea for the Christmas Caribbean cruise.

We had been wearing the same clothes—black clerical garb—since we left Notre Dame and we were beginning to get a little ripe. Some good did come of this inconvenience, however. By the time we left Fort Lauderdale, there was hardly anyone aboard ship who didn't know we were priests. I chided Ned that in the Christian spirit we had to forgive the people who failed to put our bags on the plane out of South Bend. He said that only in the spirit of the Christmas season could he bring himself to do so.

Though the Cunard Line paid our expenses for the two cruises, they were not exactly free. Ned and I were expected to earn our passage by serving as ship's chaplains. That meant not only celebrating Mass every day but also performing all the other duties that would have been expected of us had we been assigned to a parish on dry land. Also, as members of the staff, we had to defer to the paying passengers when the cabins were assigned. On the Caribbean cruise, the ship was very crowded and we ended up in an inside cabin with no porthole. It was a little bit like living in a closet. Fortunately, there were fewer passengers on the around-the-world cruise, and we were assigned to an outside cabin with two portholes.

The Christmas cruise was a real blessing. Not only did it give us a chance to learn our way around the ship and get a feel for the routine, but it prepared us to expect the unexpected. A few days into the cruise, for example, the recreation officer came to us and said he'd like us to make arrangements for the singing of Christmas carols on Christmas Eve. Ned said he'd do anything, *anything*, but sing them. Little did we know at the time that singing them would be the least of our problems.

We looked around the ship to see what we could find in the way of carols, but came up empty. We weren't concerned, however, because one of our pre-Christmas ports of call was St. Thomas, which is lined with duty-free shops of every description. Both Ned and I had been there before, so on putting into St. Thomas we knew we wouldn't mind passing up the tourist shore tours in order to shop for caroling books. The shops in St. Thomas are crammed together in a relatively small area, so it didn't take us long to find out who had Christmas carols: none of them.

In desperation we tried the Catholic church. There, to our great relief, we found about two dozen books of carols near the pamphlet rack. The only trouble was, the books weren't really for sale, and there was no one around to pay anyway. We had to have at least one copy that we could duplicate aboard ship, so I took one, slipping a twenty-dollar bill into the poor box to ease my conscience. Back aboard the QE2, we found a young woman in the purser's office to run off the necessary copies. I'll never forget her name: Sarah Halfpenny. I bought her roses for squeezing the project into her schedule during a very busy time aboard ship.

We were so busy preparing our Christmas liturgies that we didn't even go ashore on Martinique. But we really got our money's worth out of that caroling book. On Christmas Eve we had two midnight Masses, one for the passengers, another for the crew. The midnight Mass for the passengers also included the First Holy Communion of a young Mexican boy, complete with the usual sponsors, a brand-new rosary and a gleaming white candle. On Christmas Day we had two more Masses, plus an ecumenical service for the Protestant passengers and any ecumenically minded Catholics who wished to attend. All the services were well attended, and we raised about $500 for the Seamen's Relief Fund.

The ship was docked in Barbados on Christmas Day. Ned and I spent the better part of it enjoying the hospitality of Tom Cabot, father of one of our students, Jim, and later Pamela Harriman, widow of Averell Harriman and an old friend of mine. The previous year I had offered my third Christmas Mass here in Barbados for Averell, who was then ailing. It was the last religious service he attended before he died. Pamela and Kitty Carlisle did the readings and I preached. Averell put his hearing aid on the altar so he wouldn't miss a word of the homily.

Two of Pamela's house guests that evening were also old friends, Paul Moore, the Episcopalian Bishop of New York, and his wife, Brenda. Pamela's other house guests were her son Winston Churchill, grandson of the former Prime Minister, and his family. We had a traditional turkey dinner, followed by plum pudding that Winston had brought from London and a sauce that he prepared in Pamela's kitchen. So ended Christmas 1987. It was indeed a day of peace and joy.

Fortunately, there were few real emergencies on the Christmas cruise that required our services as pastors. The one notable exception was an attempted suicide the day before Christmas. About 6 A.M., shortly after we arrived in Martinique, we received an urgent phone call from a woman on board. She said that her daughter had tried to jump overboard. Ned volunteered to handle it and was involved for the better part of the day. The young woman was admitted to the ship's hospital. When we reached Barbados her mother took her ashore to receive psychiatric treatment.

The celebrity lecturer on the Christmas cruise was author James Michener, whom we came to know quite well. He showed the tape of an interview he gave to 60 *Minutes* when he was in the South Pacific, gave several talks on his books and travels, and answered many questions from his rapt audiences. I managed to corner him after one of his talks, and we spent a very pleasant hour swapping stories about our travels.

On another occasion, Michener spent an entire evening with the small group of Notre Dame people who were aboard. He proved to be a wonderful conversationalist on a wide variety of subjects, and obviously enjoyed the company of the Notre Dame group. I remember one evening in particular when we were all gathered around the piano singing "Bali Hai" and other songs from *South Pacific*. Michener and his Japanese wife, Mari, sang with a gusto equal to that of anyone in the group—no small accomplishment.

On another occasion Ned asked Michener how he became interested in athletics, the subject of one of his books. He said that his passion as a youngster was basketball and that it was only because of his talents on the court that he was able to attend Swarthmore on a basketball scholarship.

Most of the ports of call on the Christmas cruise were places that Ned and I had visited before. Neither of us, however, had ever visited Curaçao. When the ship put into port at the former Dutch East Indian colony we got off and had a good look around. Curaçao is the largest of the six islands of the Netherlands Antilles. The others are Aruba, Bonaire, Saba, St. Eustatius, and St. Martin. The islands are now autonomous parts of the Kingdom of the Netherlands.

Curaçao is about thirty miles long and five miles wide. The capital town of Willemstad dates back to 1634. It flanks both sides of the deep channel that leads to the harbor and is full of those lovely pastel buildings so typical of Dutch architecture of the seventeenth and eighteenth centuries. You could almost swear you were in Amsterdam. The main language here is Dutch, although practically all the locals speak Spanish, English, some Portuguese, and a native tongue called Papiamento. From what I head and read of it on signs, it's a mixture of all the languages spoken here, plus some African languages. It reminded me of Esperanto, the artificial world language. Most of the people were black or brown.

Curaçao wouldn't win any awards for scenic beauty. Unlike the lush tropical growth found on most of the other Caribbean islands, Curaçao's landscape is very rocky, with lots of cacti and low, scrubby trees. All the vegetation has a pronounced windblown look, caused by the strong prevailing winds out of the northeast.

Most people connect Curaçao with the chocolate-flavored liqueur that's made here. We visited the factory where they make it and sipped free samples. From there, we went to the new Seaquarium. It's right on the shore and designed so that fish and other sea creatures can swim in and out at will. If a fish lives in the sea anywhere near here, you'll probably see it in the Seaquarium.

We also toured Cartagena on the Caribbean coast of Colombia. The city was founded in 1533, fourteen years after Cortez landed in Mexico. The entrance to the bay bristles with fortresses. The Spanish built them to repulse the French, the British, and assorted pirates, including Thomas Hawkins and Francis Drake. The pirates were after the gold and emeralds that were shipped from here to Spain in treasure-laden caravels. Just before the American Revolution, the British attacked Cartagena with 23,000 men and more than 150 ships, but they never advanced past the heavily fortified harbor.

Cartagena was in those days not only an important center for shipping but also a hub of slave trading and a New World branch of the Spanish Inquisition. Those violent times produced St. Peter Claver, a Jesuit who ministered to the slaves. During a walking tour of the city, we stopped to pray at his skeletonized remains. The Jesuit church here, which appears to be the most handsome church in town, is named for St. Peter Claver. The Christmas crèche was enormous.

We also visited the cathedral and the Palace of the Inquisition with its torture chamber still intact. There were grand inquisitors here until about 1803. Not something to brag about.

Much of Cartagena's charm derives from the many well-preserved buildings that remain from the colonial era. Their balconies and beautifully carved woodwork reminded me of Bogotá. And despite its population of one million, the city is remarkably clean. We enjoyed it so much, we decided to skip dinner on the ship and dine instead at a fishing club on the beach. The restaurant was in a converted fortress. We ordered chicken and rice and enjoyed every morsel. Not much English is spoken in Cartagena. But thanks to brushing up on our Spanish during our trip to Latin America, we got along just fine.

Touring the bridge of the QE2 was a popular diversion that almost everyone took sometime during the Christmas cruise. The ship has two or three navigational systems, utilizing satellites and loran. The original steam-drive power plant had been replaced with nine diesel generators that develop enormous amounts of electrical power. This provides much better control. In the old days, it used to take the ship about two and one-half miles to slow down after being thrown into full reverse. Now it can be done in less than a mile. It's a curious phenomenon to see a ship of this size barreling through the water at 30 knots with only one man on watch and another showing passengers around the bridge. Of course, with radar, they can spot every ship in the locality up to forty miles away. It takes only a matter of seconds to plot its trajectory and change course, if necessary.

The New Year's celebration aboard ship started out in the traditional festive manner, but I thought I was getting a little too old to stick it out for the whole evening, so about 11:30 P.M., I turned in. Make of it what you will.

We arrived back in New York on the morning of January 3. That gave us exactly ten days before reboarding the QE2 for the around-the-world cruise. Ned flew back to Notre Dame to catch up on business. I flew to The Hague in Holland to attend an international conference on human rights. The conference was attended by more than forty people from thirteen different countries, the largest representations coming from the then U.S.S.R. and the U.S.A. It was put together by Ernst van Eeghen, head of a 400-year-old Dutch trading company.

The conference grew out of an idea that van Eeghen, Landrum Bolling, and I had discussed in Ernst's house four years earlier. Bolling was at the time the director of Notre Dame's Ecumenical Institute in Tantur, near Jerusalem. We thought it would be a great thing to get some Americans and Russians together to talk about things we had in common, rather than things that drive us apart. With *glasnost* and *perestroika* in the air, everything seemed to be opening up, and the timing looked just right for this conference. Dean Griswold, my former colleague on the Civil Rights Commission, gave a fine talk. We also had the wife of Giscard d'Estaing, former President of France, and Rosalynn Carter, former President Carter's wife, in attendance.

With only an hour's sleep the night before on the airplane, I was only half conscious as I gave my talk on religious liberty, a few moments after arriving at the conference, two hours' drive north of the Amsterdam airport. Fortunately, I had thought and talked on this subject so much in the past that I could have given the speech in my sleep anyway. The discussion afterward was lively, and there was a good deal of give-and-take on both sides. I found the Russians to be surprisingly open to criticism and discussion of their human rights situation, particularly as it affected religious liberty.

These were rather important Russians too. Two of them had accompanied Gorbachev on his three meetings with President Reagan in Geneva, Reykjavik, and Washington. The most important of them was Feodor Burlatsky. He used to be very close to Khrushchev, but was fired when he pushed too hard on human rights. Now he is chairman of the Soviet Commission on Humanitarian Problems and Human Rights and very close to the top man. The number two man was Aleksandr Soukharev, Procurator General and head of the Lawyers Association. The number three man was Andrei Grachev. I suspect he is also very important, as their third man generally is. Anyway, I spent a good deal of time with Burlatsky and Grachev, and I think we made a good deal of progress. At the time, I felt that something was really beginning to turn around in the U.S.S.R. regarding human rights. As a result of this meeting, a few months later 800 prisoners in jail for exercising religious freedom were liberated. Another result was that we were able to send a million copies of the New Testament in Russian to Moscow for distribution. In the past only a few Bibles could surreptitiously be brought in.

Part IV

AROUND THE WORLD ON THE QE2

WEDNESDAY, JANUARY 13, 1988
New York, New York

It's departure day on the around-the-world cruise, and this time we have our luggage with us. Still, there was one surprise: on arriving aboard around 5:30 P.M., we were told that a Mass was scheduled for 6:30. This was the first we had heard about it. Thank God we had made our shakedown cruise over Christmas, because we knew where everything was. I arrived in the theater at 6:15, recruited a couple of Filipino helpers from the projection room, and we set up the altar for Mass with no trouble. Even with all of the excitement of departure, almost fifty people showed up, so we were off to a good start.

Best news of all, they put us in a cabin with two outside portholes and a lot more room than we had before. Our last cabin was a bit like a film development room, about the same size and just as dark. It's amazing how a little sunlight can change the whole aspect of a trip. They told us we would have this cabin until Los Angeles. That's two weeks from now, so we're not going to worry about what happens after that. Another immediate change from our last trip: this time every third person stopped us to say hello and had some connection with Notre Dame or mutual friends.

We were assigned to take our meals in the Princess Grill, which turned out to be a lot better than the Columbia. First of all, it's smaller and the waiters are much quicker on their feet. Even the food tastes better. Dining here tonight, we met our fellow chaplains: Bishop Harold Robinson and his wife, Marie, and Rabbi Alvin Ruben and his wife, Ruth Ann. Bishop Robinson is the retired Episcopal

Bishop of Buffalo. The Rubens are from St. Louis. It was a real pleasure to serve with both of them, and get a chance to meet their wives. We are still good friends.

THURSDAY, JANUARY 14
En Route to Fort Lauderdale

The sea was running a bit higher when we arose this morning, and it had that curious effect that occurs when the Gulf Stream meets the colder waters from the north: steam rises in all directions as if one is walking across the moors of Scotland. It is quite an eerie sight, but beautiful too.

This morning we went to the gym to learn about the exercise apparatus. I got tired just watching the athletic young lady demonstrate it. Ned and I thought there must be an easier way of staying healthy. We never returned to the gym. In the middle of the afternoon, I went down to the computing center and spent an hour and a half learning about computers. We have ten computers aboard, a number of software programs, and an instructor.

We had about a hundred people at Mass this afternoon, which is very good considering we're only one day out and there are about twenty other things one can do at that hour. The congregation tends to build as the days pass. We're convinced that attendance will continue to improve if we give good homilies, so we're putting in some extra effort. We also worked out a schedule with the bishop and the rabbi today. No problem for the rabbi, because there is a synagogue aboard. But we have to split times with the Episcopalians. We'll have Sunday Masses at 8 A.M. and 6:15 P.M. in the theater. He'll have his Holy Eucharist at 9 A.M. in the card room and another service each week on Wednesday.

We have traveled almost 1,000 miles from New York and have another 1,000 to go after we leave Everglades tomorrow night, en route to St. Thomas. The seas have calmed down a bit and it's getting warmer. Ned and I did some high-speed walking around the outer deck after dinner tonight.

FRIDAY, JANUARY 15
Fort Lauderdale, Florida

The ship is terribly crowded. We were told that about 600 people came aboard here, which will give us a very full ship from here to Los Angeles. Once we get to Los Angeles, things should be easier. There, a good number of people will get off, and we will have only about 1,000 in the passenger group, which is about the number we have in the crew. That's why these trips are so expensive.

Father Bernard D'Arcy, a White Father from Ireland who looks like a cross between Pope John XXIII and Spencer Tracy, came aboard again in Fort Lauderdale. He was aboard when we began the Christmas cruise, but left the ship to spend the holidays with friends in Florida. He will be the chaplain for the crew.

We had a nice group of people for Mass, probably a hundred, which was better than expected since we were mixed up in the time change. I came back to the cabin to do more sailing on *The Frigate "Pallada,"* a long book I started on the Christmas cruise. It's an account by Ivan Goncharov, a Russian, of his trip around the world on a sailing ship in 1852–55. It's so full of colorful descriptions that it's difficult to read quickly. I'm now with Goncharov in Japan, where he's trying to get the Japanese to let Russians come ashore in Japan. No way!

SATURDAY, JANUARY 16
En Route to St. Thomas

As with all first days out with several hundred new passengers aboard, this was a day of meeting people. All one has to do is sit down with a book along one of the main decks and twenty-five people an hour will stop and say hello. That's a lot of names to remember. If I had my collar on, fifty would stop. Everyone is so friendly aboard this ship that it's hard to read for more than ten minutes without someone stopping by for a chat. That's all to the good, though, because we're here to be chaplains. This afternoon I did a little marriage counseling on the boat deck. I hope it was successful.

People tell me they are delighted that we can have Mass this

Saturday afternoon at 6:15, since it will count for Sunday Mass. Many of them are leaving around 8:30 in the morning to visit Charlotte Amalie, the capital city of St. Thomas in the U.S. Virgin Islands, where we anchor.

The U.S. Virgin Islands are a trust territory of the United States. They lie 1,400 miles southeast of New York, 1,000 miles southeast of Miami. There are about fifty islands in all, but only three that are inhabited to any extent worth mentioning: St. Thomas, St. Croix, and St. John. The islands are a part of the Lesser Antilles, the southern end of a 2,500-mile chain of Caribbean islands, sometimes called the West Indies, that stretch from the tip of Florida to the coast of Venezuela, dividing the Caribbean Sea from the Atlantic Ocean. Geologists and oceanographers say that the island chain was once an unbroken bridge between North and South America. Most of the islands are the extinct volcanic peaks of a great submarine mountain range; a few grew from the shallow underwater shelf as coral formations.

Columbus sighted the island in 1493 during his second voyage to the New World. He put ashore for fresh water at Salt River on St. Croix on the morning of November 14, but quickly retreated when hostile Carib Indians made it plain that visitors were not welcome. As Columbus continued sailing northward, he sighted many of the other islands in the group. So impressed was he with their number that he named them *Las Virgines*, after St. Ursula and her 11,000 companions who were reputedly slain by the Huns during the sacking of Cologne.

The first European inhabitants of the island were primarily pirates and privateers who spent their time preying on the richly laden treasure ships that passed through the West Indies on their way back to Europe from Central America. In 1671 the Danish West Indian Company began colonizing the islands—first St. Thomas, then St. John. In 1733 the Danish government bought St. Croix from the French, by which time the sugarcane industry was thriving on St. John. St. Thomas, on the other hand, was the hub of the trade routes between the Old and New Worlds, a hangout for buccaneers, and an auction block for Africans imported as slaves to work the sugar plantations.

The islands remained Danish until 1917, when the United States purchased them for $25 million in order to achieve control over the sea approaches to the Panama Canal and to prevent Germany from establishing a submarine base in the islands. Prohibition in the 1920s dealt the final blow to the sugar industry; most of the crop had gone into the manufacture of rum sold on the U.S. mainland.

Though long extinct, the sugar industry is primarily responsible for the islands' racial makeup and language. Most of the inhabitants of the Virgin Islands are descended from the African slaves and contract laborers who worked the old plantations. Because the overseers of the plantations were English, Scottish, and Irish, the workers adopted the English language.

St. Thomas is probably the best known of the islands today. Thirteen miles long and four miles wide, it comprises twenty-eight square miles, almost exactly the size of Manhattan. The capital city of the island, Charlotte Amalie, nestles above a spectacular natural harbor on the south side of the island. Yachts and sailboats swing on their moorings along the shore, and majestic cruise ships from all over the world lie at anchor further out.

The main industry of the islands today is tourism. They earn a quarter of a billion dollars on tourism every year and have a GNP of over a billion. Most of the income is due to their free-port status. Everything is sold without taxes. Tourists get a bonus; an extra $400, doubling the limit of tax-free goods on returning to the United States. Shops line both sides of Main Street for several blocks and crowd against each other in the narrow alleys that slope down to the waterfront. Good restaurants and lively bistros are scattered among the shops along the waterfront, completing the portrait of Charlotte Amalie as a busy and cosmopolitan center of commerce, government, and entertainment.

There seem to be many more Catholics aboard this time than during the Christmas cruise. And, of course, there are always others who join us, even though they aren't Catholic. The movie tonight was *Platoon*. Really bloody and full of obscenities. If they had eliminated the four-letter words, there would have been almost no dialogue at all.

SUNDAY, JANUARY 17
Charlotte Amalie, St. Thomas

This is the third time we'd been in Charlotte Amalie, so we knew where to do our shopping. We bought a couple of tropical shirts, guayaberas, for under seven dollars, some scotch for about six dollars, a few toilet articles, some more books, and a couple of very attractive little Lladros for Helen and Pat, our secretaries, who collect them.

I started another book, since it's taking me so long to get the Russian frigate around the world (I'm now in China). This is a book by Walter Burghardt, an old Jesuit friend who helped us get our Jerusalem Institute started. It's called *Preaching: The Art and the Craft.* Ned and I are going to be preaching every other day for the next hundred days, so we're going to need all the help we can get. I can tell already that Walter's excellent book is going to help a lot. Early on, he makes one very good point: the most common fault of preachers is not being well prepared. I decided then and there to concentrate especially hard on preparing my homilies.

MONDAY, JANUARY 18
En Route to Cartagena

This turned out to be the nicest day so far, and the decks were full of people sunning themselves. I took the opportunity to learn something about word processing at a lecture in the computer center. The main thing I learned was that I'll never be a computer expert. After lunch I attended a lecture by Herbert Kaplow, ABC news correspondent on *Election 88.* He answered a lot of tough questions very adroitly—demurring only when it came to predicting who would be nominated and elected. Later I spent an hour walking the deck and preparing the homily for tonight's Mass. We're now up to between 100 and 150 people every day for Mass and it's a great opportunity to preach the Word.

We had to change from our usual place in the Princess Grill tonight because someone objected to our cigars. We were moved into an area at the other side of the room where everybody else smoked cigars and welcomed us. Our friends at the old location said they were going to put on a revolution and all start smoking cigars because they didn't want us to leave. Some of them came over to have their pictures taken with us. But there is always someone who objects loudly, thinking that cigar smokers are just a notch above mass murderers.

While doing a little exercise around the deck today in high-speed walking, I ran into a couple who had six children graduate from Notre Dame. They said they just stopped me to say thanks. I thanked them!

TUESDAY, JANUARY 19
Cartagena, Colombia

We woke up this morning in the harbor, but since we had just visited here on the Christmas cruise, we decided not to go ashore. We are now en route to Puerto Limón, Costa Rica's Atlantic port, a short run from Cartagena. My greatest achievement of the day was finishing *The Frigate "Pallada."* While it is only 650 pages long, it is so closely and tightly written that it was impossible to make very much speed with it. However, I did get the author back across Siberia. He passed through Irkutsk in the center of the continent, where we I had picked up the Trans-Siberian Express from Moscow to Beijing a few years ago. At the time, a small group of Notre Dame people were arranging for peace students from the then U.S.S.R. and China. We still have them coming each year.

I've begun a new book by Jim Michener, *Sayonara.* I'm particularly interested in it because it's about a Japanese-American marriage, which is what the Micheners' is.

WEDNESDAY, JANUARY 20
Puerto Limón, Costa Rica

Some of our fellow passengers took off this morning for a four-hour bus trip into San José, the capital of Costa Rica. Since we had been there only a couple of months ago, we decided to stay with the ship and tour this port town instead. We did it on foot, which is the best way of doing it, except that it was about 90 degrees in the shade, and there was very little shade.

Puerto Limón is a typical port town with lots of trucks coming and going and huge numbers of containers up and down the docks being loaded and unloaded from ships. Outside our porthole were a number of containers from Russia. Bananas seem to be the big deal here, together with all sorts of tropical fruit. We strolled through the food market, then visited the local supermarket, where we bought such things as toothpaste, potato chips, shaving cream, shoe polish, and notebooks. Everything seemed quite cheap here, about half of what the cost would be at home.

We also visited the local church, which was very clean and neat and rather modern in design. The Christmas crèche was still up, which seemed strange on January 20. However, it was beautifully done, so we're glad we managed to see it.

My turn to preach at Mass tonight, so I've been giving some thought to what I'll say. I think I'll talk on the Mass, since we have over a hundred people coming every day and many of them have probably never heard a sermon on the Mass. People are still constantly stopping for a chat. We often turn up nonpracticing Catholics and invite them to our service. I also spent some time with a lady who is slowly dying of cancer. I'm glad that she can enjoy the sunshine we've been having today.

We are scheduled to leave here about 6 P.M. From Puerto Limón (actually Port Lemon in English), it's only a short run to the Atlantic entrance to the Panama Canal. The canal is one of the engineering wonders of the world. It spans the fifty-mile width of the Isthmus of Panama, joining the world's two great oceans. The Isthmus was known to Christopher Columbus, but it was first explored by Núñez de Balboa in 1513, eleven years after Columbus saw it. Way back in 1534, Charles V of Spain had a survey made for a canal. Nothing happened, however, until 1880, when Ferdinand de Lesseps, who built the Suez Canal, came here to start work for the French Canal Company. Nine years later, after tens of thousands of people had died in the attempt and the company had spent $300 million, it went into bankruptcy.

The United States obtained the French rights for $40 million. After the Hay-Herrán Treaty was signed in 1903, the Colombian

Senate refused to ratify it, so Panama disengaged itself from Colombia with some machinations on our part and confirmed the treaty in 1904. The treaty gave us possession in perpetuity of a ten-mile strip across Panama so that we could build the canal. We promised to pay Panama $10 million in gold and $250,000 a year forever. This went on and increased ten times over. Recently, we agreed to turn both the Canal Zone and the operation of the canal over to the Panamanians on the last day of this millennium, December 31, 1999.

As everybody knows, two colonels really were important in the building of the canal, William Gorgas, who took care of getting rid of the diseases and making life somewhat more livable during the construction, and George Goethals, who did the engineering. We put $380 million into it, not bad considering that the French put in $300 million and failed.

As for the canal itself, it's 50.7 miles long, 110 feet wide, and 41 feet deep. It has twelve locks, each of them 1,000 feet long. As the QE2 transits the locks there is just about a yard to spare at each end and six inches on each side. The QE2 pays over $100,000 to go through the canal, and generally gets preference when it arrives even though it has to make an appointment a month ahead of time.

THURSDAY, JANUARY 21
Panama Canal

We arrived at the mouth of the canal and the twin ports of Cristóbal and Colón around dawn. There were a number of ships stacked there in formation, but we entered the canal first because we pay more than anyone else and we have had a date for this hour for more than a month. In fact, today we broke the record for paying at the canal, handing over a check for more than $106,000. Since the QE2 was refurbished, there is a little more usable profitable space aboard and that is what one pays for.

It was a wonderful experience seeing this 67,000-ton vessel glide from one ocean to another with seeming ease. The transit took about nine hours. As mentioned, we entered the canal on the Atlantic side. A few miles later, we went through the Gatun Lock, which in three steps brought us 85 feet above sea level of the Atlantic. Then we traveled on our own power through Gatun Lake, which is man-made. Next was the famous Gaillard Cut, an eight-mile excavation through the solid rock of the Continental Divide. Following that, we went through the Pedro Miguel Lock, which lowered us 31 feet to Miraflores Lake. After that came the Miraflores Locks and in two steps, we were again 54 feet down to the Pacific Ocean. Four miles after that, we reached the terminus at Balboa on the Pacific.

The most interesting thing about this operation is that it is all done by water, which moves by gravity from one level to the other. For each ship that goes through, it takes 52 million gallons of water, and all of it has to come from rainwater caught either in Gatun Lake or in Madden Lake, or from the water draining into the lakes from the upper Chagres River.

We will be in the Pacific for the next two months or so until we pass through here in the other direction on our way home. Our next stop is Acapulco, a distance of over 1,500 miles from here. We'll pass the coastlines of Panama, Costa Rica, Nicaragua, El Salvador, Guatemala, and finally the Pacific coast of Mexico. We both feel very much at home here, because we visited all these countries just last September.

FRIDAY, JANUARY 22
En Route to Acapulco

This morning we woke up to as calm a sea as we have seen so far. The Pacific is living up to its name. A whole school of dolphins was cavorting off the port side as a number of ships, mainly tankers, passed by en route to Panama. Off the starboard side, we see long rows of mountains on the coastline, as well as a number of islands out at sea. It's a beautiful sunny day, with the temperature in the high 80s. I finished *Sayonara* before turning in last night, and now I'm beginning Allan Bloom's *The Closing of the American Mind* and continuing with Burghardt's *Preaching*. While I was up on the sports deck reading this morning, I ran into Herb Kaplow. We had a two-hour bull session out in the sun. He and I have known each other for a long time, going back to the late 1950s and the 1960s when I was on the Civil Rights Commission.

SATURDAY, JANUARY 23
En Route to Acapulco

We woke up to another flawless day, clear light blue sky, reasonably calm, deep blue water, and sunshine everywhere. We're out of sight of land, but we do pass occasional ships and see some porpoises skipping along to keep us company from time to time. I decided to skip two lectures after breakfast, one on computer programming and the other on Acapulco. Instead, I read the first few chapters of *The Closing of the American Mind*. At 1 P.M. today, we had an international foodfest, which meant that the largest dining room, the Mauritania, was filled with tables replete with every conceivable type of food from every culture. Several hundred people descended on it, and in almost no time everything was gone.

We continue to meet about twenty new people every day. This gets a bit difficult in the name department, since most of them will be leaving in Los Angeles. Then another 900 or so will descend upon us and we'll start learning names all over again.

SUNDAY, JANUARY 24
Acapulco, Mexico

We were met in Acapulco by Carlos Pamplona, Coca-Cola's number two public relations man in Mexico. He presented us with a wonderful copper plate depicting the Calendario, the great calendar stone of the Aztecs. He then took us to the local market, which, with three cruise ships in port, was in full swing. Mexico is in bad financial shape at the moment. The peso has fallen to a low of about 2,200 to a dollar. I remember when the exchange rate was 12.5 and it stayed there for many years.

It seemed to get hotter as the day went on. We drove around the curve of the bay down to the Princess Hotel. It's built like an early Aztec or Mayan pyramid, hollow on the inside with an enormous lobby rising up to the roof, some thirty floors up. It also has a wonderful tropical garden surrounding it and one of the most beautiful beaches one could imagine. They pump seawater through the gardens and lobby, which is quite a spectacular sight. They make the best piña coladas in the world here. We were quite dehydrated by now, so we stopped to have one. Then we drove over to Las Brisas, where we met the QE2 tour group at the beachfront restaurant. Las Brisas is a very interesting hotel too. All the accommodations are little cliffside bungalows called *casitas*, most with their own private pools.

MONDAY, JANUARY 25
En Route to Los Angeles

Today we will be crossing the bottom of the Gulf of California to Baja California, passing by those wonderful places like Las Cruces, San José del Cabo, and San Lucas, the southernmost city in Baja. I have many happy memories of this part of the world, having spent fourteen Christmas vacations down here with my friends C. R. Smith and Charlie Jones. I described these places at greater length in my last book, *God, Country, Notre Dame*. I only wish we could come closer to the shore so I could see the little church perched on the hillside above the airstrip at Las Cruces, where I offered Christmas Midnight Mass for fourteen years running.

Reading Bloom's book again, I'm finding him to be a grim prophet who somewhat overstates his case, I think. And the book is getting tougher now that he's getting into the German philosophical precedents for our current dilemma, the false prophets, Nietzsche, Weber, Freud, Heidegger, etc., not to forget Hegel and Marx. He thinks they all brought us to the moral relativity that pervades the academic scene today. Relativity is O.K. in physics, but it is the kiss of death when one gets to values and morals.

We raised $450 in church collections over the weekend for the Apostolate of the Sea. That's only slightly less than we did at Midnight Mass. The congregation seems to get bigger each day, although we only take up collections on Sunday. It will be sad to see the New York–Fort Lauderdale–Los Angeles group get off the day after tomorrow. They have been the core of our congregation and have grown steadily. As I wander around the deck in a pair of white trunks and a guayabera, almost everybody says, "Hi, Father." This morning I talked to some people who were having spiritual problems. I am sure it would look peculiar to the Fathers of the Church to see me discussing prayer, marriage, alcoholism, and a variety of other things clad only in a guayabera and a pair of tennis shorts. However, the important thing is the message, not the messenger, or what he's wearing.

TUESDAY, JANUARY 26
En Route to Los Angeles

When we turned out this morning, it was about twenty degrees colder than the 85- and 90-degree temperatures we've been used to, and windy. For the first time in weeks, I put on a jacket. It's amazing how a change in temperature alters the whole tempo of life on this ship. When it's hot and balmy, the decks are full of people lying around in shorts and bikinis getting sunburned. The moment the temperature drops, the decks are deserted and people are inside taking advantage of all the indoor activities aboard the ship. There is bingo with a $5,000 final-day pot. There are lectures on everything from astrology to investments. There is the library and the wonderful 10,000 books that go with it. There is the Golden Spa, which offers a wide range of athletic activity. There's even a course on what one might expect in Los Angeles. This is in addition to about fifteen other activities of various kinds, and about ten bars. My answer to all of this is to get two good books and my Breviary and go up on the deck, get my prayers said for the day, light a good cigar, and start reading.

We had a fine Mass today. It was Ned's birthday and the last day aboard for the passengers who were getting off in Los Angeles. I gave a nostalgic sermon, telling those who were leaving us in Los Angeles how much we had enjoyed seeing this Christian community spontaneously form on board. They really are an extraordinary group. They sang "Happy Birthday" to Ned at Mass and gave him a cake. After Mass, many of them came up with other gifts to help us along the way.

We have to change cabins tomorrow. Our new one is one deck down and smaller, but at least it's an outside cabin. The rabbi and the bishop are being changed too, and we're now all together along the same corridor, which the crew calls "the Holy Land."

WEDNESDAY, JANUARY 27
Long Beach, California

I looked out of the porthole at 5:30 A.M. The tugs were pushing us into our anchorage in Long Beach. Actually, it's San Pedro. It's like parking in the middle of a city. Anyway, today is moving day. It took us about two hours to get all of our accumulated stuff down a floor to our new cabin. I had a call from one of our alumni who took care of us in Mexico City, Juan Cintrón. He said that they were putting thirteen cases of wine aboard. Juan is joining the ship in Singapore with fourteen of his colleagues, but he said we should feel free in the meantime to dip into the wine that is arriving here from his company, New World Wines, Inc., out of Tustin, California. There is no way on earth we could possibly get thirteen cases of wine into this cabin. In fact, we couldn't get one in, since the little wine we have is stashed in the bathroom at this moment. Anyway, I think we have conned the baggagemaster into putting it in a corner of his storage room, although he's pretty tight with stored things in there at the moment.

When we came in to dinner we found we were changed back to our original places on the other side of the Princess Grill. Who is sitting next to me but Ruby Keeler of Hollywood fame. She just came aboard and will be giving a lecture or two. She's getting along in years now, but who could ever forget Ruby Keeler and her dancing? We even hummed a couple of songs together, but Ned said that's what got us thrown out of this place the last time when they moved us to the other end of the grill, not our cigars. Anyway, we're back. We've decided to give up cigar smoking in the restaurant voluntarily, even though it's allowed. We were planning to give up cigars for Lent anyway, as a small bit of penance.

When we leave L.A. we will begin the longest leg of our journey so far. It's 3,561 nautical miles between here and Papeete, Tahiti, our next stop. It will take us all of five days and nights to get there.

THURSDAY, JANUARY 28
At Sea

I finally got through the second of three sections in Bloom's *The Closing of the American Mind*. It's very philosophical and every page seems to be replete with Rousseau, Kant, Hegel, Nietzsche, Marx, and Descartes, and a host of others. Bloom is trying to lay the philosophical foundations for the current state of mind in America. Again, I had the impression, as in the first part, that he is probably overdoing somewhat and stroking it with too broad a brush. But it was interesting, if difficult reading. He really blames Weber and Freud for bringing in the nihilistic ideas of Nietzsche to American minds and educators and thus leading us into a kind of new nihilism, without values, without philosophical foundations that are demonstrable and even without reason, not to mention faith. His third part is on the university and I'm sure I'll find that a lot easier going.

Ned and I both are trying to eat as lightly as possible; practically no breakfast, lunch something like today's V8 juice, quiche, and a bit of carrot cake without the frosting. Tonight we're having some Dover sole which they bought in Los Angeles. Nothing alcoholic until after Mass in the evening before dinner. I just did a number of turns around the deck, which are a fifth of a mile each time. It's the best exercise aboard ship, unless you like riding a stationary bicycle, which I don't, even though I once did over 3,000 miles on one, to strengthen my knee muscles. Ugh.

FRIDAY, JANUARY 29
En Route to Papeete

It was overcast again today, which is probably good for our collective skins, since we've been getting a lot of sun in the past week or so. There was also a bit of quartering wind out of the northeast. At noontime, the closest land, 600 miles to the east, was Cabo San Lucas, Baja California.

This morning the rabbi, the bishop, Ned, and I invited everyone who was interested to come to the Queen's Lounge, where we introduced ourselves and then broke up into four groups, one in each corner of the room, to get to meet some of the passengers more intimately and to get some of them to meet each other. Out of that little encounter came two persons with problems who stayed behind after the others left. I had planned on going to hear Waldemar Hansen talk on the South Pacific (he's our onboard expert for the lands we're visiting), but it seemed more important to spend the time with my two new "parishioners." An hour or two later we had both situations under reasonable control, I thought. Always good to talk out problems with a third party.

I managed to read the opening chapters of Robert Hughes's *The Fatal Shore*, a beautifully written book on Australia.

We had a great conversation with Ruby Keeler tonight. She told us a great deal about her early days in New York and how her career started. During the course of the conversation we decided that all of the top show people are either Catholics or Jews.

The captain, who is spending a good deal of time on public relations, introduced the rabbi tonight as Father Ruben. He made a good recovery, though, saying, "I'm sorry he's not really a father, but he is a grandfather." Alvin said to us, "Is that a promotion or demotion?" All I could say was "We're glad to have you."

SATURDAY, JANUARY 30
En Route to Papeete

Another cloudy day as we head into the doldrums, which extend 10 degrees north and south of the equator. I believe we're about 9 degrees north at the moment. We've been traveling on the northeast trade wind, which is perfect for us because we're going southwest. The trade winds run on both sides of the doldrums, and the stronger they blow, the less wind there is within the doldrums. That made for great difficulty when sailing ships depended on the wind alone. They could languish here for days, even weeks. We are plowing through the doldrums at about 27 knots, being now just a little over 1,000 miles from the first of the South Sea islands, the Marquesas.

We had two lectures on the painter Paul Gauguin today, one by Waldemar Hansen and a second by an art historian on board. Both were excellent, and of particular interest now, because we're headed toward Tahiti, where Gauguin painted a lot of his pictures. He was broke most of his life. Ironically, his paintings now sell for $40 to $50 million each.

The farther we are from port, the more activities there seem to be aboard ship. Today, in addition to the two Gauguin programs, there was a fashion show, a lecture by sports broadcaster Win Elliott on how to root for the Chicago Cubs, a course in carving, all kinds of athletic activities, a Spanish class, and lectures on computers, bridge, and financial planning. If one didn't skip about 90 percent of the activities on this ship, life would really get hectic.

At the French cocktail party this noon, I met a woman who told me she'll be dead from cancer within a year or two. That makes two such persons in two days. Both are facing it quite well. I hope I helped them face it even better. One needs to be at peace with God and oneself, to cherish every day of life, and to live each day to the fullest, even as we are trying to do in retirement.

SUNDAY, JANUARY 31
En Route to Papeete

We had some excitement at noontime because we officially passed the equator, where we are at 0 degree. From now on, everything is south of the equator, beginning at 1 degree and increasing to 90 at the South Pole. I calculate that we'll get to 45 degrees south as we go around New Zealand and Australia. It's about the latitude of Patagonia and southern Chile, although those places stretch another 12 degrees farther south, almost to 60 degrees.

Crossing the equator is always a time for great fun. We all gathered on the aft deck by the swimming pool. Men and women members of the crew were brought out under guard and presented to King Neptune and his queen. He ordered them to kiss a dead fish, which in this case was a salmon, presumably from the kitchen. Then they were doused with ketchup, mustard, eggs, whipped cream, and a variety of other gooey concoctions, shoved into a seat, and dumped into the pool. At the conclusion of the festivities, we all got certificates saying we were pollywogs, people who had crossed the equator. It's about the twentieth time for me.

Between halves of the Super Bowl, which we had on radio, I had a call that a woman who was a patient in the ship's hospital wanted a rosary. When I took it to her I could see that she was failing. We talked for a while and she seemed more at peace. Interesting about the rosary, just praying it and moving from bead to bead is settling, to say the least. I was told that her son would be flying out to Tahiti to take her home.

MONDAY, FEBRUARY 1
En Route to Papeete

Today we reached the Polynesian triangle, which is an enormous sweep of islands, thousands of miles across and thousands of miles down, with three basic divisions, mainly ethnic. Imagine an enormous triangle with its points in Hawaii, New Zealand, and Easter Island. This is the Polynesian triangle, Polynesian meaning "many islands." The people here have a very similar culture and are generally lighter-skinned and with black wavy hair. To the west of Polynesia is Melanesia, also a Greek word, meaning "black islands." Here the people are darker and have frizzy hair. To the north of Melanesia and, of course, west of Polynesia, is Micronesia, the Greek word for "small islands." We will be visiting Polynesia, which contains Tahiti and Mooréa in the Society Islands, under French political control, and Rarotonga in the Cook Islands, related to New Zealand. We were originally scheduled to go to Fiji, but because of political unrest there we are going instead to Rarotonga. To the south of all these islands, which can be designated by a generic name, Oceania, lie the two great islands of Australia and New Zealand, with the smaller island of Tasmania below Australia to the south of Melbourne in the state of Victoria. Many of these islands are now independent countries; others are related to Australia, New Zealand, France, England, or the United States.

TUESDAY, FEBRUARY 2
Papeete, Tahiti

I looked out the porthole at 7 A.M. and already we were entering the harbor of Papeete, skirting the reef. Mooréa was miles behind us, its volcanic top rising up out of the sea. Tahiti has two volcanoes joined by the narrow isthmus of Tarawa, which gives it a real figure-eight shape. After looking at the rolling sea for six nights and five days, those volcanoes look startling and very beautiful against the early morning sky. I was reminded of the first time I came here. It was in 1969 with Doc Kenna, my provincial. Because I had done the whole island tour, I didn't take the tour this morning. It is the first visit here for Ned, however, so he went.

About 10 A.M., I left the ship and started to walk into Papeete, which is a couple of miles from the dock. It was about 100 degrees in the shade and there wasn't any shade along that dockside road. I wasn't sure I would make it, because it kept getting hotter and hotter and the black asphalt didn't help any either. Everything is very expensive. I stopped at the bank to change twenty dollars into Polynesian francs and had to pay a three-dollar service charge on the transaction. A mai tai, a tropical drink, cost eight dollars.

Around noon, I met some people from the ship and we decided to have lunch together at a little French restaurant up on a hilltop. Everything was wonderful until the bill arrived—$250 for the five of us. A bit much, even considering that we had a round of mai tais in addition to the wine. I had planned to take Ned out for dinner at one of the reefside French restaurants this evening, but after a look at the prices, we decided to stay on board. Tourism declined 30 percent here last year and it is supposed to go even lower this year. Perhaps the prices have something to do with it, or perhaps this reflects the falling dollar. Despite the prices, however, there's no denying that this is one of the most charming and exotic places in the world.

A lot of Tahitians came aboard tonight to put on a cultural show on the top deck. The music was so-so and the dancing was typical hip gyrating, the Tahitian equivalent of Egyptian belly dancing, both of which are more athletic than aesthetic. However, it was a lovely evening with a full moon and bright stars shining down from the black vault. The night sky out here has a very special charm.

WEDNESDAY, FEBRUARY 3
Mooréa

We left Papeete around 6 A.M. and crossed to Mooréa. The bay here was immortalized in the musical *South Pacific*, and it's easy to understand why. Mooréa has to be one of the most enchanting islands in the South Pacific. With its glistening white beaches, fringed by coconut palms, banana trees, and high serrated mountains, it is truly an idyllic place. Like many of its sister islands, it was born about six million years ago as a huge volcano.

Ned left early on the official tour and I went in with one of our launches about an hour later. I had no sooner disembarked from the launch than I spotted four Americans getting into an outrigger. The man at the tiller was a Frenchman. I had no idea where they were going, but since I had no plans, I asked them if they had room for one more. The Frenchman called out a friendly *"oui"* and welcomed me aboard.

The four Americans were two retired couples. The Frenchman was a Parisian named Oliver. He told me he had come to Tahiti with his wife seven years ago and had reconstructed an entire native village, using all the original materials and native craftsmen. He was taking the four Americans, and now me, to visit it. Oliver stayed inside the reef as we sailed along the coast. At each village we passed, he would take out a conch shell and blow it to announce our arrival. At one village a woman came out and waved. Oliver brought the outrigger in as close as he could, then jumped out, waded ashore, and carried the woman back to the boat. When we reached the village, two stout workers came out and did the carrying.

Oliver took us all around the village to show us how the Tahitians lived. He even climbed a sixty-foot coconut tree and threw down some fresh green coconuts. We split them open, then drank the milk and ate the meat. Both were delicious. Next came one of those Polynesian dancing shows, which always anesthetize me. I managed to stay awake, but I was glad when it was over. After the dancing we strolled along the beach. It was a great spur-of-the-moment outing, but I was glad to get back to the ship and shower after spending the morning in 100-degree heat.

THURSDAY, FEBRUARY 4
En Route to Rarotonga

The highlight of today's shipboard activities was a showing of *Forty-Second Street*, with an introduction by Ruby Keeler. She told us that this was not only her first movie but also the first movie of her co-star, Dick Powell. They made fourteen more movies together after that, so the box office return was obviously very good. It was sad to see the way Ruby practically had to be carried on and off the stage; sadder yet to realize that she was once the sparkling young tap dancer in the movie. She was a real trouper to endure the awkwardness of it all. I'm sure her presence must have reminded everyone of the ravages of time on the human body. But at the same time, we could all take a lesson from Ruby's indomitable spirit. She was the embodiment of the old show business adage that the show must go on.

FRIDAY, FEBRUARY 5
Rarotonga

This is supposed to be the most beautiful of the Cook Islands, which are named after the famous captain who first discovered them in the 1770s. The fifteen islands in the group are scattered over a vast expanse of 850,000 square miles. Fewer than 20,000 people live on the islands, and about half of them, most of whom are Polynesians, live in Rarotonga. The islands belonged to the British until 1901, when they turned them over to New Zealand. In 1965, they became internally self-governing, although they are, in fact, a kind of protectorate of New Zealand, which takes care of their defense and foreign affairs, and provides certain subsidies, as well as jobs. There are actually more Cook Islanders living in New Zealand than there are in the Cook Islands.

We woke up just before the ship reached its anchorage outside Rarotonga reef. After breakfast, we boarded the first ship's tender going ashore. Two things struck me right away: how friendly the people were and how clean the town was. I found out later that cleanliness is taken very seriously here. Every house on the island is officially inspected every three months. If it is not clean and well kept, the occupants receive a fine and a mention in the local newspaper, as well as on the radio.

Ned and I visited the local Catholic church and school, where we met Father Paul Farmer, a New Zealander, and a friend of John Mackay, the former Bishop of Auckland, who is a Notre Dame Ph.D. Father Farmer had us talk to his high school students, who were in the middle of a geometry class. I tried to persuade them to do very well in school and come to Notre Dame. I'm reasonably sure that we've never had a student come to Notre Dame from here.

Rarotonga, the name means "down south"—is oval-shaped. The whole island is surrounded by a coral reef, but there are two openings in it where ships can enter. One is near the town of Avarua. The other, to the south, has a beautiful sandy beach with a ring of very small islands outside it.

We drove around the entire circumference of the island, which is a journey of about nineteen miles. It's covered with jagged volcanic peaks interspersed with deep valleys and tropical forest. One sees beautiful tropical flowers everywhere, mostly red and yellow, such as hibiscus and frangipani, both of which come in more than fifteen different varieties. In gardens and on large farms there were trees laden with breadfruit, bananas, and pineapples. There is good fishing off the south coast of the island. They catch mainly snapper, mackerel, and mullet inside the coral reef. Fortunately, most of the sharks stay outside.

We also visited the island's first Christian church, which was built in 1835 and has some very interesting tombstones, both in Polynesian and in quaint English. On our way back to the anchorage, we stopped at the Rarotongan resort hotel, very tropical and very nice. There we saw an hourlong show by some local singers and dancers. They began with a prayer and ended by singing the Our Father in Polynesian, which was very beautiful indeed. On the whole, it was the best performance we've seen so far.

As on the other islands we have seen, the London Missionary Society got an early start and most of the people are Protestants. There are, of course, Catholic churches on all of these islands, but priests are rather rare. There were none on Mooréa, although there were two Catholic churches there. We met a young seminarian here today. He told us that there are about a hundred young men in the seminary in Fiji, all from this vast area of small islands.

Just to give some idea of where we are in relation to other places we have been and are heading for: Papeete, which we left two days ago, is 816 miles east-northeast of here. Auckland, to which we now head, is 2,155 miles south-southwest of here. Sydney is 3,699 miles southwest, and Tokyo is 6,810 miles northwest. This is indeed an isolated little island far from everywhere, but it has a beauty all its own and a kind of peace that can't be found in cities. In the whole history of the islands, only five murders have been recorded. Jails are rare, and those they do have allow prisoners to go home on weekends to be with their families.

We have an interesting theological problem for Friday Mass tonight. There won't be any Saturday, since we jump from Friday to Sunday at midnight crossing the international date line. Question: Does Friday night Mass count for Sunday? I say it does if you're passing the date line and losing Saturday entirely. But the question is largely academic, because most of our 100-plus parishioners will come to Mass again on Sunday anyway.

SUNDAY, FEBRUARY 7
En Route to Auckland

Ned was up early this morning for Sunday morning Mass. He tells me he had a good congregation too, despite another half-hour change in time last night. Keeping up with local time becomes quite a problem because the international date line, which we crossed today, is not exactly at the 180th meridian all the way north and south. Out here they stretch it 10 degrees east so that Fiji and the Tonga Islands can be within the same time zone. Thus we will cross the international date line at 170 degrees, rather than at 180. From Greenwich, England, from which all time and longitudinal lines are reckoned, 180 degrees is exactly halfway around the world. We are now a bit more than 25 degrees south of the equator, going through the Tropic of Capricorn.

Today we watched *O'Hara's Wife*, a prize-winning film by Bill Bartman, who eats at the table next to ours in the Princess Grill. It provided me with a closing thought for my homily tonight. Bill's film was so well done generally that I've invited him to come to Notre Dame to advise us on films for the International Peace Institute. After dinner, we escorted Ruby Keeler down to the theater lounge, where four Australian-Irish players and singers were performing. Because of her stroke, she has great difficulty in walking. Her left leg and left arm are almost useless, but with her cane and some help from us, she managed quite well.

We had some rain this afternoon and evening. It's practically the first rain we've seen since leaving New York. The weather has been spectacular, as it was all summer and fall when we were traveling through the West in the United States and later in Latin America. So far, we can count the bad days on the fingers of one hand. There have been many blessings on this trip, but the incredibly good weather stands out.

MONDAY, FEBRUARY 8
En Route to Auckland

We passed 30 degrees south early this morning. By 9 A.M. the winds for the first time switched around to west-southwest, hitting us just off our port bow. We've had helping trade winds thus far, but now we're in the variables, where we will probably pick up some head winds. We've come some 1,046 miles since leaving Rarotonga a day and a half ago, leaving us 565 miles yet to go to the Bay of Islands, which is outside Auckland, New Zealand. Despite the strong wind, I worked up a sweat just walking the deck for a few rounds this morning. The temperature is about 76 degrees and heading up toward 80.

I finally finished Robert Hughes's The Fatal Shore this morning, all 602 pages of it. It is a brilliant history of what was called "the system." It ended on January 10, 1868, eighty years to the month since Captain Arthur Philip brought the first convict fleet to its anchorage in Sydney Cove. Over 160,000 convicts, in fact lifelong slaves, were shipped to Australia, 45,000 of them being Irish political prisoners. They were sent to Australia because American independence prevented them from being sent to America.

The system had a deep effect on the history of Australia. At its first centenary in 1888, the country buried that part of its past and celebrated the future. No doubt Australians will have even more to be optimistic about when they celebrate their second century shortly.

We Americans have our own sad memories of slavery. Legally it began to end, in the South, in 1863 with Lincoln's Emancipation Proclamation. But it did not end institutionally until the Civil Rights Act of 1964, better than a century later. Even today the painful effects of our system linger on in the plight of so many of our black population. Slavery, white or black, is institutionalized injustice and it's not easy for the victims to escape its long-term effects. But we must keep trying and I am sure we will. This is what the civil rights revolution in America was all about during the 1960s.

TUESDAY, FEBRUARY 9
En Route to Auckland

I spent most of the morning on deck reading Bloom. It was beautiful sailing weather because there was intermittent sunshine behind high clouds with a nice breeze. Also, there were lots of islands in view once we approached the Bay of Islands. It was our first contact with New Zealand. As we left the bay and headed into a new channel, we coasted along the northeastern shore of New Zealand, all the way to Auckland Harbor. There were many islands strung out along our path, mostly rugged and rocky. At noontime today, we assembled all the Notre Dame alumni for a cocktail party. They all reminisced about their happy years at Notre Dame, and Ned and I filled them in on our hopes for the future.

I was back on deck right after lunch with my copy of Bloom's *The Closing of the American Mind*. I must say, I find it hard to believe that the million-odd people who bought this book really read it, especially the long central philosophical part. As I mentioned earlier, his analysis is somewhat overdone as he looks at intellectual life in America today. His third section, which is on the university today, was quite well done, although again, I think, exaggerated. I couldn't find a great deal of resonance with university life, its teaching and values, as I am familiar with it at Notre Dame. Perhaps it's different at state universities. Bloom himself is at the fine private University of

Chicago. In any event, I'm glad I read the book. It did raise some important questions.

We came into Auckland Harbor about 5 P.M. Just about everybody was on deck as we made the long approach, twisting and turning in the channel. Thousands of boats, large and small, had turned out to meet us, plus airplanes and helicopters. Obviously, the arrival of the QE2 is considered quite an event in this part of the world.

New Zealand is made up of two large islands, North Island and South Island. Between them, the two islands are over 1,000 miles in length. They are located 1,400 miles southeast of Australia and exactly midway between the equator and the South Pole. The Dutchman Tasman found New Zealand in 1642, but it was rediscovered by Captain James Cook in 1769. This was part of Cook's commission to find a continent in the South Pacific. It was just assumed that there had to be one, because the earth could not otherwise have stayed in balance.

After Cook had mapped New Zealand's outlines, he found Australia, specifically at Botany Bay, which was the landing point of subsequent convict ships. I can't think of any story more exciting than Villiers's account of Cook's two voyages, which I read on my first trip out this way in 1969.

When the settlers first came here, they met the Polynesian Maoris, who had been here since the middle of the fourteenth century. New Zealand became an independent dominion in 1907 and a member of the British Commonwealth in 1931. The population of New Zealand is 3.3 million. Of that number, more than 800,000 live in Auckland and about 342,000 in Wellington, the capital. Most of the population is European, although 8 percent are Maori, descendants of the original inhabitants. As to religion, 29 percent are Anglican, 18 percent Presbyterian, and 15 percent Catholic. There are more sheep on these islands than people. They also grow grain and fruit crops and catch fish. Big game fishing is very good among the 144 islands of the Bay of Islands. Some of the largest black marlin in the world are caught here.

After dinner tonight, Ned and I took a walk along the dockside for several blocks. It was quite warm, and we both had to shed our coats. The QE2 looks even bigger than it is when you see it in the harbor silhouetted against the city skyline.

Auckland has grown tremendously since my last visit here in 1969. There are new buildings everywhere one looks, and derricks to mark the locations of yet others under construction. The city is often compared to Corinth, because it is built on an isthmus between the Tasman Sea and the Pacific Ocean. This port is so large that it could easily accommodate a whole flotilla of the world's navies all at once.

We returned to the ship around 10 P.M. Ned went to the movies. I caught up on this diary, worked on tomorrow's homily, and turned in early. Tomorrow several hundred Australians will come aboard to sail on the QE2 back to Sydney as part of the Bicentennial celebration of Australia.

WEDNESDAY, FEBRUARY 10
Auckland, New Zealand

This was a day to remember. I was up at 8 A.M. on the nose because we had arranged a breakfast with the Catholic port chaplain, Father Jack Sloane. He turned out to be a Marist Father. We had something in common, since his former Superior General, Father Joe Buckley, had obtained a Ph.D. in philosophy at Notre Dame after the war. I learned from Father Jack that only about 15 percent of New Zealanders are Catholic, but that many of them live in Auckland.

We were off the ship around ten and met Meredith, our driver, who was provided by Coca-Cola. Then began a very busy day. First, we went to the museum. It presents everything from the history of the Maoris to both world wars to English furniture—you name it. After that, we went up to Mount Eden, where one can see the whole city in all directions. Then we went to the aquarium to see a wide range of fish, especially a lot of sharks and stingrays. Then it was back into the city for lunch at the top of one of the tallest buildings. There were great views in all directions.

After lunch, we bought some jade stones, looked at a pair of kiwis in the zoo, toured the university, and prayed at the Catholic cathedral. We then visited Mount Victoria, from which one gets another whole perspective of the bays, the harbor, and all of the buildings in Auckland. After crossing the bridge, which opened up a new housing section to the north of Auckland, we went to another mountain spot where again we had a wonderful vista of the whole city, the bay, and the harbor. About this time, it occurred to us that we had twenty minutes to get back to the ship if we were going to sail on her. There were a few tense moments getting back across the bridge, but we finally made it with about four minutes to spare.

It was my turn to preach tonight and, believe it or not, I preached on the obtuse spirit. A lot of the people aboard, given their age, are worried about death and dying, retirement and inactivity, loss of power, etc. It is probably all too much to categorize under the concept of the obtuse spirit, but I gave it my best shot. I have no idea whether I brought it off or not. At least, no one fell asleep.

As we left Auckland Harbor, hundreds of boats surrounded the ship and ran her out to sea like a pack of sheep dogs. As we rounded the corner of the bay, we encountered the Pacific swell and the ship began to sway from side to side. This will probably go on until we arrive at the entrance to Wellington Harbor tomorrow, arguably the windiest place on earth. Also, we have a 20-knot following sea from the northeast, which creates a low swell and gives the ship a constant rocking motion, but thankfully a fairly mild one.

THURSDAY, FEBRUARY 11
En Route to Wellington

I spent two and one-half hours on deck today reading *Ministry*, a new book by Father Dick McBrien, then chairman of Notre Dame's theology department. I found it very balanced and quite helpful. Like everything else that Dick writes, it is wonderfully clear and orderly. When one considers the history of ministry in the early Church and all of the permutations in its conduct over the centuries, it's wonderful to live in an age when the Church is beginning to see its mission as service to the Kingdom and the people of God who constitute the Church. We're all part of the people of God—the people in the pews, the ordained ministers and bishops, even the Pope.

Lest I forget to mention it, Ned has been doing yeoman service in keeping our bills straight, doing a great deal of telexing to spots ahead where we hope to meet the alumni, and generally keeping our affairs in order. He's much better at this than I am. But then, he is a CPA and I don't even count well.

About 4:30 this afternoon, we came into the narrow entrance to Wellington Harbor, Cook Bay. Hundreds of small craft came out to greet us, including three tall ships, one from Spain, one from Poland, and one from Ecuador. Also, two fire boats came out into the harbor and sprayed water in all directions. It was a very festive occasion.

We had orange roughy for dinner. It's become a very popular fish in the Midwest and, believe it or not, it comes from here. It lives deep in the ocean and was not known as an eating fish until fairly recently. It's very good and it was nice to get it right here where it is caught.

FRIDAY, FEBRUARY 12
Wellington, New Zealand

We were up reasonably early this morning, again to a bright, sunny day as well as a hot and humid one. Once again we were taken in tow by a representative from the Coca-Cola organization. First we went west out of Wellington and then north along the west coast. About twenty-five to thirty miles out, we climbed a mountain above a town called Paekakiriki. From there, we could see south across the strait to South Island about twenty or thirty miles away. We'll be passing this way tomorrow on our way to the west coast of South Island and Milford Sound. We saw a lot of rough country populated mainly by sheep, goats, and horses, plus large areas that had been reforested. Coming back into Wellington, we went through the town and up to Victoria Hill, which offers the best view of the city. From there we could see the QE2 swinging at its moorings, plus the magnificent bay which we entered yesterday afternoon. We couldn't help noticing how much the scene resembled San Francisco, with bright white houses climbing up the green-clad hills and many smaller bays going inland from the main harbor. The only element missing was the Golden Gate Bridge.

Shortly after noon, our driver dropped us off at the residence of Cardinal William, whom we found to be young, bright, and progressive. We enjoyed a traditional lamb dinner, followed by a three-hour conversation on things both ecclesiastical and secular. This is really a remote part of the world, about as far away from Rome as one can get and far from many other centers of action.

The New Zealand government prohibits U.S. warships from entering the harbor because of the nuclear weapons they carry. Yet during our short stay here we discovered that many New Zealanders don't agree with the ban, nor with New Zealand's dropping out of ANZUS, the Australian, New Zealand, U.S. mutual defense group. Most were aware that the United States saved New Zealand during World War II—and would probably have to save it again if it became necessary. New Zealand's military consists of a navy with thirty smallish ships, an army of a few thousand, and an air force of ten outdated airplanes.

In any event, this is one of the most friendly places we have visited. It's really amazing how good-natured New Zealanders are when you consider that they have to pay $130,000 for a modest house, 24 percent interest on mortgages, and impossible taxes, such as the 50 percent tax on American automobiles.

SATURDAY, FEBRUARY 13
En Route to Milford Sound

We awoke to another slightly overcast day, about 75 to 80 degrees on deck, but getting warmer. The sea is calm. There is only a slight 5-knot wind coming in from the east. We are cruising down the west coast of South Island, having come almost 500 miles since leaving Wellington last night. We're moving along at 28.5 knots.

This morning we passed Mount Cook. At about 12,000 feet, it is the highest point in New Zealand. As we made our way down the coast toward Milford Sound, the coastline was about twenty miles off our port side, very mountainous, like the coast of Chile, with some snowcapped peaks as well.

Rudyard Kipling called Milford Sound the eighth wonder of the world. It was formed many millions of years ago when the sea flooded a giant glacial valley. It's really a fjord that is dominated by a miter peak over a mile high. Pembroke Peak is even a bit higher. From these two peaks, precipitous rock walls plunge deeply into the water. The water is 180 feet deep at the entrance to the sound and 1,680 feet deep at its head.

Fog descended down off the peaks, along with rain, as we approached the head of the sound. Nevertheless, we were able to make out the Milford Sound Hotel and most of the outstanding sights along the way. The scenery was quite spectacular, much like the Norwegian fjords. When we reached the middle of the fjord, we turned around and retraced our route. At 45 degrees south, Milford Sound is the farthest south we will sail on our journey across the world, although we'll come close to this latitude as we round the bottom of Australia near Melbourne.

Two pastoral consultations took about an hour and a half today. With this many people and particularly the age group, which seems to average around sixty-five, one encounters a wide variety of problems—but opportunities too. Ned and I generally wear a cross on our coat collars, as military chaplains do, so people will know what we're about, even if they have no need for our services. Cardinal Suahard of Paris expressed it very well, I think, when he spoke of the effect one can have merely by being visible. He called it "the apostolate of one's presence." Or as my old Holy Cross friend Charley Sheedy used to say, "Just being there helps."

SUNDAY, FEBRUARY 14
En Route to Sydney

There was a considerable weather disturbance about 300 miles south of us and, as a result, we picked up some heavy swells during the night. Even in moderately heavy swells, this ship rides pretty evenly, although it has a tendency to sway a bit from side to side when being hit by waves on starboard or port side, as happened today.

We had good attendance at both the morning and afternoon Masses today. The Sunday Gospel tells of Christ curing the leper, so I decided to preach on the Sacrament of Reconciliation or, as we used to say, Confession. We collected about $350 at our Saturday night and two Sunday Masses, which is not bad. It all goes to the Apostolate of the Sea, an international organization that has houses for seamen in almost every major port and helps them when they're in trouble, besides providing spiritual care.

MONDAY, FEBRUARY 15
Sydney, Australia

At about 6:30 this morning, we were already heading through the massive rocks that mark the kilometer-and-a-half entrance into Sydney Harbor. This has to be one of the greatest harbors in the world. There are twenty-one square miles of enclosed anchorage, including a great number of small bays full of private sailing yachts.

This is the most cosmopolitan of all Australian cities. It has a larger population, 3.4 million, than all of New Zealand, yet the people enjoy a whole range of outdoor activities not normally associated with large cities. There are, for example, fifty-four beaches along the various shores of the harbor bays.

We had lunch at the top of the Needle, which soars 1,000 feet above the city. We settled on lamb and the local red wine, both of which are highly regarded here, and we weren't disappointed. After lunch, we visited the cathedral, a large English Gothic building, which is as beautiful as any cathedral on earth. It certainly equals the great English Gothic cathedrals I've seen, and I've seen a lot of them. We made a brief stop at the botanical garden, then walked around the campus of the University of Sydney, the best of the three universities here in town. Its central building is very reminiscent of the buildings one sees at Oxford and Cambridge.

Ned had caught a cold a day or two before we arrived here and wasn't feeling well, so our driver dropped him back at the ship. I continued on to Bondi Beach, which has the best combers in the world for surfing. I had our driver, Sam, stop at a sign that displayed the name of the place where the Navy is quartered. It said "Woolloomooloo," which I took to be an Aboriginal word. We also visited the famous Sydney Clamshell Opera House, which is only a few hundred yards from where we are docked. Besides the Taj Mahal, it will probably turn out to be one of the most photographed buildings in the world. It was designed by a Danish architect who estimated that it would cost about $15 million to build. It ended up costing $112 million.

There was an enormous party after Mass tonight as part of the Australian Bicentennial celebration. Among the several hundred important people on hand was a large complement of government officials and the U.S. ambassador to Australia. Needless to say, the cocktails were flowing and there were special banquets in each of the ship's dining rooms, followed by entertainment and a dance, all very formal.

TUESDAY, FEBRUARY 16
Sydney, Australia

We were up at 5:30 this morning, even though at midnight we were still watching the Bicentennial fireworks display, which was fantastic. By 7 A.M. we were off to Canberra, by air this time.

It's only a thirty-minute flight from Sydney to Canberra, the Australian capital. The name Canberra comes from an Aboriginal word meaning "the meeting place," a pretty good title for a capital. Canberra is about halfway between Sydney and Melbourne. It's located on the inland side of the Blue Mountains, the coastal range here, and is the largest inland city in Australia.

On the way into town from the airport, we passed the Royal Military College, which, interestingly, is based on the West Point model rather than Sandhurst in England. Everything here is English and one would expect Sandhurst to be the model. However, they asked General Kitchener to make a planning report on it and he recommended West Point as the best model. Besides this, one has the impression that Australians favor Americans over the British because we came to their defense during World War II.

Australia was not federalized until 1901. Until then, each of the states was a separate colony of England. In 1912, there was a worldwide competition to lay out a federal capital for the country. The winner was an American, Walter Burley Griffin, a landscape architect from Chicago. Nothing really happened after that until 1957, when a commission was finally appointed to proceed with the construction. What we saw today was what was done since then.

Ironically, though Griffin's overall layout was followed, none of the buildings he designed was ever built. One of the biggest things that Griffin did was to get the rivers dammed up to create some artificial lakes around the capital. Also, his plan called for four satellite cities, three of which are already built and the fourth now abuilding. The only private dwelling in the federal district proper is the house of the Anglican archbishop.

After a quick trip around the city, we went to Tralee Station, where they raise the best of all sheep, the merino, which comes from Spain. Bernard Morrison, the manager, showed us how to throw boomerangs and how to guide sheep dogs that control the sheep. The dogs are very important because there are 160 million sheep here in Australia. Believe it or not, a single dog can control 1,000 sheep! Before leaving the ranch we had a marvelous barbecued steak. After only a continental breakfast, followed by several hours of touring, it really hit the spot.

Our next stop was the new Parliament building, which will be dedicated by Queen Elizabeth on May 7 of this year. It took them seven and one-half years to build it. Once again, there was a big competition. A New York firm submitted the winning design, and most of the people we talked to said the New York firm deserved to win. The building is truly spectacular. But it is also difficult to describe, so I won't try, except to say that it cost over a billion dollars, a tidy sum for a country of 16 million people.

Another impressive sight was the War Memorial, which honors all the Australians who fought in wars going back to World War I. Australia suffered almost a quarter of a million casualties in these wars, a terrible price for any country and all the more so for a small one.

At the end of this busy day, we rushed to the airport, caught the plane back to Sydney, and reboarded the ship just in time to grab a bite to eat before the Mardi Gras celebration. Lent is coming at the right time, given the wonderful choice of food and drink on this ship. I trust it will help to keep us in fighting trim.

ASH WEDNESDAY, FEBRUARY 17
En Route to Melbourne

Today was uneventful compared with yesterday. I spent about three hours reading Andy Greeley's *Patience of a Saint.*

It's about 500 miles from Sydney to Melbourne and another 500 from Melbourne to Adelaide. That gives us the better part of twenty-four hours at sea on both this leg and the next one. I also did a lot of walking the deck and thinking about my sermon for Mass this afternoon. Since this is Ash Wednesday, I'll talk about the need for penance. And I also have to decide what I am going to give up for Lent. You can't preach it if you don't practice it.

Ned had about fifty at Mass this morning and I had close to a hundred this afternoon. Father D'Arcy also concelebrated with us today. He knows a good number of the people who are repeaters on the world cruise, as he is.

It was a nice day for walking the deck and reading outside because the weather has been in the 60s, not too windy, and a very moderate swell on the water. It has always amazed me how people who are very irregular in their church attendance never miss receiving ashes on their foreheads on Ash Wednesday or getting their throats blessed on the Feast of St. Blaise. It really brings everybody out of the woodwork.

I told the congregation that one good resolution for Lent would be to come to Mass every day, since it is so convenient here on the ship. I submitted that they would find giving up food and drink difficult, given the menu and nine bars aboard this ship. The Anglican bishop came by to receive ashes on his forehead from Ned this morning. Then he took some of our ashes for his service at 10:30 A.M., since he didn't have any. We're really ecumenical here.

THURSDAY, FEBRUARY 18
Melbourne, Australia

It was another bright, sunny, and quite warm day as we arrived in Melbourne. This is the second-largest city in Australia, with a population of almost 3 million. It has been described as stately, sedate, and snobbish. It is also an important financial and commercial center, an arbiter of artistic and cultural values for Australia, and the home of three universities. If Sydney is the New York or London or Paris of Australia, Melbourne would have to be its Boston. At the same time, the city has begun to lose some of its stodginess. There are many more glass-and-steel skyscrapers than there were when I last visited here nineteen years ago, as well as large influxes of Greeks, Italians, Turks, and other Ethnic groups, who have helped to liven things up.

Once again, Coca-Cola furnished us with a car and driver. We began our tour at the War Memorial, which overlooks the city. Then we went to see Como, a house built by an Englishman who made fortunes in wool both in England and in Australia. Next came the high-rent district of Toorak, where houses cost a minimum of a million apiece. The old money here comes from either sheep or gold.

At the conservatory we saw some wonderful multicolored begonias and had lunch at Fitzroy Gardens. As we were walking along a path on the way to the restaurant, we turned back to the car to pull our jackets out of a bag we were carrying. While we were putting them on, a giant limb came crashing down on the exact spot where we would have been walking had we not stopped. That stroke of good luck, or God's mercy, was all that prevented our trip from ending under a branch at Fitzroy Gardens in Melbourne. We also saw Captain Cook's house here. It was transported all the way from Yorkshire, stone by stone, and reassembled in the park.

We continued our tour with a visit to the University of Melbourne. This university of 18,000 enrollment includes Newman College, which used to be for men, and St. Mary's College, which used to be for women. Now both are coeducational, with about 250 students each. There are no Catholic colleges per se in Australia. Instead, they follow the English system of having Catholic houses at the state universities. We learned from the rector of Newman College, Father Bill Uren, a Jesuit, that there are also Catholic houses at the universities in Brisbane, Sydney, Adelaide, and Perth. Most of them are run by the Jesuits, who keep three or four priests there for tutoring help and program direction. They also have chapels with daily Mass.

Today was the twentieth anniversary of my mother's death, so we offered Mass for her today, as well as for my dad, who will be twenty-eight years dead in ten days, and my sister Mary and her husband, Al

Lyons, both of whom died at this time of year too—Mary in January twenty-nine years ago and Al in early February nine years ago.

FRIDAY, FEBRUARY 19
En Route to Adelaide

We woke up this morning to a quite high sea with the wind coming out of the southwest at about 25 knots an hour, hitting us on the port quarter as we headed almost due west. We've been riding about twelve to fifteen miles off the coast and intend to come in closer at noontime so we can touch the harbor of Portland, which is putting on a big celebration for the Australian Bicentennial. They want us to at least make an appearance. The temperature is about 60 degrees because we are right on the edge of the Roaring 40s, our present position being about 39 degrees south. It really took some doing to walk the deck this morning with the starboard side soaking wet and the port side sporting a wind that almost kept one from walking forward. One just leaned into the wind and pumped.

We passed Portland at noon. Many of their tugs and vessels, decorated with flags, came out to meet us tooting their horns as we slowly cruised by to help them celebrate their Bicentennial. I started a new book this afternoon, Mikhail Gorbachev's *Perestroika*.

SATURDAY, FEBRUARY 20
Adelaide, Australia

Around 10 A.M., we left the ship and met our guide for the day, Kay Kelly Lindberg, a Notre Dame master of arts in the class of 1964 and a student at St. Mary's College before that. Her father and her brother are also Notre Dame grads. In town, we met her husband, Janis, a Latvian.

The first order of the day was to find opals for our secretaries, Helen and Pat. Both of us found exactly what we were looking for with no trouble. This is the opal capital of the world. Ninety percent of the world's opals come from Coober Pedy, some 590 miles northwest of Adelaide. I think opals are one of the most beautiful stones around, and this is the place to buy them.

The Lindbergs own a couple of racehorses, so they took us out to Victoria Park to watch them run. In the first race, the horses came in third and fifth. We had them to win, so we came up empty. In the second race, we picked a horse whose name described the weather we'd been blessed with most of the time so far, Sunny Welcome. This time we got lucky. We bet him to win or place and he placed. With all of one dollar on the line in each race, neither had any appreciable effect on our financial status.

We then drove up into the hills behind Adelaide. We had a wonderful meal at a place called Ducks Inn, where you can get everything but duck. Ned ordered an entrée of kangaroo meat, much to my surprise, and let me sample it. I found it very tasty, much better than steak or venison. Other orders around the table included rabbit, lamb, and beer-battered fish.

After lunch we continued up to the top of the mountain, where we toured the Cleoland Park and Zoo. Ned and I had our pictures taken with a koala bear hanging on to us for dear life. We also saw some dingo dogs, the ones that were tamed by Aborigines here to help them in hunting. They are a small dog, but very intelligent.

We were back at the ship in time to wash up, finish our prayers for the day, and run six flights upstairs for Mass in the theater. Among other things, I've given up elevators for Lent. Climbing stairs is the best exercise of all. I'll be doing about fifty flights a day.

SUNDAY, FEBRUARY 21
En Route to Fremantle

By the time we woke up, the ship was well into the Great Australian Bight. This is an enormous bay—600 miles from east to west—that covers the bottom of Australia where it bellies inward to the north. There was a light southeasterly wind coming up behind us and a very gentle swell, although the bight can be rough when the Roaring 40s continue up this way with a clear sweep all the way from the Antarctic to the southern shores of Australia.

Ned had almost as many people at Mass this morning as we had last night. I believe that Lent is pushing up our attendance somewhat, not only on Sundays but also during the week.

As we cruise along the southern coast this quiet Sunday afternoon, I'm taking a break from reading Gorbachev's *Perestroika* to record a few unrelated facts about Australia. First of all, it is the only nation that occupies an entire continent. It is also the flattest and smallest and driest inhabited continent in the world. Antarctica is drier, but uninhabited. Less than 10 percent of the land is arable in Australia. But the country is certainly not dry in terms of alcohol consumption. Among English-speaking nations, Australia holds the record for consumption of beer and whiskey.

Australia is also one of the oldest of the world's landmasses. Some fragments of the earth's crust here are 4.3 billion years old. One hundred sixty-five million years ago, Australia, together with North and South America, Africa, and most of Asia, was part of a landmass called Gondwana. Then Australia and the current continents began to drift away. Eventually, Australia and Antarctica separated and drifted farther from the center of what is now India. This explains why the flora and fauna of Australia, having developed separately over millions of years, are unique in all of the world. Even the human remains here go back 40,000 years, considerably older than any yet discovered in the New World.

Australia is about the size of the continental United States. It is one of the least populated countries in the world, averaging only five people per square mile. There are ten times as many sheep here as people. This is why they produce 30 percent of the world's wool and export the second-largest amount of mutton, almost 300,000 tons a year. Australia appears to be very healthy economically. Its per capita income of $11,200 is one of the highest in the world and 70 percent of Australians own their homes. Workers have from four to six weeks' vacation annually. On the downside, the Australian dollar has lost 50 percent against the Japanese yen in the last three years. As a result, there is heavy Japanese investment here, just as there is, for the same reason, in the United States.

Since 1950, the number of college students in Australia has grown from 30,000 to 180,000. There are now a few private universities, but higher education is mostly public and free, although there is a current move toward privatization of higher education. But all is not perfect. Only 40 percent of the seventeen-year-olds are in school, compared with 92 percent in the United States. One of five teenagers is unemployed.

Australia was originally populated only by Aborigines, an estimated 300,000 of them. But with the coming of the whites, most of the Aborigines were killed off. Now there are about 60,000 left. About 30,000 live on reservations. Another 30,000 are mixed into the general population. We were told today that $2 billion has been paid in welfare for Aborigines in recent years.

It wasn't until 1973 that Australia was open to immigrants who were not white. Seventy-five years before that, the all-white policy governed all immigration. Today, one of every three immigrants is Asian, much like the current pattern in the United States. There is a very strong Irish influence in Australia, especially in the Catholic Church. Of the 162,000 convicts who were transplanted to Australia, 45,000 were Irish, mostly political prisoners. Today, of the 16 million-plus Australians, 2.5 million are Irish. Enough for statistics, but this is a very unusual country, little understood by most of the world.

Tonight I read the last two of eight tracts that Karl Rahner, the famous Catholic theologian, wrote on the Sacraments and the Vows. Good theological insights. So came the end of Sunday in the Great Australian Bight.

MONDAY, FEBRUARY 22
En Route to Fremantle

We're so far away it's hard to believe that this is Washington's birthday. It's been a fairly quiet day with exercise, walking the decks, and reading Gorbachev's *Perestroika*. At four this afternoon, we had a meeting of the bishop, the rabbi, Ned, and me regarding our chaplaincy work aboard the ship. We laid a few long-range plans and generally agreed that things were going much better than they were at the beginning.

TUESDAY, FEBRUARY 23
Fremantle-Perth, Australia

We arrived in Fremantle Harbor right on the nose at 8 A.M. Most people, if they've heard of Fremantle at all, remember it as the place where the America's Cup race was held in 1987. On that occasion, the United States won the cup back from the Australians, who had taken it away from us in Newport in 1983. It's a great little port town with a population of only 25,000 people. The much larger city of Perth is eleven miles up the Swan River from Fremantle.

Perth, the capital of the state of Western Australia, is about the size of Adelaide, nearly 1 million people. That's two-thirds of the people who live in the state. It's a bright, fresh-looking city, expanding faster than any other Australian city. But it is terribly isolated, being closer to Singapore than to Sydney. Even Adelaide, our last port of call, is almost 2,000 miles from here. Perth is spread out along both banks of the Swan River. This city has spawned many of the great entrepreneurs in Australia. This state is four times the size of Texas, and it contains vast amounts of iron ore, coal, oil, gold, silver, and many other minerals. It also has some of the best vineyards in Australia. One of them belongs to Denis and Tricia Horgan, who gave us a tour of the area.

Denis and Tricia first drove us all over Fremantle showing us properties that Denis had recently acquired with the thought of building a Catholic university here. Also, we took a quick look at Perth and the University of Western Australia, which is very attractive. We then went to Denis and Tricia's house, which is located on a hill overlooking the Swan River, about halfway between Perth and Fremantle. There we were joined by Peter Tannock, a classmate of Denis's, who has his Ph.D. in education from Johns Hopkins and is director of Catholic education for this state. He's working with Denis on the Catholic university project.

When we had finished our coffee, we went down to the heliport and boarded Denis's helicopter for a trip about 125 miles south along the coast. There are miles and miles of clear sand beaches. As we rounded Cape Leeuwin, the most southwesterly point of the continent of Australia, we came along rocky beaches with enormous surf pounding in from the south and surfers being thrown end over end 100 feet below us.

Our next stop was the Margaret River, which is the center of the wine district. There we flew farther inland, landing at Denis's Leeuwin Estate, which comprises about 2,000 acres. We had a splendid gourmet lunch there, accompanied by three or four excellent local wines. Denis owns 200 acres of grapes and produces about 25,000 cases of wine a year. Though relatively new in the business, he told us his wines were beginning to win some awards. The winery was originally a joint venture with Mondavi of California.

All the way down and all the way back and while there, our nonstop conversation went on concerning the feasibility of building a Catholic university in Western Australia. I think we came to the cautious conclusion that it was a good thing to do. I suggested that they give the university a Catholic name so that it would be unmistakably Catholic and totally committed to remaining Catholic. (They eventually decided to name it Notre Dame Australia, with our law dean, David Link, as its first two-year vice chancellor.) I also suggested that it be conceived as a Pacific Rim university which would take a third of its students from Western Australia, another third from the rest of Australia, and a third from the other Pacific Rim countries. That would give it plenty of potential students to draw from. Two-thirds of the world's population currently lives in Pacific Rim countries. Most authorities agree that it will be the great trade center of the future.

We returned to the Horgan home for dinner. Among the other guests were the Archbishop of Perth; Bill Foley, the head of St. John of God Hospital; and Sister Columba Howard, a very distinguished doctor here. Denis served some of his best wines, which went well with the pink snapper.

When we returned to the ship, we discovered that fuel handlers all over Australia had gone on strike. As a result, though we were scheduled to leave at 11 P.M., we couldn't. The worst part was being berthed next to a large Saudi Arabian ship. There were 100,000 sheep on board and we were downwind of them. If you've ever lived in a stockyards town, you can imagine what it was like.

WEDNESDAY, FEBRUARY 24
Fremantle, Australia

Instead of waking up a couple of hundred miles out to sea, as scheduled, we woke up again in Fremantle. The captain spent most of the morning negotiating with the strikers. Normally, the loss of a few hours on a cruise of this duration would not have been of great concern, but with the QE2 in port, it was. The ship was paying a docking fee of $10,000 per hour, so by the time the strike was settled and we got underway, it had cost the Cunard Line $120,000. That made it a very expensive twelve hours. But at last we were on our way to Mauritius, 3,600 miles away off the coast of Africa. We were leaving with many pleasant memories of Australia. The sheep, however, were not among them.

I read more Gorbachev this morning and continue to be surprised at the openness of his language and the way he invokes a Christian vocabulary with words like "human rights," "social justice," "the dignity of man," "high character," "spiritual development," and so forth. They are words you don't expect to hear from a Communist.

THURSDAY, FEBRUARY 25
En Route to Mauritius

A beautiful day today with a small following wind in a calm sea. We have the engines cranked up to about 28 knots, so we're making up for the time we lost in Fremantle. The navigator says we'll arrive in Mauritius on time. The temperature is about 67 degrees and will rise to the middle 70s during the day. We're just a few miles north of a trench in the Indian Ocean where the depth is 22,000 feet.

I'm getting in the habit of doing about one and a half miles around the deck each morning after breakfast when there isn't too much traffic up there and before the day gets too warm. Ned generally does a couple of miles in the afternoon. It's enough to raise a sweat, and they tell us that exercise is no good if that doesn't happen. The heart has to do a bit of pumping.

We heard a fine lecture by Waldemar Hansen, our on-board cultural lecturer, on the history, geography, anthropology, politics, and culture of Africa. A large subject, but he compressed it well. After lunch, I donned shorts and went up on the absolutely top deck to get some sunshine and finish the Gorbachev book, which I did. In my opinion, it should be required reading for anyone who has any dealings with the Russians today. I suspect that several people had a hand in its writing, such as Georgi Arbatov, but it's fairly obvious that the best parts of the book come from Gorbachev himself because the message is the same one he's been espousing ever since he was elected General Secretary almost three years ago. I have a hunch he will either be deposed or change the face of Russia in our time—perhaps both. (This was prophetic, because it happened. I've had the opportunity to meet and converse with Gorbachev three times since reading *Perestroika*. I continue to admire him and his present program of action.)

After Gorbachev, I read a hundred pages or so of *The Peacock Throne* by Hansen. It's a great history of the Mogul Empire in India just before and after the time that the Taj Mahal was built. Ned has been trying to organize a trip to the Taj Mahal, because the regular tours are sold out. I encouraged him to do it on his own by plane and then go to Dhaka to see our Holy Cross operation there.

I had an interesting pastoral experience shortly after the afternoon Mass. A gentleman in the sick bay had asked for a priest. I went down, spent some time with him, and, at his request, heard his confession. When we were finished, he said as I was going out the door of his room, "By the way, I'm not a Catholic." I answered, "You may not be a Catholic, but you've just had all your sins forgiven."

FRIDAY, FEBRUARY 26
En Route to Mauritius

We did a bit of rolling during the night, but not too bad. All you have to do is think rock-a-bye-baby and go to sleep. The day dawned hazy with a sharp wind from the southwest that is kicking up the waters. Between here and the Antarctic there's nothing to slow them down. It's really a vast and almost empty ocean.

It was a quiet afternoon with another hundred pages or so of winding my way through the Mogul Empire in India. The war of succession there was really something, with three brothers battling each other to the death for the job of emperor. The whole dynasty there began in the fifteenth century with Babur, who was a descendant of Genghis Khan and Tamerlane. The story really begins with Shah Jahan (Khurram), who ruled from 1628 to 1658. He wanted his favorite and eldest son, Dara Shikoh, to take over from him, but the three younger brothers, Shuja, Aurangzeb, and Murad, took a dim view of this. Aurangzeb won out by either imprisoning or killing off the other brothers. He ruled from 1658 to 1707. There was a lot of battling going on in Europe at this time, but nothing more fierce or more full of intrigue than life in the Mogul court, where the Muslims and Hindus added a religious dimension to the squabbles. This division continues to resonate into our own time with Pakistan and Bangladesh for the Muslims and India for the Hindus. The drama has not yet totally unfolded.

Ned administered Extreme Unction, or the Sacrament of the Sick, to a Catholic woman whose doctor has told her she is terminally ill. She seemed greatly consoled by the ceremony, which we had right after the evening Mass with her son also present. The new ritual is much more meaningful and beautiful than the old one, another of the many blessings of Vatican Council II.

This evening we had a cocktail party in the Yacht Club for the four Notre Dame couples aboard, the Bob Bauchmans, the Bordas, the Dirksons, and Bart and Shirley Ramsour. It turned out that Bart and Bob Bauchman had been classmates and even played in the band together at Notre Dame. We also asked Ernie Secoy and Faye Beauchamp to join us, since they are from Indianapolis and are near neighbors. They are practically alumnae now. Also good bridge players and daily Mass attenders, although neither is Catholic.

SATURDAY, FEBRUARY 27
En Route to Mauritius

We covered about 650 miles yesterday and have now traveled close to 2,000 miles since leaving Perth. That's better than halfway to Mauritius, where we'll arrive on time. The captain has been pushing the ship along at about 29 knots an hour, which is about the limit of its speed without using another 50 percent more fuel to get it up to 33 or 34 knots.

Ned and I put on a cocktail party this noon for all of the chaplains, the rabbi, the bishop, Father D'Arcy, the captain of the ship, and all of his top staff so that the religious personnel would have a chance to mingle freely and talk a little policy with the other staff officers. It worked out very well. We try to keep good relationships with the captain and his top people because they're our bosses and we need to go through them whenever we want to do anything beyond our usual duties.

SUNDAY, FEBRUARY 28
En Route to Mauritius

This was a quiet and sunny day of reading on deck and walking the deck for some miles. I read *Life in the Afternoon: Good Ways of Growing Older*, by Ed Fischer, former professor of journalism at Notre Dame and a classmate of Ned's. Fischer retired from teaching about five years ago at age sixty so that he could write some books. He's written at least six or seven since then, half of which I've read, and with great enjoyment, I might add. He started writing this one after his seventy-first birthday. It offers a lot of sound advice on how to grow older gracefully.

I also read about half of Genesis in French today. It's the only Old Testament version I have. I am preaching on Abraham tonight and his total following of the will of God and what that meant for him and all of us who are his descendants—that is, those who believe in one God: Jews, Christians, and Muslims. Given the squabbles we've had through the centuries, it's often difficult to believe that we share such an important common heritage. I also began reading James Clavell's *Whirlwind*, the fourth book of his that I've tackled. I'm not sure I'll finish this one, though; it's more than 1,300 pages long.

Ned turned in early and I read for a while after that. He's getting very good at sleeping with the lights on.

MONDAY, FEBRUARY 29
En Route to Mauritius

I looked out the porthole at about 7 A.M. and there was Mauritius with its tall peaks soaring upward. It was a welcome sight after 3,600 miles at sea. Mauritius is the main island of the Mascarene archipelago, 3,650 miles west of Perth, 1,120 miles southeast of Mombasa, and 500 miles due east of Madagascar, the large island off the east coast of Africa. Mauritius is home to Indians, Creoles, Muslims, Chinese, and Europeans—about 1,100,000 of them in all.

Mauritius was practically unknown before the late sixteenth century, except to some Arab sailors and Portuguese explorers. The Dutch were the first settlers here (1598–1710). They let it go to the pirates. Later the French East India Company took over and called it Ile de France. In 1810, Great Britain seized Ile de France by sailing into the harbor with two British warships flying the French flag. When they got broadside of the two French warships in the harbor, they opened up their gun ports. Then they ran up the British flag and took down the French. It was the end of the French on Mauritius, although their language and culture still dominate. Finally, in 1968, Mauritius became independent.

I was here once before about ten years ago. I had just spent twelve difficult days in South Africa with an American educational group meeting university educators there to discuss apartheid. I came to Mauritius to dictate my report, and did most of it under a tree on the beach. My secretary, Helen, said it was the best dictation she had ever transcribed, because, unnoticed by me, the birds were chirping loudly during the several hours of dictation. For this and many other reasons, it's really a beautiful island.

Ned took the full tour. I decided just to mosey around Port Louis, the capital. On the trip in to shore on the tender I ran into Father D'Arcy. We hailed a cab and went into town together to the cathedral, where we visited with Archbishop Jean Margeot. I had met the archbishop during my earlier trip. He is the first native Mauritian to be bishop here. The place was first evangelized by the Benedictines from 1819 on and then by the Holy Spirit Fathers from 1916 on. The latter came mostly from France, Ireland, and the U.K. (Archbishop Margeot has since been named a cardinal.)

It was hotter than you know what in town, but we went to an air-conditioned Chinese restaurant and had a great duck dinner with beer. After that, the archbishop's chauffeur took us on a little tour, which included the botanical gardens and a brief stop to visit the Sisters of the Good Shepherd.

TUESDAY, MARCH 1
En Route to Mombasa

We're now at 16 degrees south of the equator. As the day went on, the temperature rose to about 100. Ned went to lectures on Kenya and I spent most of the day reading Clavell's *Whirlwind* (about Iran) and *Our Common Future*, which is the report of the World Commission on Environment and Development. We invited Ernie and Faye of Indianapolis to join us for dinner and played three rubbers of bridge with them afterward.

WEDNESDAY, MARCH 2
En Route to Mombasa

We rounded the northern tip of Madagascar this morning. By 8 A.M. we'll be in Mombasa, Kenya. I had a telex last night from Father Tom McDermott, one of our Holy Cross priests in Nairobi, who says he will meet us at the ship. Our Coca-Cola contact there telexed a similar message. So while Ned goes off to see the animals in Tsavo Park overnight, I'll have plenty of company in Mombasa.

J. W. Canty III, an Episcopal priest on board, was feted tonight for being one of 2,000 or so nominees for the Nobel Peace Prize. Not many people came to the party, but I thought I should, and did. After the evening Mass we had a final get-together with the Bauchmans for some wine before dinner. Three of our four Notre Dame couples leave the ship tomorrow.

THURSDAY, MARCH 3
Mombasa, Kenya

We arrived in Mombasa at 8 A.M., right on schedule as always. The Arabs and the Portuguese used to expel each other from this port with great regularity. Finally, the British intervened and took over Kenya, which became a Crown Colony in 1920 and an independent country in 1963, though still remaining a member of the British Commonwealth. The national patriot was Jomo Kenyatta, who spent a good deal of time imprisoned by the British. But he became President of the country and remained so until his death in 1978.

Mombasa is the largest port along the east coast of Africa. The country of Kenya is about as big as France, with a population of 22.5 million people. About half a million of them live in Mombasa. The main language of the country is Swahili, but almost everybody speaks English as well.

I'm sure a lot of people aboard are going to be disenchanted with Africa when they make their two-day trips inland. When I first came to Kenya in 1958, there were animals everywhere. Then came independence and the natives acquired automatic rifles. They quickly killed off about 90 percent of the wildlife. Can they now preserve enough of the wildlife to still attract people to Africa? That's an open question, and the jury is still out on the ultimate answer.

Regarding religion in this part of the world, it is judged to be 27 percent Protestant, 26 percent Roman Catholic, 6 percent Muslim, and 19 percent animist, the original African religion. Our Community, Holy Cross, has missions in Nairobi and also in the diocese of Fort Portal in Uganda. It's a difficult mission, but so far we seem to be holding our own.

We were met by Father Tom McDermott and two other Notre Dame graduates, John Kraft and Sanjeev Tak. We had a great reunion and then met Jon Belcher, who runs things for Coca-Cola in five East African countries. With him were the local bottler and his wife. We split up into two cars and set out on a driving tour. Our first stop was Fort Jesus. It was built by the Portuguese in 1593, then taken over by the Arabs in 1698, and eventually by the British in 1895. From the fort we went down through the old city, which looks centuries old. Then we headed for the countryside and the Tamarind Restaurant, which was right on the beach. After walking along the beach for a while we went into the Tamarind and had a marvelous fish, shrimp, and crab dinner.

About 3 P.M., I parted from our Coca-Cola friends to get a haircut. It cost $2.50, as against almost $20 on the ship. I found myself speaking Italian to the Hindu barber, who told me he learned the language from a friend at night after work. He spoke it very well. I then brought our Notre Dame group back to the ship for a tour and Mass. After that, we got back into one of the cars and drove up the coast for about 100 kilometers to a sports hotel. We had a great lamb dinner and made arrangements for a boat trip to the reef in the morning.

FRIDAY, MARCH 4
Mombasa, Kenya

We were up about six this morning, just in time to behold a beautiful sunrise across the sea. Then we boarded boats for a trip out to the reef and some scuba diving. The reef was beautiful and teeming with equally beautiful tropical fish. The hotel where we stayed, the Ocean Sport, is the center of blue and black marlin fishing here. They had two stuffed marlins in the bar that ran over 750 pounds apiece. Various kinds of sharks and tunas are also caught just outside the reef. The cost of the whole trip for the four of us—meals, hotel, and diving—came to $150, so bargains are still available in Mombasa.

SATURDAY, MARCH 5
En Route to the Seychelles

We have just over 1,000 miles to go between Mombasa and the Seychelles, where we will arrive Sunday morning. We're moving almost due east in the face of a northeast wind of about 20 miles an hour. That, together with the speed of the ship, produces more than a 40-mile-an-hour wind across the deck. As a result, my usual two-mile walk became a fairly strenuous exercise.

After lunch, we played bridge with Ernie and Faye. As soon as the game was over, I taped an interview with the ship's TV director, Liam O'Murchu, which is Irish for Bill Murphy. He asked me a lot of questions about world affairs as several hundred people looked on. The interview will be shown next week on the ship's TV.

SUNDAY, MARCH 6
Seychelles

We arrived in the Seychelles about 8 A.M., anchored about five miles out, and took a launch into Victoria, the capital. The islands are approximately midway between East Africa and Bombay, India. It's about 1,000 miles either way. The Seychelles are an archipelago of about a hundred small islands. The main one is Mahé, which is seventeen miles long and three and a half to five miles wide. There are about 100,000 people here, a quarter of whom live in Victoria. The main languages are English and French, but French seems to predominate. Ninety percent of the people are Catholic, 8 percent Anglican.

The French first settled the islands in 1756 and started plantations of cinnamon, cloves, nutmeg, and pepper. In 1794, the British Royal Navy forced the French to surrender. The Seychelles were ceded to Britain in 1814 by the Treaty of Paris. In 1903, they became a British Crown Colony, and, in 1976, an independent country.

After a quick tour of Victoria, we boarded a small De Havilland Otter STOL (short takeoff and landing) for a fifteen-minute flight to Praslin Island. It's second to Mahé in size, and the only other island with any inhabitants to speak of. The people spoke French or Creole when conversing among themselves, English when they spoke to us.

We traveled by minibus to a nature preserve. There we saw two things this island is famous for. The first was a tree called the coco-de-mer (the sea coconut), which grows only on this island and another one adjacent to it. It is also the largest coconut tree in the world which comes in male and female form. The male tree grows to a height of about 130 feet, and both trees can live as long as 1,000 years. The other thing this island is famous for is the black parrot, which builds its nest in the coco-de-mer palms. There's also a spice tree here that has four different spices in its bark and on its leaves—namely, vanilla, pepper, cinnamon, and clove. Perhaps this is why these islands are sometimes called the Spice Islands.

I couldn't help wondering what it would be like to live on this island, only seven miles long and three miles wide. The palms, the parrots, the glistening white sand beaches, and the blue-green lagoon would be nice, but unless you were a contemplative given to continual prayer, or an intellectual with a first-rate library, life would probably get boring after a while.

MONDAY, MARCH 7
Seychelles

While doing forty minutes around the deck this morning in 80-plus heat, I ran into George and Eleanor McGovern. George, of course, is the former senator from South Dakota who ran on the Democratic ticket for President in 1972. Both he and Eleanor are nice, interesting people. I told them I'd be at George's lecture this afternoon.

The first lecture today was by Hansen on India. He did a wonderful job of compressing about 4,500 years of history into an hour. His lecture tomorrow is on the subject he wrote about in *The Peacock Throne*, which I read. That lets me out of class tomorrow. George lectured on American foreign policy, doing very well both in his talk and during the question-and-answer period following. This is a largely Republican group, as one might imagine given their age and wealth. But George told it as he saw it, and I think most of them admired him for that. After Mass, Ned and I had cocktails with Eleanor and George.

TUESDAY, MARCH 8
En Route to Bombay

This morning I ran into a man from Richmond, Indiana, whom I hadn't seen in about a month. That gives you some idea how big this ship is. As we stood there chatting on the deck, he lighted a very good cigar and offered me one. I told him I had sworn off them for Lent. He said, "Well, O.K., take one for Easter." I agreed, and calculated that I'd be able to smoke it by the time we reached Osaka, Japan.

Later this morning I spent an hour in the library. I must have looked at several hundred books before finding a wonderful account of the Amundsen expeditions in the Arctic and Antarctic, together with some original photographs. I also found a book called *The Great Journey*, by Brian Fagan. It's on the anthropology of ancient America.

We were invited to a noon-hour cocktail party by Terry and Bobby Conroy in the general manager's dayroom. The purpose was for us to meet Al Van Ness, the executive vice president of Trafalgar House, which owns the Cunard Lines. He arrived with his wife, Nancy. They turned out to be a delightful couple. In the afternoon I attended another session by George McGovern. This one was all question-and-answer, principally about the upcoming presidential election. As before, George gave a very good account of himself. Later he came to Mass, though, like quite a few others who attend, he is not Catholic. After Mass, Ned and I had a nice visit with George and Eleanor over cocktails and dinner.

In the surprise department, I ran into Trudy Rumely, a woman I had known when I was chaplain of Vetville, Notre Dame's post-World War II village for married veterans. She was living there with her husband, Lee, now deceased. Though forty years had passed since we had last talked with one another, we resumed the conversation as if it had been yesterday.

WEDNESDAY, MARCH 9
En Route to Bombay

Ned has a lot of bureaucratic red tape to cut through this morning. He finally got the Indian government to promise him a visa. They had turned him down in Mombasa, claiming that he was a missionary, and therefore would need special permission to enter India. That's a large joke when one thinks of the 4,000-plus Indians we've educated to doctoral degrees at Notre Dame, free of charge.

The Indians want all kinds of documents regarding cameras or binoculars or anything else brought ashore. This has got to be the most red-tape-bound government in existence. The bureaucracy, of course, has its roots in the days of empire when the British kidded the Indians into thinking they were still running the country by having them shuffle papers by the hundreds of thousands. That, in fact, is how the use of the words "red tape" originated. They would take all these papers and wrap them in bundles. Then they'd secure the bundles with yards of red tape. Finally, they would stack the red-taped bundles of papers against the walls of the offices, where they remained, unread. Ever since then, the words "red tape" have stood for the slow, senseless, and infuriating paperwork that bureaucrats love—and everyone else hates. The British are long gone, but red tape remains a staple of the Indian government and, to be fair, many others.

Waldemar Hansen lectured on Bombay today. With 8.5 million people it's the second-largest city in India after Calcutta, which has over 9 million inhabitants. Eighty-three percent of the Indian people here are Hindu, 11 percent Muslim, and only 3 percent Christian. While Hindi and English are the two official languages, there are fourteen other main languages spoken and recognized by the Constitution, and there are at least 300 dialects in use.

Bombay, known as the Gateway to India, was the headquarters for the East India Company. It is located on the Arabian Sea and is made up of seven islands linked by causeways and bridges. Its location undoubtedly has much to do with the fact that it contains a good cross section of all the Indian ethnic groups, religions, and languages.

We played bridge this afternoon and I continued my run of absolutely atrocious cards. My partner for today, Faye, did likewise, so Ned and Ernie murdered us by a couple of thousand points. I should add in fairness that they played well too, and that I would never make a living as a bridge player. Ned will be off in the morning for ten days to Agra and the Taj Mahal, Delhi, Katmandu, Nepal, and Dhaka and Bangladesh. We'll join forces again in Bangkok on March 20.

THURSDAY, MARCH 10
Bombay, India

Having had three Indian immigration officials aboard since Mombasa, we thought things would go smoothly upon landing in Bombay. But we had seriously underestimated the Indian bureaucracy. Just as everybody was lined up and ready to go ashore on the tenders, it was announced that we all had to get temporary landing cards, even though we would only be touring around the city of Bombay. That meant landing cards had to be made out for about 1,000 people and stamped by the appropriate officials, of whom we now had about thirty on board. It was 10:30 A.M. before they were finished, and by that time we were two and a half hours late for our tours. So even before we could begin our introduction to India, the score was red tape 1, visitors 0.

The tour I was on began with the Prince of Wales Museum, where they have some wonderful Mogul miniatures in color. They look like the illustrations you see in medieval books. We continued with such well-known landmarks as the Hanging Gardens and the Silent Hills, where the Parsi laid out the bodies of their dead to be eaten by the vultures so they wouldn't pollute the four elements of earth, sky, water, and air.

We also visited the house where Gandhi lived on and off between 1917 and 1924. The house contained some wonderful pictures of the high points of Gandhi's life, as well as his floor-level bed, writing table, and spinning wheel.

Every Indian city I've ever visited leaves me with one overwhelming impression: how crowded with people the streets are. Bombay is no exception. Its population density is four times that of New York City. The population of the country is over 800 million, and will probably be a billion by the time anyone gets around to reading this.

When the bus stopped at the Taj Mahal Hotel, I abandoned the tour and decided to have lunch. I ordered shrimp tempura, which tasted exactly the same as it would have in Japan. I also bought the new *Time* magazine and a couple of bars of soap. Soap is provided on the *QE2*, of course, but it comes in small bars and I like something larger in the shower.

I had a somewhat diminished group at Mass tonight, since about a third of our congregation is over in Agra to see the Taj. Ned obtained his visa at 10:30 this morning and had his tickets in hand about an hour or two later. I hope he made the plane to Agra. He's not here, in any event, so I'm on my own, at least as far as the chapel services are concerned, for the next ten days.

I've been thinking all day today about my old friend Dr. Homi Bhabha, who was head of the Indian Atomic Energy Commission. I saw him frequently during the fifteen years I was the Vatican's representative to the International Atomic Energy Agency. The annual meetings of the agency were always held in Vienna. Homi was on his way to one of them when the Air-India plane he was riding in crashed into Mount Blanc. Everyone aboard was killed. The last time I was in Bombay, I had dinner with Homi, who was not only a brilliant scientist but a great artist. He gave me some of his original pencil sketches. They now reside in the Notre Dame library.

This evening I preached on faithfulness, a good theme for a very faithful congregation. It was cool and fresh after Mass—rather unusual, because we're only about 19 degrees north of the equator. But it's a nice change from the intense heat we've had over the past couple of weeks.

FRIDAY, MARCH 11
Bombay, India

This morning our tour group boarded buses for the twenty-five-mile ride north to the Caves of Kanheri. Buddhist monks carved 109 caves here. They picked this site because it was on the north-south trade route and close enough to the city so they could beg for their food there. Buddha, a Hindu, founded his new religion 600 years before the time of Christ. In India it petered out around 1100 A.D., to be replaced by Islam and the Hindu religion, but it is still strong in places like Thailand, Indonesia, China, and Japan. Today, Hinduism claims the most adherents in India, while Islam flourishes in Pakistan and Bangladesh.

These caves were begun in the fourth century B.C. and continued until about the fifth century A.D. One would guess that in the heyday of the caves, well over 100 monks could have lived here.

Back on the ship, I walked my usual two miles and prepared a sermon on charity. Ed and Helen Halluska, our bridge instructors aboard, joined me for cocktails after Mass. Ned and I are off scotch for Lent, so cocktails are reduced to white wine. By seven, despite another delay visited upon us by the Indian bureaucracy, we finally got underway and headed for Penang, Malaysia, 2,133 nautical miles away.

There were a lot of new people in our dining room tonight. On my right were two couples from Bombay who spoke in Gujarati during the meal. It was a new language for me and I took the opportunity to learn a word or two of it. Right across from our table was a black couple from Chicago. He's a musician and will be entertaining the passengers between here and Singapore.

The ship's daily bulletin has been exciting interest in the upcoming solar eclipse. We will be in a perfect place to see it. The guest scientists tell me I have to take some part, but what part hasn't been figured out yet. I'm no astronomer. Maybe they'll want me to pray for clear weather.

SATURDAY, MARCH 12
En Route to Penang

After breakfast, I did my two miles in the company of Ralph Gilbert, a typical world traveler, of whom there are many aboard this ship. Ralph is retired, so for a fourth of the year he travels with Linblad (whom he calls a great explorer and poor businessman) on the *Society Explorer*, plus the Cunard Line and the *Rotterdam*. Like me, he has almost run out of new places to see. While he has been on the fringes of the Antarctic, he has not yet been to the South Pole, so I'm one up on him in that department. However, he has a few places on me too, such as Tibet.

Today begins a round of special events in connection with the eclipse, even though it won't take place until after we leave Singapore next week. We have five scientists aboard: Dr. Edward Brooks, a leading eclipse meteorologist; Owen Gingerich, who is an astrophysicist at the Smithsonian Astrophysical Laboratory and a teacher at Harvard; Donald Goldsmith, a professor at the University of California; Stephen Maran, Senior Staff Scientist at the NASA Goddard Space Center; and Kenneth Bercher, professor of astronomy at Boston University. Ken acts as the coordinator of this group. He has also asked me to join the group for some of their seminars dealing with the meaning of man and the universe and the possibilities of extraterrestrial intelligence. What one does as chaplain! Ken introduced everyone today with cleverly drawn caricatures of each of them, including me.

SUNDAY, MARCH 13
En Route to Penang

We had two good lectures today on the eclipse. First, Don Goldsmith talked about the search for life in the universe. He said that there may be a million forms of life out there, but that the distances are so vast, even within our own galaxy, that we're not likely to make contact with other life forms, nor they with us. Next, Stephen Maran talked about the sun, the planets, and what's involved in exploring the solar system. The scientists are also conducting star watches out on deck each evening.

Tonight I preached on the *unum necessarium*, the one necessary element of life—namely, to achieve salvation. I came down a little heavier than usual because when you're on a ship like this one you can easily get caught up in a million silly little things that have nothing to do with this ultimate necessity. Curiously enough, one gets very little reaction from sermons, even though Ned and I have preached every other day since leaving New York. The few reactions we have had are very good, but most people don't react at all. We're not used to that, because Notre Dame students always let you know what they think of your homilies, good or bad.

I just counted the collection for Sunday—$296. That's a bit less than usual. There was only one twenty-dollar bill in the collection; normally we get three or four of them, plus an occasional hundred-dollar bill. Tonight the collection was mainly characterized by ones and fives, with a few tens. Maybe I was too tough in the sermon and they were voting with their donations. No matter, my task is telling them the truth, not what will produce the biggest collections.

MONDAY, MARCH 14
En Route to Penang

We are now coasting along at 5 degrees north above the equator in an easterly direction. We just passed 90 degrees longitude, which puts us halfway between Greenwich, England, and the international date line in the Pacific. We'll be coming up on the northern tip of Sumatra this evening and then head south toward Penang, which is 511 miles north of Singapore on the western coast of Malaysia.

One of the ship's scientists, Ken Bercher, gave a talk today entitled "Do Black Holes Really Exist?" He doubts that they do, although plenty of other good scientists, including Stephen Hawking of Cambridge, hold the opposite view.

During lunch, the Sicilian wife of George Kirby, the well-known comedian, came up and handed me a generous donation. I told her I would offer a Mass for her and George today. They're very nice people, and George is a great comedian. After lunch, I decided that it was time for some sunshine, so I went to the top deck and read the book I had checked out of the library on aboriginal life in America. Later there is a lecture by Professor Owen Gingerich of Harvard entitled "The Mysterious Nebulae and the Southern Sky." I'm going to hear this one from the balcony so that I can beat a retreat without being seen if it turns out to be too nebulous. I didn't really expect so much education in astronomy on this trip. Fortunately, the scientists are all first-rate, as well as extremely friendly.

Tonight I was invited to dinner in the Queen's Grill and had a wonderful time conversing in English and Spanish with the mixed group at the table. The social life keeps picking up and it's even more demanding now because Ned's not here to share the invitations.

TUESDAY, MARCH 15
Penang, Malaysia

We came into sight of Penang about 10 A.M., as I was pounding the decks on my two-mile walk. Malaysia is about the size of New Mexico, although it's stretched out long and thin, almost like a cobra with a hooded head. There are 16 million people in Malaysia, 1 million of whom live in Kuala Lumpur. Penang has approximately 300,000. Fifty percent of the country's inhabitants are Malay, 36 percent Chinese (they really run things), and 10 percent Indian. They have their own language, called Malay, but many speak English, Chinese, and some Indian languages.

Coming into Penang was a bit of a surprise. One would expect thatched tropical huts clinging to the side of the hill. Instead, twenty or thirty high rises lined the shore, obviously vacation villas. In the middle of George Town, the city here, was a building at least forty to fifty stories high. We visited a Chinese temple and a reclining Buddha temple, then drove along the north beach, where all the resort hotels are. It's hard to believe they will fill all of them, but then the Japanese and the Australians do come here in large numbers on vacation.

WEDNESDAY, MARCH 16
Kuala Lumpur, Malaysia

Kuala Lumpur means "muddy river mouth." It lies at the junction of two rivers. When the British granted independence to the Federation of Malaysia, Kuala Lumpur became the capital. It is now a metropolis of 1 million people, replete with modern architecture, though the distinctive Muslim domes and minarets remain.

Our first stop was the palace of the Sultan of Selangor. There are nine sultans in the country, one for each of the nine states. They take turns serving as king, each sultan serving a five-year term when it's his turn.

Another stop was at the Blue Mosque, which had just been dedicated on March 11. It's probably one of the most beautiful mosques in the world, with a 400-foot-high dome. We were told it cost $160 million to build. We then went to the National Museum, where we saw excellent exhibits on anthropology, geology, and history.

After lunch at the Regent Hotel, we visited a batik factory, where I bought a couple of great tropical shirts, somewhat wild in pattern and color but perfect for the kind of weather one experiences in the tropics. The one I bought many years ago in Indonesia simply wore out at the beginning of this trip, or perhaps it was the Notre

Dame laundry that did it in. We then visited another Hindu shrine, a large natural cave 700 feet high in the side of the limestone cliffs outside of town. Only four of the thirty-six of us made the climb. Lastly, we visited the Selangor pewter works, which has been in business since 1885 and is reputed to be the best pewter company in the world. Pewter is mainly tin with some copper and arsenium alloy. I bought a small cup here that I can use as a chalice in my traveling Mass kit.

THURSDAY, MARCH 17 (ST. PATRICK'S DAY)
Singapore

Singapore is the world's busiest harbor. Over 30,000 ships call here each year, with one leaving every ten minutes. Singapore was literally nothing until the visionary Sir Stamford Raffles arrived here in 1819 and got the ruling sultan to allow the British East India Company to establish a trading post at the mouth of the Singapore River. A few years later, the British had control of the whole island.

Singapore enjoys the second-highest standard of living in the Orient after Japan. Of the total population of 2.5 million, 77 percent are Chinese, 16 percent Malay, and 5 percent Indian. About 1 percent are Eurasians. The main languages here are Malay, Mandarin Chinese, and Tamil (spoken in southern India and parts of Sri Lanka).

Our tour today began with a ride through downtown streets full of high rises and luxury hotels. Because of the scarcity of land, 85 percent of the population here lives in high-rise apartments. Over 60 percent of the population is under the age of twenty. The average family here has about two children. As one goes over the long causeway, one can look to the right (eastward) to the Pacific Ocean and the South China Sea. To the left (westward) is the Indian Ocean and the Strait of Malacca.

Our first stop was the old palace of the Sultan of Johore (presently king of Malaysia). It makes the White House look like an outhouse. We then visited the mosque, always a major landmark in any Muslim country. Here the Muslims make up about 55 percent of the total population. We visited a rubber plantation, where we saw the rubber flowing from the trees. Then we went to a rubber factory to see how they form the latex into big white blocks of rubber. From there we moved on to visit plantations where they grow cacao, coffee, bananas, and palms for palm oil.

After lunch at a Holiday Inn in Johore Bahru, we stopped at a memorial to those who were killed in World War II, then went back to the ship for Mass. I had Liam O'Murchu, alias Bill Murphy, give a homily in honor of St. Patrick. Bill is the only authentic Irishman on board, so I thought he should do the talking. I'm only half Irish, and Ned is in Katmandu. Anyway, Bill gave a great homily.

FRIDAY, MARCH 18
En Route to Pattaya, Thailand

At 7:30 this morning we stopped near the island of Serata to view the big event we'd been anticipating—the total eclipse of the sun. As the moon gradually interposed itself between the earth and the sun, the sun gradually took on the shape of an ever-narrowing sickle. Then came the total eclipse with bright flares coming out of the corona at the top and bottom of the sun. The total eclipse occurred at precisely 8:32, an hour after the partial eclipse began, and lasted three minutes. I think we were in the best place on earth to see it. Fortunately, the sky was very clear and, needless to say, all the astronomers on board were ecstatic. We were very lucky, because later on the sky clouded up.

This afternoon the three scientists and I held a seminar on science and religion. One said he was an atheist, another an agnostic, and the third, I think, was probably a theist, a vague believer in God. Anyway, I hope I held my own with the three of them regarding religion and science, faith, and a lot of other related and very important questions. I think it was important that we had this conversation after all these days of science and enlightenment. At least a number of the passengers seemed gratified that it took place, and that's enough for me. Regardless of our intellectual differences, all the scientists and I remain good friends.

SATURDAY, MARCH 19
En Route to Pattaya, Thailand

There were a lot of lectures scheduled for today—by the astronomers, by a psychiatrist, and by a few others besides. I've attended almost all of them in the past week, plus making the shore tours, so I decided to stay aboard and read today instead. After delving into some more of *The Great Journey*, by Brian Fagan, I came away convinced, as are most of the experts, that the earliest humans in the Americas were those who crossed the Bering Strait toward the end of the late Wisconsin ice age. That took place about 15,000 years ago, when the Bering Strait was dry land and North America and Russia were connected.

Father D'Arcy and I got together this afternoon to plan our Holy Week services. Over the years, I've done all of the services in my brother's parish of Corpus Christi in Pacific Palisades. This year we'll be doing them en route to Japan and in Osaka.

SUNDAY, MARCH 20
Pattaya, Thailand

We were in the harbor with the hook down before dawn. There was a large crowd at the eight o'clock Mass because almost everybody was off to shore to get the buses for a two-hour ride into Bangkok. I made the homily brief so they could get going as soon as possible. I went ashore later, waited around for a while, and was finally met by Len Harvey, a vice president with Coca-Cola. He'd come by earlier when I was still aboard. We gathered up his wife, Ann, who was down the beach, and drove to the Dusit Thani Hotel, where Coca-Cola had made reservations for Ned and me. I was hoping that Ned would have made it on his flight from Dhaka, Bangladesh. In fact, he had already checked in a few minutes ago and had Pao Sarasin with him, a Notre Dame MBA graduate. Pao is a member of a prominent Bangkok family, and they were feting us at the family compound, where they had invited seemingly every Notre Dame graduate in the city. We enjoyed a wonderful Thai meal and returned to the hotel tired but grateful for another cordial Notre Dame reunion.

MONDAY, MARCH 21
Bangkok, Thailand

Pao picked us up shortly after 7 A.M. to take us back to the family compound for breakfast. On the way, he provided us with a kind of Who's Who of his family, all of whom have both Thai names and catchy nicknames. His brother Por is studying at the Police Academy. His sister Pia is at Boston University working on an MBA. The children's father is Pow, head of the national police. Pow has three brothers—Pong, Thailand's Deputy Prime Minister and head of Coca-Cola bottling here; Pook, Thailand's ambassador to the United States; and Pake, a businessman. The patriarch of the family is Pote, a former Prime Minister, now eighty-three and retired.

There are now 53.5 million people in Thailand, of whom 75 percent are Thai, 14 percent Chinese, and 3 percent Malay. Bangkok has a population of about 5 million. The main languages here are Thai (Siamese), Chinese, and English. Ninety-five percent of the population is Buddhist and 4 percent Muslim, quite a contrast with neighboring Malaysia.

Pao and Pet, his wife, took us to the national Buddhist shrine, which is absolutely fantastic and indescribable as well. Then Pet went back to work at Thai International Airlines and Pao drove Ned and me to Pattaya, about a two-hour trip. It was my impression that about half the buildings we passed along the way displayed the elephant logo of the Siam Cement Company, Ltd., the company Pao has been working for since receiving his MBA degree from Notre Dame. In Pattaya, we had a superb Thai meal at the Royal Cliff Hotel, and then reboarded the ship.

TUESDAY, MARCH 22
En Route to Hong Kong

Bishop Harold Robinson came to the cabin to discuss an ecumenical service from 2 to 3 P.M. on Good Friday. It looks like I'm going to give a ten-minute sermon. He and the captain are going to do everything else.

By noon today, we were coasting by the southeasterly point of

Cambodia on our way to the Mekong Delta, where the great river enters the South China Sea. At this point, we will head east-northeast toward Hong Kong. We'll pass within about eighteen miles of Vietnam, but no closer because of the danger of running aground on the many shoals and rocks in this area. The names along the shore are familiar and sad—Saigon (now Ho Chi Minh City), Cam Ranh Bay, Haiphong, Hanoi.

Ned has been trying to talk me into going to see the movie *Cocoon* tonight. So far, I have resisted his blandishments. He said it was a gerontological comedy. I said, "At this point, that's just what I don't need." In the end, he went and I didn't.

WEDNESDAY, MARCH 23
En Route to Hong Kong

Hong Kong, our next port of call, continues to be a British Crown Colony until 1997, when it becomes part of the People's Republic of China. Currently, it is the greatest duty-free port in the world, so the Chinese will be well advised to leave it alone if they want the revenues to keep rolling in.

The total population of the area is 5.5 million people, mainly Chinese. The Cantonese dialect is spoken here, but almost everyone understands English. When I first visited Hong Kong, it was full of refugees. One of the main tasks of the American missionaries here, mainly Maryknoll, was to take care of them. The flow of refugees began during the 1937 invasion of China by Japan. Restrictions were introduced in 1974, but the flow continued even after that because of the Vietnam War.

I have a session after lunch with Father D'Arcy to get all of our ducks in a row for Holy Week. Then comes bridge for an hour with Ernie and Faye. Incidentally, Ernie has taken care of all of our excursions ashore, which come to about $3,000. We tried to put her off on this, but she was not to be denied. Ernie and Faye took Ned and me to the cleaners at the bridge table this time. I should have said earlier that they are both Indiana widows, and very competent bridge players.

THURSDAY, MARCH 24
Hong Kong

Hong Kong Harbor is as exciting and crowded as ever with sampans, junks, ferries, tramp steamers, and cruise ships. As soon as the gangway was attached, I went off on the dock where they have an enormous shopping arcade for duty-free merchandise. I had about five items I needed, and found them all quickly and at terrific prices. One was a replacement for a Sony radio I'd had stolen some time ago in Brazil. It was priced at $300 in New York. I found the same one here for $84. Five rolls of film cost $10 less than they would have in the duty-free shop aboard ship. I also bought a small alarm clock for $14, five new blank tapes for my Dictaphone, a copy of *Time*, and some of Ned's favorite brand of chocolate, his Easter present.

Back on board, I bumped into the tailor, Sam, who had measured us for some lightweight suits when he was aboard ship, crossing to Australia. Now we were to have our second fitting. By and large, it was almost perfect the first round. That also means, Thank God, that we haven't put on weight in the last month. Thank Lent for that.

Some friends of ours in Hong Kong, Australian Peter White and his wife, Sun Ling, took us to the American Consulate so we could phone the American ambassador in Beijing, Winston Lord. We want to arrange a visit there, if possible. From the consulate, we rushed over to the American Club, where we both gave short talks to about twenty or so Notre Dame alumni. In the evening, Ned went off to dinner with some of our Latin American friends, and I hosted a dinner ashore for Peter and Sun Ling, University of Michigan professor and Notre Dame alumnus Al Bailey and his wife, Mary, and Brian Callahan, who was student body president at Notre Dame in 1984. Ned had run into him on the street earlier in the day while out shopping for T-shirts.

FRIDAY, MARCH 25
Hong Kong

We got up before 7 A.M. to make the short trip to the island of Macao. In the early days of exploration, the Portuguese passed up Hong Kong for Macao. They settled here in 1557 when the island (in fact, a small peninsula) was ceded to them by China. Now, almost 450 years later, 85 percent of the population is Chinese, only 2 percent Portuguese. As with Hong Kong, the island will soon revert to Chinese control, but here it will take place in 1999, two years later.

Macao is only a little over two square miles, but it has a population of more than 500,000 people. It is attached by a very thin land spit to mainland China. Macao's chief income producer is gambling. Manufacturing is second and tourism is third.

On our tour, we visited three Buddhist temples. They were burning incense at all of them and by the time we reached number three our eyes were burning. The house of Sun Yat-sen, first President of China, was also on the tour. When he lived here he was practicing medicine. He died in Beijing in 1925 and is buried in Nanjing (Nanking).

Next we saw the façade of St. Paul's Church, a marvelous Jesuit cathedral, built in 1602, burned in 1835. Fortunately, they let stand the only thing left—namely, the façade—which contained the 195 statues of St. Ignatius and other Jesuit saints. There is also a sturdy fort here. From behind its thick walls the Portuguese repulsed the Dutch in 1662.

After lunch in a delightful cafe on a hill above the harbor, we went to one of the five gambling casinos. It was an incredible experience to see literally thousands of young Chinese crowded around every kind of gaming table from baccarat to twenty-one, not to mention a few thousand slot machines. The frenzied atmosphere was almost unreal. Many of the players seemed obsessed as they bet hundreds of dollars on a single turn of the dice or a card.

It was a fast hydrofoil ride back to Hong Kong and the ship. En route, I had a long talk with a Chinese girl who wanted to know what it meant to be a Christian. No sooner were we back aboard than we received a phone call that we were being ousted from our table in the

Princess Grill because they were oversold. This meant that for the time being we'd be eating our meals in the Columbia Restaurant, where the food is about ten cuts below that of the Princess Grill. They did say, however, that we'd be moved back into the Princess after things eased up in Yokohama or Honolulu. In any event, we've had two-thirds of the trip in this wonderful dining room and one couldn't ask for more, especially when one is not a paying customer.

Six hundred people left the ship at Hong Kong and another 600 boarded, mainly Chinese and Japanese. We're off tomorrow for another tour, this time to Lantao Island, where, wouldn't you know, we're going to visit another Buddhist monastery.

SATURDAY, MARCH 26
Hong Kong

We were up about seven this morning and off soon afterward to Lantao Island. Of all the 235 islands (over 200 uninhabited) in the Crown Colony, Lantao is the largest, about two and one-half times the size of Hong Kong. However, only 40,000 people live there. It took us a little over an hour to get there by motorized junk. We learned that there are still about 30,000 Vietnamese refugees on Lantao. They take English lessons and learn trades so they can go to the United States and earn a living. On the other side of the mountain, there is a Trappist monastery. Most of the monks are Americans and Europeans, and the only way you can get there is to take a junk from another island.

Next we went to Tai O, a 200-year-old fishing village at the western end of the island. The population is about 7,000. We spent an interesting hour walking down the narrow streets, lined on both sides by shops selling just about everything. The dominant smell, of course, was fish. From there, we drove 2,000 feet up a mountain to the Buddhist monastery of Po Li, which means "precious lotus." Though I wasn't particularly impressed with some of the other Buddhist temples and monasteries we had visited recently, I enjoyed this one. It was cleaner, more beautiful, and its mountain location made it more appealing. It will become even more impressive when the giant statue of Buddha is placed on a huge platform at the very top of the mountain. They're working on it now.

At noon the monks served us a tasty vegetarian lunch in their lovely courtyard. Afterward we toured the monastery, then reboarded the junk for the return trip to Hong Kong.

SUNDAY, MARCH 27
Xiamen Island, People's Republic of China

During the night we sailed from Hong Kong to Xiamen Island. Like Hong Kong, it is set up in a whole nest of islands. It is the one closest to the mainland of China and is connected to it by a causeway, which makes it a kind of peninsula. Xiamen has only sixty square miles of territory, but 588,000 people live here. Ned had Palm Sunday Mass at 7:15 and finished by 8 A.M. using the short Passion. We had to get out of the theater by then because the 500 people who were going ashore had to come to the theater first for their instructions. We were going too.

At the landing, we were met by a large group of children gaily dressed and lining both sides of the passageway from the dock to the main street. There were about 300 or 400 of them waving bunches of flowers in one hand and a bright balloon in the other. As we passed by, they performed a little dance for us. They were very cute kids, and everyone was thoroughly charmed by them.

Our first stop was Xiamen University. It has about 8,000 students, twenty-eight departments, and four colleges—not unlike Notre Dame. Students come from all over the country and from about 150 foreign countries. They live in dormitories, about six to a room, and hang their laundry out the windows, not a pretty sight, but a common one in this part of the world. They have a good sports facility, a stadium that would appear to hold about 15,000 people, a hospital, and, unlike most universities, a beach.

From there we went to the Buddhist shrine. It hasn't been that long since religion was largely repudiated and the government relocated the monks on farms. Now these Buddhist shrines and temples are full of studious young monks learning about Buddhism, and all these buildings are being restored to their former glory. This particular temple is called Potuo and is about 1,200 years old.

A stop at a public park gave us an interesting glimpse of the daily life and recreation here. People were doing Tai Chi exercises, practicing martial arts, and performing all sorts of classical dances. One of the most fascinating groups consisted of about a hundred kindergartners, who were dancing under the direction of two teachers. Finally, there was a classical Indonesian dance being performed by little boys and girls in classical Indonesian sarong outfits. I began talking with the female guide and a woman reporter from the *China Daily*, the local newspaper. They had good questions about education in America and particularly about Notre Dame. When they asked me what I was, I said I was a Shenfu, which is Chinese for Catholic priest.

MONDAY, MARCH 28
En Route to Tianjin

We woke up this morning to what was probably the worst weather we've experienced. The sea was full of whitecaps, the wind was strong, and the rain was pelting down as we passed offshore of Shanghai. To make matters worse, there was fog in all directions, so we couldn't see anything.

Played bridge for an hour and a half this afternoon, and for a change Ernie and I beat Ned and Faye. I can't claim it as a great victory, though, because in over 4,000 points scored on both sides, we won by only 30.

The captain invited us to dinner in his private dining room tonight. We had been invited once before, but couldn't go. This time we did, and it was very nice. As a memento of the occasion, each of us received a necktie with the Cunard logo. This captain understands and practices public relations as well as anyone I've ever met. He'll be a hard act to follow. (Unfortunately, he died of cancer within a year.)

TUESDAY, MARCH 29
Tianjin, People's Republic of China

When we woke today, the sea was much calmer, but muddy. Perhaps that explains why this is called the Yellow Sea. We are just coming in to dock at Xingang, which is about an hour's drive from Tianjin. This is also the entry point for Beijing, which is about a two-hour train ride from Tianjin. Over 500 of our passengers are going off to Beijing for a day or two. They'll also see the Great Wall and the Ming tombs. Having seen all these places twice before, I've decided to take a pass and go to Beijing on my own for a visit with the American ambassador.

As the tour groups disembarked they were greeted by another large group of attractive children waving flags. Also, a band was playing and about 200 pigeons were let go. I was told I couldn't go to Beijing because the Chinese had impounded all our passports and wouldn't let anyone in unless they were with the group, which I wasn't. I had to settle for a phone call from the ambassador instead. We had a nice chat and he suggested I keep trying. I said I would.

When I went up to the ship's manifest office, one of the staff members said, "Why don't you just go and talk to the Chinese themselves? They are all up in the cardroom." It sounded like a good idea, so I went up there. There were four of them. I explained that the ambassador was a friend of mine, and I just wanted to go into Beijing to have lunch and a chat with him. We lived halfway around the world from one another and this was as close as we would get to each other in many months, perhaps years.

When I had finished making my case, the chief officer, to whom I was making my case, simply sat back and said in a rather complacent way, "You have not complied with our law. There is no way you can go to Beijing without a personal visa stamped in your passport. You are confined to this ship. You're not going anywhere."

He said this as if he were the Emperor Constantine himself, which really got my Irish up. I told him that the university with which I was connected had spent $1 to $2 million a year to give scholarships to train Chinese students in a wide variety of subjects so that they could come home and teach their own people all that was needed for their advancement. I told him that many of our alumni had important jobs here, including the secretary-general of the Science Academy for many years and directors of the Institutes of Chemistry, Physics, and Metallurgy. I then added that many of the top Chinese, such as Vice President Feng Yi, had given me a dinner at the Great Hall of the People when I was last in town. Both his son and daughter were at Notre Dame. In addition, the new vice president of the National Science Foundation was a Notre Dame graduate, and the vice president of the Chinese Academy and the president of Hubei University had sons at Notre Dame. Then I said, "You may think you are correct in administering these laws with such authority, but when all of these important people hear that you have kept me from going to Beijing simply because of a paper that could be written in a few minutes, you may be in deep trouble."

He replied that I could buy a visa for $500. I told him to forget it. After that he and his associates had a heated conversation in Chinese, after which he said, "Maybe something could be arranged if you were on a group visa." I said I was already on the group visa. He wanted to see it for himself. I went down and got the papers from the manifest office, and there I was, No. 353. Clearly, he was now worried. He said I could get off the ship and go to Beijing, but I had to take my passport. That involved telling the manifest officer of the QE2 that he had to give me my passport. The manifest officer objected, saying that he had been told by another Chinese official to impound all the passports. This fellow told the manifest officer to give me my passport and he did. He then told me to leave the ship and go to Beijing, although I still had no visa, nor anything else in my passport that would make my trip to Beijing legal. No one wanted to put anything in writing.

I quickly returned to the cabin, offered Mass, packed a bag, and then went down to leave the ship. When I reached the gangplank, the Chinese officer in charge stopped me and said I couldn't leave without a visa. I asked him to get in touch with his officer on the upper deck, saying that I had just been over that matter for about the last hour and a half. There ensued another thirty minutes of conversation by walkie-talkie between the gangplank and the upper deck, after which I was told I had to see the Port Commander and he would give me a yes or no on going to Beijing. At this point, I really didn't care whether I went or not, but I had my dander up and decided I would see it through.

I dickered with a taxi driver over the price of the four-and-one-half-hour ride to Beijing. He wanted $100. We settled on $70. I then went to the Port Commander's office, and after a few more rounds he said I could go to Beijing, but again no visa was put in my passport, so I was completely illegal as I left.

After everything I'd been through just to get off the ship, the ride to Beijing was very pleasant. Spring was in evidence everywhere, with sycamores starting to bud and people preparing the fields for planting. There were also the great contrasts that one sees in a country like this. For example, on one side of the road there was a miserable broken-down brick apartment building, on the other an ultra-modern nuclear plant generating electricity. There were people riding bicycles, buses, and little tractors and driving horse-drawn wagons.

We had to stop at several checkpoints, but fortunately for me they checked only the driver. I slumped down in the front seat with my Mao cap pulled down over my eyes. When we arrived in Beijing, we pulled up right in front of the Great Wall Hotel, where Win Lord, the ambassador, had made my reservation. I gave the driver a large tip, since he would be deadheading back to the port of Xingang. I checked into the hotel, which is a Sheraton, and then decided I would go downtown before eating dinner. First I went to the Friendship Shop to buy some Easter presents for our bridge partners. Then to the railroad station, which is an absolute zoo, but I was somehow able to get tickets back to Tianjin on tomorrow's midafternoon express train. Nobody spoke English but my meager Chinese worked, as it had with my taxi driver all afternoon.

WEDNESDAY, MARCH 30
Beijing, People's Republic of China

I offered Mass for all of the people of China while looking out over this great city of Beijing and hoping that somehow the Good News of Christ might one day come to all of them. Breakfast, which was orange juice, coffee, and a croissant, cost me $7.00. The ticket I had bought to Tianjin on an express train was less than $3.00. My one and one-half hours in the taxi last night to the Friendship Shop, the railroad station, and back here, with the driver waiting twenty minutes in each place, cost me only $6.00. Pretty inexpensive when you consider what these same things cost in many other parts of the world.

I went back to the Friendship Shop and bought twelve beautiful little porcelain figures of animals for less than $2.00 that would be great around the Christmas tree. Nice little sketches of Chinese scenes were very reasonable, and one beautiful cloisonné bracelet I priced was only $1.50. I bought nicer ones for our bridge partners.

At the embassy, I spent an hour with the science attaché on a wide variety of subjects of interest to the university, and another hour with the cultural attaché going over the new Chinese thinking on sending students to America. It had been reported in the New York *Times* that they were going to cut back, but apparently they are still going to send 20 to 30 percent of all their overseas students to America. The main difference is that they will send more postdoctoral research students rather than beginning graduate students who can string their courses out for six or seven years. There is also a fear that students who stay that long might become enamored of democracy in America and never return at all. Also, there was the good news that they are now going to accept Peace Corps volunteers, the first Communist country to do so. I have worked many years for this. (Unfortunately, the incident at Tienanmen Square later squelched this.)

Shortly after noon I went to the ambassador's residence, where he and his wife, Bette Bao Lord, who has a Notre Dame honorary LLD, greeted me. We had a wonderful conversation and a splendid lunch. All too soon, it was time to catch the train, and Win's chauffeur whisked me there in good time. An hour and a half later I was in Tianjin. Back on the ship, I learned that an eighty-six-year-old Brazilian passenger had suffered a heart attack while I was gone. Ned had anointed the man and he had died a few hours later. The body is being flown back to Brazil.

Ned and I had dinner with Ernie and Faye in the Queen's Lounge. Now they are watching a special performance by some Chinese acrobats and I'm down here trying to catch up with the diary. I forgot to mention one of the things I picked up in Beijing. It was a book that Bette Bao Lord wrote years ago for children, entitled *In the Year of the Boar and Jackie Robinson*. It will be interesting to read a children's book for a change.

Some reflections on China: One cannot easily write off a quarter of the human race. There are more than one billion people in this land. Their history for the last century has been terribly complicated and terribly cruel for vast segments of the population, many millions of whom have died as a result. Today they are trying very hard to move ahead, with all kinds of internal tugging and pulling on the part of both the conservative and the liberal elements in the government. I find that the Chinese tend to be pragmatists, rather than doctrinaire ideologues like some of their Communist brethren. What is the future? God only knows, but I'm glad that Notre Dame is doing something to help lead it in the right direction, with more than a hundred mainland Chinese students on our campus. Perhaps some of the things they've learned and felt on our campus will enable them to help their country in the years ahead.

I finally finished James Michener's *Legacy*, which is a fictionalized account of the Constitution and the various amendments to it. I thought I knew a lot about this subject, but I learned a great deal more in reading this book. At the end of the story, he reproduces the Constitution and all of the amendments. It would do every American a lot of good to sit down periodically and read the Constitution and all of the amendments. We tend to forget what a wonderful document it is.

HOLY THURSDAY, MARCH 31
Xingang, People's Republic of China

Ned was off at 8 A.M. to visit Tianjin. I did my two miles on deck and thought about what I would say in my homily tonight, as well as at the Good Friday ecumenical service tomorrow afternoon and then again at our own evening service.

After all the rushing around trying to get to Beijing and then making the trip, it was nice to have a restful, uneventful day. I spent most of the day reading *Yamani* by Jeffrey Robinson. It's about the sheik of the same name who was dropped as oil minister of Saudi Arabia. I knew him and like him and was surprised at his ouster. Robinson's book cleared up some of the mystery. Tonight we had a fine Holy Thursday service with all three of us concelebrating.

GOOD FRIDAY, APRIL 1
En Route to Osaka

Curious day today. The very calm Yellow Sea is covered with a light fog, light enough so that the sun comes through and makes it a bright, rather than a dull gray fog. Even so, as I did my two-mile walk on deck, the ship's foghorn sounded every thirty seconds. They had also closed all of the watertight doors beneath the waterline. This is standard procedure in this kind of weather. If we were to run aground or into another ship, the ship couldn't fill up suddenly and sink, as the *Titanic* did. Seamen have long memories. By midmorning the visibility was, perhaps, 300 yards, as opposed to the 100 yards it had been earlier.

Another problem is the large number of small boats in these waters, which don't show up on radar. Few of them would be able to do any damage to us, but we could do a lot of damage to them. I'm sure that if one of these Chinese fishermen in a small sampan saw the QE2 bearing down on him out of the fog, he'd die of fright before he drowned.

We had the ecumenical Good Friday service from 2 to 3 P.M. with the captain, the bishop, and myself. More than 300 people came, almost a full house. It came off very well and all who attended seemed to appreciate it. Ned did the evening service with Father Bernie and me assisting. Rabbi Ruben had a seder tonight. We couldn't go because they were serving chicken and Good Friday is a day of abstinence. However, I did go to the seder for the regular blessings and greeted the rabbi after that. Tomorrow is the last day of Lent, thank God. It will be good to have some scotch and cigars again.

HOLY SATURDAY, APRIL 2
En Route to Osaka

There were light rain squalls as we walked the deck this morning. Let's hope we get some sunshine for Easter. We played bridge for an hour and a half this afternoon. Faye and I were partners and just barely beat Ned and Ernie. Our Easter Vigil Mass was switched to the Queen's Lounge, the second-biggest hall aboard ship, but a deck down from the theater. That meant we had to move everything one level down, but it actually worked out better than it would have in the theater. About 150 people came to the services, most of whom received Holy Communion. After Mass, Father D'Arcy came down to our cabin, where we all broke our fast with some scotch. I had bought a great Monte Cristo cigar in Hong Kong to use up my leftover Chinese money. After dinner I enjoyed it on deck.

EASTER SUNDAY, APRIL 3
Osaka, Japan

Ned has a cold, so he went to bed and I went to Osaka by myself. It turned out to be a beautiful day, the first in a week. I took the shuttle bus to the new Otani Hotel, then walked to Osaka Castle, which dates back to about the time that Columbus discovered America. It's quite formidable, with a large moat and high walls. The castle is about eight stories high with square roofs diminishing in size as you go up, in the Chinese fashion. The castle is surrounded by a very large park. I drifted through it with a couple of our shipmates and joined them for a beer. We decided to get adventurous on the way back to the ship, so we took the subway. The station where we got off was just two blocks away from the ship.

Everything is very expensive here in Japan, partially because the yen is now almost on a par with our currency—120 yen to the dollar. The bus ride we took this morning cost $30. A meal that our waiter and his girlfriend had in town last night at a very simple restaurant cost them $170, and the cab that took them there cost $30. Roses are $3.00 a stem. I priced a medium-sized bottle of shampoo and it was $8.00. Not surprisingly, no one is shopping here.

MONDAY, APRIL 4
Yokohama, Japan

We were greeted on arrival by a band and all kinds of geisha girls in bright kimonos. The *QE2* is an especially big deal here because it will return for ninety days next year to help the city celebrate its 130th anniversary. This is a very busy port. Everywhere one looks, one sees cargo ships and tugs. The tugs are the biggest we've seen so far, real oceangoing ones. The ship is crawling with Japanese. Every time one turns a corner, there is another TV crew. At one point coming into port, we had five TV crews circling overhead in helicopters.

We've been invited to an alumni gathering here. Unfortunately, Ned is still sick and won't be able to make it. I was escorted to the event by Andy Shilling, who met me at the dock. He told me that he had been a language major at Notre Dame and that he and his wife, a St. Mary's graduate, now both work for the United States Information Agency here. We took the train from Yokohama to Tokyo and then switched right across the platform to a subway which took us within a couple of blocks of the U.S. Embassy housing section, and the apartment of Jim Moynihan, where the party was. Jim had done our Tokyo program at Sophia University. Walking to his apartment from the subway, we passed a Franciscan church and school, where one of the priests, Father Eric, was sitting out in front wearing a Notre Dame sweatshirt. He was quite surprised when we went up and introduced ourselves.

More than twenty alumni showed up for the buffet dinner. Afterward I gave a talk on international studies at Notre Dame and some of our new institutes for peace and human development. It was, as these gatherings always are, a wonderful evening. Our alumni are doing good work all over the world. In the embassy alone, there are six Notre Dame graduates, products of our Tokyo program, operating all day in Japanese. Father Peter Moriwaki, a Ph.D. in chemistry from Notre Dame and former chairman of Sophia University, also joined us.

On the way back to the ship we stopped at a foreign-book store in Tokyo to pick up a copy of *Time*. While I was looking for change, Andy paid for it. I said, "You can't do that." He said, "I met you once in the Detroit airport when I was on my way to Notre Dame to visit my bride-to-be. You bought me a hot dog that day, so we're even." Well, not really. *Time* costs over $5.00 here. I'm sure I didn't pay that much for that hot dog in Detroit.

TUESDAY, APRIL 5
Yokohama, Japan

About 7:30 A.M., I received a call from Jim Grant in New York. He and his wife, Ethel, had gone to India to visit their son John and his wife, Maria. While they were there, Ethel suffered a massive heart attack and died. Ethel Grant was a wonderful woman, an able mate for Jim Grant, whom she joined in China right after the war when Jim was doing relief work there among the starving millions. Over the years, she was at his side in India, Turkey, Egypt, and in just about every trouble spot one could think of on earth. I stayed many times at their home in Washington when Jim was president of the Overseas Development Council and I was chairman. I will offer Mass for this exceptional woman today.

Ned was feeling better, so he got dressed and joined me for the trip into Tokyo with a driver from Coca-Cola. We met John Hunger and Kimura Sato, the top Coca-Cola people here, for a delicious steak and shrimp tempura lunch. We then drove to the American Embassy, where we were met by David Wallace, Notre Dame class of 1971, who works in the political section. When he was at Notre Dame he led a group of students who worked with victims of Down's syndrome at Logan Center, a local provider of services to the mentally retarded.

Later we talked with Ambassador Mike Mansfield, who had just returned to Japan after a triple bypass surgery in the United States. He looked a little wan, but was in good spirits and sharp as a tack at age eighty-five. Mike said all six Notre Dame graduates at the embassy spoke Japanese and performed extremely well in a variety of tasks. He said he was very proud of them and, needless to say, so were we. We all had a good time reminiscing about the commencement at which he received Notre Dame's Laetare Medal. President Jimmy Carter received an honorary degree at the same ceremony.

Our next stop is Honolulu, over 3,900 miles away. There are

another 600 Japanese on board now. The Japanese love Hawaii, both as a travel destination and as an investment. They already own $3 billion worth of real estate in Hawaii, and the figure will undoubtedly continue to climb.

WEDNESDAY, APRIL 6
En Route to Honolulu

With several days on the open ocean in front of us, I decided to make the most of the time by reading on deck. I've read more than 925 pages of James Clavell's *Whirlwind* but still have 400 pages to go. By the time I'm finished I'm sure I'll know more about the Ayatollah than I care to. Ben Gingiss and his wife, Rosalie, put on a cocktail party before dinner tonight. He's the tuxedo czar from Chicago. I read some more after dinner, then went to bed. The ship was rolling and pitching all night.

THURSDAY, APRIL 7
En Route to Honolulu

We have a 15-mile-an-hour wind, which when added to the speed of the ship creates a wind of 40 to 50 miles an hour across the deck. I did my usual two-mile walk, but it wasn't easy. Many people had it worse. They were seasick.

I read some more of the Clavell book and worked on a memorial for Ethel Grant, to be given to Jim and their three sons.

FRIDAY, APRIL 8
En Route to Honolulu

The wind is not as bad as yesterday and the sea has flattened out a bit as well. Ned and I were partners today at the bridge table. We had terrible cards and Ernie and Faye beat us badly. Perhaps they would have anyway.

FRIDAY, APRIL 8
En Route to Honolulu

My watch says it is the ninth, but since we just went over the date line at 180 degrees east of Greenwich, we have to do Friday, April 8, twice. At noon today we were eighty miles north of Midway Island, which saw the turning point of World War II when we knocked out four of Japan's carriers. They were the same ones that took the planes within striking distance of Pearl Harbor. From here we're 1,231 miles from Honolulu.

I witnessed a great personal grace today that grew out of the beauty of the Easter liturgy. Miracles of grace happen even in the middle of the ocean. Someone who was away from the Church for many years came home. At 2:30 A.M. I finished the Clavell book! I hope he doesn't write another book soon.

SATURDAY, APRIL 9
En Route to Honolulu

The wind was force 7 on deck this morning, which is over 30 miles an hour. When you add the 30 miles per hour that the ship is doing, it's next to impossible to walk into it. After leaning into the wind and pumping three lengths of the port-side deck, I capitulated and finished my walk on the lee side to starboard. Today we had a county fair for charity. There were something like forty booths in operation and they raised over $30,000 for handicapped children. The affair wound up with a tug-of-war among various groups aboard the ship. The waiters in the Mauritanian Restaurant won, taking special delight in whipping the officers' team. I started reading a new novel today, *Presumed Innocent* by Scott Turow.

SUNDAY, APRIL 10
Honolulu, Hawaii

Ned returned from the early Mass and immediately took off on a nine-hour island-hopping air trip. Having done this when out here with the Navy in 1947, I went ashore and phoned Tom and Ruth Flynn. Tom is our oldest alumnus in the islands. The Flynns picked me up and took me to their new apartment, then to the Waialeale Country Club for lunch. Afterward they showed me one of the high-rent districts and told me that it was not uncommon for wealthy Japanese to buy new million-dollar homes, then tear them down and replace them with even more expensive homes built in the Japanese style.

The economy here on the main island is somewhat slack, but tourism is booming. The population of the islands is about 1 million, of whom 700,000 live on Oahu, and most of those in Honolulu. Hawaii, better known as the Big Island, is six times bigger than Oahu but has only 80,000 people. The other main islands are Maui with 55,000, Kauai with 40,000, and, of course, Molokai with only 5,000. We toured Pearl Harbor, with its memorial of the battleship *Arizona*. Then I brought the Flynns back for a tour of the ship. When we were finished, I bade them goodbye and got ready for Mass.

The Royal Hawaiian Hotel used to be one of the most prominent landmarks here, but there's been so much high-rise construction in recent years you can hardly find it now. Ned and I had dinner tonight with Ernie and Faye and some of their Honolulu friends at La Mer Restaurant in the Halekulani Hotel on Waikiki Beach. The meal was superb and Ernie insisted upon picking up the rather substantial tab. We protested, but to no avail. We were back on the ship around 11 P.M. and left harbor for the island of Maui around midnight.

MONDAY, APRIL 11
Maui, Hawaii

This was once the whaling capital of the world. The great whales would come down from Alaska to breed and give birth between

November and May. At the height of the season, as many as 500 whaling boats would be present at one time.

We decided to take the tour, which will be our last one until we reach Martinique in the Caribbean. As we drove, our guide filled us in on the volcanoes here. Actually, they are the highest mountains in the world. They begin 18,000 feet below the ocean surface and rise 10,000 to 14,000 feet above the surface to form these islands. On the island of Hawaii, the two volcanoes, one still active, are over 32,000 feet high when measured from the sea floor. Everest, the highest mountain in the world by traditional reckoning, tops out at 29,028 feet.

Lao Valley State Park, very green and very rugged, has huge trees growing right out of the lava and many species of gorgeous tropical flowers growing everywhere. Some, such as hibiscus, come in three different colors. Kaanapali impressed us for quite a different reason— its many luxury hotels and condos.

Shortly after noon we headed back to the ship, and by 2 P.M. we were on our way to Los Angeles. Once we left the lee of the islands (you can see six of them from here) the wind whipped the sea into a mass of whitecaps. We saw whales blowing and flipping their huge tails. Next month they'll start traveling back north again.

I read on the top deck for a couple of hours. I am about two-thirds of the way through Turow's *Presumed Innocent*. Turow is a lawyer, and his knowledge of the law and the way the courts work lends a lot of authenticity to the tale he spins.

TUESDAY, APRIL 12
En Route to Los Angeles

This is going to be a big social day. I had my first warning while walking on deck—invitations on all sides. There are always many more of them when we're at sea with no shore tours to take.

WEDNESDAY, APRIL 13
En Route to Los Angeles

I did my two miles around the deck, then some praying and paperwork. After lunch I reread the ending of the Turow book on the murder trial. It's quite subtle and the denouement comes fairly suddenly. I had to reread it for all the nuances. It would make a great movie. This afternoon I began Barbara Tuchman's *The March of Folly*. I can tell from the first two chapters that it's going to be a great book.

After dinner Ned and I watched the film *Guess Who's Coming to Dinner* with Spencer Tracy, Katharine Hepburn, and Sidney Poitier. Ned had never seen it, but I had seen it once. It's one of the relatively few movies I would watch a second time. Another one is *The African Queen*.

THURSDAY, APRIL 14
En Route to Los Angeles

This is our final day en route to Los Angeles. For some reason, they cut off the buffet breakfast early, so I had to do my two miles on a cup of coffee. Normally, I have juice and a little cereal too. There was a reception–cocktail party at noon for many of the passengers who don't have English as a basic language. Everyone who spoke Spanish, German, Portuguese, or French was invited, and it was a lot of fun to move from group to group.

Ernie and Faye are getting off in Los Angeles and flying back to Indianapolis, so our bridge game with them today was our last. We changed partners every time we played, so there was no winning team during the cruise. But I'd guess that Ernie would be the individual winner, with Ned next and either Faye or myself last. Though neither of them is Catholic, they came to Mass practically every day, and they're very good company as well.

We were told that about 500 passengers will get off in L.A. but almost 1,000 will get on. So we'll have about 500 more passengers from L.A. to New York than we do now.

FRIDAY, APRIL 15
San Pedro Anchorage, Los Angeles, California

As soon as we went ashore I called Helen, my secretary. She told me that we had to be back at Notre Dame by May 5 to participate in the groundbreaking for the Hesburgh Center for International Studies. Ned and I hadn't planned to be back until June. We were going to have our trusty RV meet us in Fort Lauderdale, then wend our way back to Notre Dame in leisurely fashion. Well, we could live with the change in schedule, especially since Joan Kroc was going to give us $6 million to build the new center and would be there for the ground-breaking. We wanted to be with her, to thank her.

Tonight is the first night in a long time we haven't had a cocktail party with some of our friends aboard. Many of them are now winging their way home. As we left the harbor, we were escorted out to sea by hundreds of small craft amid much excitement.

SATURDAY, APRIL 16
En Route to Acapulco

The day dawned just as one would wish it to—bright blue sky, fuzzy cumulus clouds throwing shadows on the dark blue waters, a bit of breeze, but not too much, and off to the east the rugged mountain spine of Baja California. I put on shorts for the first time since Pattaya, and spent two hours in the sun reading Barbara Tuchman's *The March of Folly*. It's extremely well written and makes the point that political leaders are often their own worst enemies, doing stupid, destructive things to themselves and their countries when there are much better alternatives at hand. She presents a list of examples as long as your arm, but singles out Troy and the Trojan Horse, Renaissance Popes, and Vietnam as prime examples of folly.

We almost filled the theater for Saturday night Mass, which tells me that a lot of Catholics must have boarded in Los Angeles. I preached on the encounters between Jesus and His Apostles at the Sea of Galilee and how we're on a journey too, not only on this ship but as we travel through life. We picked up about $300 in the collection tonight. Adding what will come in tomorrow, we should do pretty well for the Seaman's Fund.

SUNDAY, APRIL 17
En Route to Acapulco

After breakfast I walked about three miles on deck, the last one with one of our non-Catholic parishioners, who had some problems he wanted to talk about. It never ceases to amaze me what a vast collection of joys and tragedies we all carry around. Tonight I preached on the Mass, something I've done every time we had a new group come aboard. That gets their interest right away, and I think it's the reason many of them keep coming back. When the group got off in L.A., many of them, especially those who came to Mass every day, told us that the cruise had been almost like a retreat for them. I also think there is something about the vast expanse of sea and sky out on the ocean that encourages reflection about the things that are really important in life.

We're having cocktails and dinner with Jody Gamble tonight. Though not Catholic, she has attended many of our services, and this morning gave me a check for the Peace Institute at Notre Dame. Her doctors have told her she has only a year to live, and I don't know anyone who could be bearing up any better. She's already booked passage on next year's around-the-world cruise. (She made it too, and the next one as well.)

We have an old gentleman aboard, Jimmy Powers, who will be eighty-nine in August and who is one of the greatest Notre Dame fans around, having gone to practically all of the Notre Dame games this year, as well as to a lot of other places. He also makes all of the monthly alumni luncheons in Los Angeles and goes on many of the Notre Dame foreign tours. He must have an understanding wife.

We watched the last half of *The Treasure of the Sierra Madre* on our cabin TV tonight. As you know, it stars Humphrey Bogart and Walter Huston and still has a lot of meaning for our time. Ned fell asleep well before it was over. It wasn't Bogart's fault. Ned was just tired.

MONDAY, APRIL 18
Acapulco, Mexico

At the dock we hired a cab for half what it would have cost us for the scheduled bus tour. As I had learned many other places, there's really no substitute for speaking the language, especially when you're discussing price. We told the driver to take us to La Quebrada, the famous place where daring divers plummet into the water from 130-foot cliffs. They are called *clabados*, perhaps because they clobber themselves if their timing is the least bit off.

Acapulco's history is often dated to 1564, the year that Miguel López de Legazpe led an expedition from here to the Philippines. He reclaimed those islands for Spain, and for the next 250 years, Spanish galleons carried Mexican silver from Acapulco to the Orient; and silk, spices, porcelain, and ivory from the Orient back to Mexico. There are few reminders of those times in Acapulco, save Fort San Diego, built in 1616 as a defense against pirates, as well as against the English fleet, which found the lumbering galleons to be easy prey. (The fort was largely destroyed by the 1776 earthquake and rebuilt in 1784.) We paused at the fort briefly, our only educational stop of the day.

The galleon trade ended with the Mexican War of Independence in 1821, when the Mexicans captured Fort San Diego from the Spanish. From that time on, nothing much happened in Acapulco until the jet setters discovered it in the 1950s. Ever since then, its reputation as a premier resort has never been in doubt. The hotels alone are reason enough for coming here. To take just one example, the Princess has about five swimming pools between the hotel and the beach. Water seems to be everywhere, pouring over low cliffs and sparkling quietly in man-made ponds. We had a piña colada here before returning to the ship.

After dinner and a walk on deck with a cigar, I went back to the cabin and caught the second half of *Huckleberry Finn*. This must be the week for old-time favorites.

TUESDAY, APRIL 19
En Route to the Panama Canal

During my walk around the deck this morning I met Vincent Price, who must have boarded yesterday in Acapulco. He told me he still has a book I autographed when he visited Father Ned and me at Notre Dame some years ago. He also told me that five years ago he became a Catholic. Tonight he gave a lecture entitled "Villains" and introduced his movie *Laura*. The theater was packed, and everyone seemed to enjoy the movie, including me.

WEDNESDAY, APRIL 20
En Route to the Panama Canal

I started a new book this morning, *The Great Circle*, by Sam Llewellyn. It's a fictional account of a sailboat race around the world. And I must say it's something of a relief after all the heavy stuff I've been plowing through.

The captain hosted a cocktail party tonight. That meant formal dress, which the ladies love and the men hate. But that's the British tradition on the *QE2*, and it's strictly enforced. When they say informal on this ship, they mean coat and tie.

THURSDAY, APRIL 21
Panama Canal

There's an air of excitement aboard whenever a cruise ship enters the Panama Canal. The *QE2* is no exception. The excitement is running especially high this time because of the events surrounding the Panamanian dictator Manuel Noriega. We were told that he had soldiers watching us all along the canal as we passed through it, but we never saw any of them. The only mishap we had was blowing an electric fuse, which stalled us at the entrance to one of the locks. It took us about half an hour to get going again. We're now cruising along the northern coast of South America. Our next stop is Caracas, Venezuela.

I had prepared a sermon on St. Paul, mistakenly thinking that his feast day was today. I didn't realize my goof until I was on my way to Mass. St. Paul's feast day is tomorrow. There was no time to prepare a substitute homily, so I just winged it with a homily on marriage. Afterward, one of the passengers stopped me and said it was the best homily I'd given since the beginning of the cruise. So much for preparation. I give all credit to the Holy Spirit.

FRIDAY, APRIL 22
En Route to La Guaira

We've slowed down a bit to about 23 knots, although even at that we made almost 500 miles yesterday, with another 450 yet to go. We were coasting off Colombia at noontime and should be arriving at La Guaira, Venezuela, tomorrow morning at eight. I had a telex from Ricardo Marchant, the Coca-Cola manager in Venezuela. It said that his secretary, Cristina Pico, would be at the wharf tomorrow at eight. Also, we received another telex saying that the manager of Coca-Cola in Martinique, Gabriel Levy, and his wife, Sylvia, will meet us there on Sunday morning. They will be our last two Coca-Cola meetings. We are certainly grateful to the company and to Don Keough, president of Coca-Cola and chairman of Notre Dame's Board of Trustees (now chairman emeritus), for the wonderful treatment they've given us along the way.

I finished Sam Llewellyn's *The Great Circle* this afternoon. It was a great race around the world, a little more trying than the cruise we've had. I think I've about run out of books, so it's a good thing we're coming down the homestretch.

SATURDAY, APRIL 23
La Guaira, Venezuela

Our Coca-Cola guide, Cristina Pico, took us up over the hills to Caracas. We made quick stops at two universities, Andrés Bello, which is Catholic, and the Universidad Centro, which is public. Our ultimate destination was the home of Rafael Caldera, a leading Latin

American intellectual, former President of Venezuela, and founder of the Christian Democratic Party in this hemisphere. Rafael is about seventy-three years old now, but he's still full of ideas. He took us to lunch at a very fine restaurant, where the food was great, but the service was slow. Normally, this wouldn't have mattered to us, but the ship was sailing at 4 P.M. and we were quite a distance away from it. Then, after we got underway, we hit heavy traffic in the middle of town. When we reached the ship, they had already taken up the gangplank and we had to enter through the crew's door in the rear. That was our closest call so far.

SUNDAY, APRIL 24
Martinique

Martinique has been called the Jewel of the Antilles, since it is in the center of a long necklace of small islands stretching along the eastern perimeter of the Caribbean. A lot of famous people were born here, including Napoleon's Josephine. Gabriel and Sylvia Levy, our Coca-Cola contacts, were waiting for us with their daughter Silvana. To our surprise, he was a Nicaraguan of the Notre Dame class of 1967, so we had many mutual friends among our Nicaraguan alumni.

The Levys drove us down the Atlantic coast to the end of the island and past the spot where the great volcano had buried a whole town at the turn of the century. We then came up the Caribbean side of the island through a rain forest. The whole trip was very scenic, with colorful tropical flowers on all sides.

We arrived back at their home, met their two young sons, then drove to a restaurant on the beach. Besides some excellent French cuisine and two French wines, we also had some rum and Cokes and brandy. I probably should have skipped some of the libations in deference to the fact that it was my turn to preach tonight, but, even so, I thought my homily came off pretty well. I talked about Christ, our Way, our Truth, and our Life and tied it in with the life of Tom Dooley, a Notre Dame alumnus who became a medical doctor and devoted his life to the service of the poor. It's always been my feeling that very little theology gets through unless you can put it in real-life terms.

MONDAY, APRIL 25
St. Thomas

About 90 percent of the passengers went ashore because this is our duty-free port and the second-to-last port of any kind before Fort Lauderdale. We went ashore ourselves, but only to buy some Macanudo cigars and a roll of twine to tie up our books. Ned had to buy a duffel bag to accommodate his purchases during the cruise. This is our last night aboard. We figure we've done from 25,000 to 30,000 miles on this trip and raised over $5,000 for the Seamen's Fund at our Sunday Masses.

One of our daily communicants surprised Ned tonight. He had been going to Mass and receiving Holy Communion every day for the past three months. He told Ned that prior to the cruise he hadn't been to Mass in ten years. The Lord continues to work in strange and mysterious ways.

TUESDAY, APRIL 26
En Route to Port Everglades

Our last day aboard, like so many others, was appropriately bright and sunny. I didn't see any reason to change anything else, so I did my usual two miles on deck. As I walked I tried to put together an outline for the talk I'll have to give at Notre Dame when we break ground next week for our new Center for International Studies. Then I had coffee with Father D'Arcy, who was such a good cruise mate on this trip. He expects to be back on the Atlantic run come August, after taking a couple of months off in England and Ireland.

After that, I began organizing the last items to be packed and making some difficult decisions. What does one do with two koala bears, each a foot high and six inches thick? I then climbed to the top deck to enjoy a final afternoon of sun and do some reading. If you can believe it, I read the National Geographic. It contained articles on train rides in China, the past, present, and future of Alaska, and the Falkland Islands five years after the war, and I read them all. I guess I can never get enough of travel, even the vicarious kind.

WEDNESDAY, APRIL 27
Fort Lauderdale, Florida

We docked about 7:30 A.M. and were off the ship shortly after ten. Faithful Marty Ogren, our driver at Notre Dame, was there with his friend Joe Yonto and Ned's Buick. We quickly loaded our luggage into the Buick, waved goodbye to Marty and Joe, and headed north toward Notre Dame. Marty and Joe flew back.

POSTSCRIPT
On the Way Home to Notre Dame

En route back, we visited Ned's brother Jack and his wife, Cele, in Sea Island, Georgia. The next day while visiting a Notre Dame Trustee, Jane Pfeiffer and her husband, Ralph, in South Carolina, I received some sad news. My sister Anne's husband, Jack Jackson, had died. I had married them forty years ago last year and considered him a good friend, as well as a brother-in-law. Naturally, I cut short the homeward leg of the trip so I could fly to Syracuse in time for the wake and funeral. Ned drove back alone. It was an easy homily at the funeral Mass because Jack was such a good man. His life spoke more eloquently for him than my words ever could. May he rest in peace.

Part V

ANTARCTICA

Both Ned and I thought that the QE2 trip was the end of our sabbatical year. Then, out of the blue, in early fall we had a letter from the Society Explorer organization saying that they had enjoyed our company on the Amazon and wondered if we would be interested in being chaplains on the "Little Red Ship" going to the Antarctic over Christmas.

I had been on the other side of the Antarctic continent at McMurdo Sound, below New Zealand, and even the South Pole in 1963. That was a fascinating trip, but this was a chance to see the other side of the Antarctic, the Palmer Peninsula, now called the Antarctic Peninsula. Also, this time it would all be made by boat, equipped with rubber zodiacs for trips ashore. Ned, being a good Southerner, has always been fascinated by snow and ice.

It took us a few milliseconds to agree to their offer. Here is our trip.

WEDNESDAY, DECEMBER 14, 1988
Notre Dame, Indiana

After the usual flurry of Christmas business and wrapping up the old year, Ned and I finally left for the airport in the early afternoon. At last we were off for Ned's first trip to the Antarctic, my second.

However, it's going to be a different one because this time we're going to the other side of the continent from McMurdo Sound.

Things started off badly. Piedmont Airlines, unlike them, were half an hour late leaving South Bend with a forty-minute connection for the Miami plane in Dayton. However, that was late too, and in addition made an unexpected stop in Gainesville to pick up some people who were stranded there. That got us into Miami over an hour late.

The good news was that our baggage was there. We transferred it to Lan-Chile for the trip to Santiago. We also learned that tonight was the maiden voyage of a Boeing 747 that Lan-Chile has leased from Aer Lingus. The flight lasted about nine hours and was the worst either of us could remember. We were wedged in like sardines. The people ahead of us put their seats back, so that our knees dug into them all night. It was almost impossible to get in and out of our seats. St. Teresa of Avila once said that hell was like a night in a bad hotel. She was speaking of medieval Spain. I have a new one: hell is an overnight flight in economy class on an overcrowded airplane.

THURSDAY, DECEMBER 15
Santiago, Chile

Santiago was beautiful and sunny and summery as well. There was a bit of a hassle for an hour getting the baggage together, but it all showed up, and we then drove through town to the Sheraton Hotel. Ned and I offered Mass at the hotel. Since we had only slept about an hour the night before in our sardine can, we took a nap after lunch.

Around six o'clock, three of our Holy Cross priests, George Canepa, Joe Dorsey, and Charles Delany, came to the hotel. They took us out to St. George's, where we saw the new Community residence that is being built adjacent to the old Casa Santa María.

About eight o'clock, we went to a restaurant that George had heard was pretty good. It turned out to be almost nonoperating because there was a bus strike scheduled for that evening, and the cook and several of the waiters had gone home already. All things considered, we had a pretty good meal and a lot of good conversation before we returned to the hotel around 11.

FRIDAY, DECEMBER 16
Santiago, Chile

We had a wake-up at five o'clock. Ned and I offered Mass and were down at breakfast about 5:45 and then off to the airport for our flight south to Punta Arenas (Sandy Point). It was a three-hour flight, and we did not see much of the Cordillera because the mountains are less high here and the clouds covered them and their ice fields. Punta Arenas was quite a bit colder than Santiago, but this is coming into early summer and the sun is quite bright, even at 30 degrees temperature.

Soon after arriving at Punta Arenas, we had another plane ride to Puerto Williams. Puerto Williams, beyond the Strait of Magellan, is a rather new military installation that has been set up there to guard the Beagle Channel. As everyone will recall, the Argentinians and Chileans were arguing for years about three small islands in the Beagle Channel. The Vatican was set up as arbitrator and recently settled the matter in favor of Chile. One wonders what the fuss is about when one sees these islands. Apparently, there may be some oil under the ocean floor here and that's probably the point of the argument.

We had lunch in Puerto Williams and then walked down the road a mile or so to the town. They have a nice little church dedicated to Our Lady of Carmen. There are about 1,000 people, mostly military, living here at this southernmost town on the continent. Argentina is right across the Beagle Channel on the other side, a few hundred yards away. We stopped by to see the priest and say hello, since he must be fairly lonely here. However, he was in Punta Arenas on business.

About 4:30 P.M., we boarded the "Little Red Ship" again, the *Society Explorer*, the same ship we took down the Amazon a year ago November. It seemed like coming home. It had just returned from the Antarctic Peninsula, so we also met some of the people who had just finished the early December Antarctic trip.

There were several reunions with old friends, including Peter Harrison, who is the best bird lecturer in the world, as well as being a fine bird artist. Our expedition leader is Micheline Place, a French woman who was with us on the Amazon as well. There are very few of last year's crew aboard, but we did meet a few who remembered us, one being the bartender!

As soon as everyone was aboard, we swung away from the dock and started down the Beagle Channel. The channel is named after the ship that took Charles Darwin around the world, especially to this part of the world, where he worked on his theory of evolution, which has had an enormous effect on human culture. The captain of the *Beagle*, figuring that he had contributed to the delinquency of Darwin by leading him into an evolutionary theory which was repugnant to Christian fundamentalists, finally committed suicide. I should have mentioned that there was also a fine little museum in Puerto Williams, which we spent about an hour visiting. The Indians here go back some 5,000 years. There are about a dozen or so of them left after they were wiped out by the white man's diseases. They hover around the dock as we board the ship trying to sell us woven grass baskets at $3.00 apiece. A sad scene.

We were up on deck for a while watching the sights. The sun does not set until about 11:30 P.M. this far south. We went to bed about 11:30 and were quite tired because we have not had much sleep the last two nights. We won't have a good deal tonight either, since reveille is at five in the morning.

SATURDAY, DECEMBER 17
Cape Horn, Chile

The call went out to rise and shine at five this morning, a second day in a row for that. At 5:30 we arrived at Cape Horn, where there is a Chilean radar station on the top of a large hill at the very tip of the continent. After a quick orange juice and coffee, we were all bundled up and down the side of the ship and into one of our seven zodiacs. The sea was fairly rough, and the tide was low, which meant that we came in as far as we could over the rocks and then had to jump out of the boat and climb over slippery rocks to the shore. Fortunately we were all wearing high rubber boots. Then it was a series of steps that must have been built for giants and across a high muddy field that led to the top of the hill and the radar station. There was also a little chapel there called Stella Maris, "star of the sea."

The wind was chilly, but the temperature fairly decent. There were some penguins cavorting around the shoreline. After an hour or so on top, everyone came back to the ship, where some had breakfast and others a cup of coffee to take off the chill. Ned seems to have picked up a cold during the night, but he went ashore nonetheless. He's now trying to sleep off the cold.

As soon as everyone was back aboard, we pulled up the anchor and cruised around the very end of the island we have been exploring. There is a high, rugged, cathedral-like cliff, which is the one always seen in photographs of Cape Horn. A good number of ships have foundered here, where the Atlantic and Pacific oceans meet and the weather generally is horrible. The Roaring 40s (the worst winds from 40 degrees south) come in from the Pacific to be met by the winds racing north from the Antarctic and then from the Atlantic to the east. After toasting the Cape, we headed directly south to Antarctica. This is one of the stormiest passages in the world, called the Drake Passage after the pirate who cruised these waters, the most famous of the east-west and west-east ocean routes, looking for plunder.

Already we are surrounded by seabirds, even some albatrosses with a wingspread of eleven feet, the largest of any bird. We saw many petrels as well; the largest of them has a wingspread of seven feet. Things were quite rough until after lunch, when the wind seemed to subside. If this keeps up, we're going to luck out and have a reasonably calm and not too bouncy trip through one of the worst marine passages on earth. The sun came out this afternoon. That is unusual down here, and we continue to have our ship surrounded by wheeling birds, beautiful and graceful. They are right at home here, although some of them nest as far as 16,000 miles away in the Arctic.

We had a lecture on the history of the Antarctic this afternoon. Having been an Arctic-Antarctic buff for years, I didn't learn very much new, although it was good to review the history of this fantastic continent. Antarctica is the fifth-largest continent in the world, the driest, the highest, and the only one permanently uninhabited, because there simply is no food here, except in the waters surrounding the shoreline.

Before supper tonight, we had a recap on all of the day's activities. There are almost a hundred passengers aboard. We fill the Explorer's Lounge just before supper each night and have a great session on everything that happened all day, plus questions and presentations of what's going on tomorrow. One thing that was mentioned tonight is that Ned and I will have Sunday Mass at 9:30 A.M. tomorrow in the Penguin Lounge, another large meeting room on the ship. It will be interesting to see how many show up. There is one thing that we can figure out already—namely, that there are many more Catholics aboard in this group than there were on the Amazon last summer, when one could count them on the fingers of one's hand. All in all, it's a very congenial group, judging from our conversations thus far.

Tonight is the first night since we left home when we might get more than three or four hours of sleep.

SUNDAY, DECEMBER 18
En Route to Antarctica

It wasn't all that restful a night, although it was longer than usual. We continue to luck out on the sea, which is giving us a good roll, but no pitching. The best word to describe sleep in this situation is "intermittent."

About half of the passengers were at Mass this morning, practically filling the lecture hall. A good number of crew were there as well. About half of them received Communion, so I assume the other half probably weren't Catholics.

We have three lectures today. First, "The Antarctic by Sea and by Ice," by Richard Rowlett, one of our four lecturers aboard. At 2:30 this afternoon, there will be another one, "Deception Island: Where Rocks and Penguins Come Down from the Sky." Later, at 4:30, Peter Harrison is presenting "Ocean Nomads: The Gentle Giants." That means albatrosses, at which he is very good indeed. As usual, Peter was spectacular. He illustrates most of his lectures by giving various birdcalls. At the same time, he is a superb artist who has done the best book on seabirds of the world with his own illustrations. He's a rare talent.

Tonight is the captain's cocktail party, followed by the captain's dinner. It's the only time on the whole trip that we have to dress up a bit. We've made such good time through the benign seas of the Drake

Passage (a spectacular bit of luck) that we may even be able to make a landing tonight to see nesting birds.

This is really an eager group. We hurried through the captain's reception and dinner, and by 8:30 P.M. we were on the zodiacs going through the icebergs to shore. It was a much easier landing on smaller rocks than at Cape Horn the other day. Everywhere one looked, one could see nesting chinstrap penguins, one of the very numerous rookeries of some 7,000 birds. They make quite a racket too, and, of course, the place stinks to high heaven because they are eating fish and krill, the one coming out white guano, the other red. Both stink equally.

We also saw some ordinary seals and one Weddell seal. It was close to 11 P.M. when we started back, but, of course, it doesn't get dark here until around midnight and then only for a couple of hours. Farther south, it doesn't get dark at all.

We're learning more about penguins than we really have to know, but since we've got such great experts here, we might as well learn all we can. Tonight we'll be traveling from Nelson Island, where we're currently anchored in this South Shetland group, over to the next island, Deception. I'm sure we'll get there by about six o'clock tomorrow morning, and they will have us tooting off in the zodiacs about five minutes later.

MONDAY, DECEMBER 19
En Route to Antarctica

We picked our way through the ice all night and arrived at Deception Island about 6:30 this morning, when reveille sounded. It was a quick breakfast, a quick getting dressed, although there is no easy way of getting into all of these clothes, and then off to shore with a much easier landing than the last time. The beach was really lava sand with small pebbles. Within view was a chinstrap penguin rookery of about 500,000 birds.

Deception Island is one huge volcano. The island itself is almost like a doughnut with the caldera in the middle full of water. It is also the site of an old whaling station. One enters the inner bay or caldera through a place called Neptune's Bellows. The beach we visited this morning is just to the right of that. Some of our folks walked over the top of the mountain and slid down through the snow to the other side to Whalers Bay, where we'll be meeting them in a couple of hours. The atmosphere is unbelievably clear. The nearby mountains on adjacent islands which are probably fifty miles away look about two miles away. We've been fortunate in having a lot of sunny days, something they had only once on the last trip out here. Everywhere one looks, one sees these great tabletop icebergs, or "tabular," to use the official word. Most of them are about a half mile long and about 300 feet high. All the icebergs that we're seeing look huge, but one must remember that this is only one-seventh of the mass of the iceberg we're seeing, the rest being underwater.

All of the colors here seem pastel because of the translucent atmosphere and a predominance of white snow and ice. They have some very interesting names for these places. The beach we landed on is called Bailey's Head. A cut in the mountain is Neptune's Window, and the passage we came through into the caldera, which, of course, is now like an enormous lake surrounded by mountains, is called Neptune's Bellows or the Devil's Throat. Once inside the lake, we pulled into Foster Landing, which is where the whaling station once was. One could still see the large tanks that held the whale oil that had been rendered. The oil was stored here for transport. There is also a British installation and a rudimentary airfield, last used by Lincoln Ellsworth when he was down this way. It must have been quite an explosion when the whole center of the island went up and then caved in, leaving this caldera very much like Crater Lake, but filled with seawater, which poured in through the Devil's Throat.

At around eleven o'clock, we went ashore again to see the whaling station with its dilapidated buildings and even a hangar which still has the remains of an old Otter airplane. This must have been one of the southernmost airports in the world. Jacques Cousteau was here years ago. In fact, one of his men was killed here when hit by the rotor blade of a helicopter. His crew camped in these dilapidated buildings for several weeks. Some of these buildings were struck by huge stones thrown out of the volcanic eruptions here in 1968. There were also eruptions in '69 and '70. We'll be visiting the crater after lunch, but that's another short cruise up the bay.

Our only alumni couple aboard, Bob and Ruth Leibin, are

celebrating their forty-sixth wedding anniversary, so we had Mass for them at four o'clock this afternoon. Between lunchtime and then, we went up to Telefon Bay, from which we walked into the crater formed when this island exploded in 1969. We climbed up a sloping hill for about a mile to the mouth of the crater, which was quite deep. Back to the ship in time for the Mass and renewal of marriage vows. I told Bob and Ruth that it was rather unique to be celebrating their forty-sixth wedding anniversary in Antarctica, with a couple of Holy Cross priests, in a cabin of a small red ship, as we cut our way through the ice to the shore, where some of our shipmates are now swimming in hot springs. This has to be the southernmost swimming pool in the world.

In addition to all of the volcanic explosions mentioned above, the Chilean station was destroyed here by a 1967 volcanic eruption and the British station here was destroyed by the 1969 explosion.

All in all, it's been a busy day, from our first view of a rookery for a half million chinstrap penguins, to the beautiful entrance to this caldera through Neptune's Bellows, to the visit to the ruined British station and whaling station, to the craters themselves, and then a swim in the hot springs. We did all but the last. While I was inspecting the ruins, Ned climbed up to Neptune's Window on the other end of the bay to a rookery for pintado petrels, a black-winged bird with white designs, no design being similar to that of any other bird in that species. These are a kind of bird fingerprints, if you will. Now it's goodbye to Deception Island. Tomorrow, I gather, more islands.

About 6 P.M. we came back through the Devil's Throat, or Neptune's Bellows, if you prefer, and started south along the coast of the Antarctic Peninsula toward a series of other islands we will be visiting tomorrow. If this sounds confused, it is for us too, because we've never been this way before and it isn't quite like going to Chicago or New York.

As we finished supper tonight, we suddenly sighted some humpback whales and have spent the last hour chasing them around the ocean. I think they are having as much fun as we are. It's like a game of hide-and-seek, but they win as often as we do. One of these humpbacks is about 100 feet long, which is a fairly large whale. God knows how much it weighs. There are about five humpbacks in this pod.

It's ten o'clock in the evening, but the sun is still fairly high in the sky, and we have beautiful snowcapped mountains off in the distance. They seem more spectacular than usual at this time of day, with the late evening sun lighting up all of their icy pinnacles. This is really a beautiful part of the world.

TUESDAY, DECEMBER 20
En Route to Antarctica

They let us sleep a little bit later today, about 7:30. Looking out the porthole gave us an incredible view of the mountains, snow, and ice bathed in bright sunlight with a beautiful blue sky, which was to dwindle as the day passed and the clouds moved in. However, it was a great wake-up sight.

After a quick breakfast, everybody was on deck to see the sights on both sides as we passed down the Neumayer Channel. About 10:30 A.M., we suited up again for the umpteenth time. The process doesn't get any shorter. Then it was back into the zodiacs to make a landing at Port Lockroy. It's an old British base and has the look of abandoned places, especially in the Arctic and Antarctic. Actually, the base was an island called Weincke, which is a rookery for gentoo penguins and the blue-eyed cormorants. Gentoos are the rarest species of the Antarctic penguins. This is the only place we've seen them.

There was one chinstrap penguin in the rookery, but all the rest of them had the beautiful white covering over their eyes and arching across the top of their skulls. Gentoos are a very distinctive bird and easy to identify, as are the chinstraps, who have a black line like a chinstrap keeping a hat on. Gentoos also often have more red-orange-colored beaks and feet. There were a number of small chicks already born in the last day or two and the rest were doing their final session of sitting for more than a month on the eggs. Their nests are made out of small pebbles about an inch or two long which they pile up all around them. On the way to the rookery, we passed three large Weddell seals on an ice floe. They really look lazy and helpless out of the water, but they are very graceful in the water. They are a large mammal about eight to ten feet long and, I would guess, about as big as Fatty Arbuckle, if anybody remembers him.

This island was named after a seaman, Carl Weincke, who fell overboard on one of the early expeditions at the end of the last century. The mate dove in after him, but he was already gone, so they named the island for him. One can only last a minute or two in these waters before getting hypothermia. We all wear life vests when we go ashore, but, even so, I wouldn't want to be in the water very long, despite all of the clothing we're wearing, the rubber pants and knee boots with several pairs of socks underneath. Add some wool shirts, sweaters, and a parka to all of that and one would really weigh a ton when soaking wet.

After the visit, we plan to have a Mass in the lecture room, the Penguin Lounge, before a late lunch. Then we'll be sailing down the Le Maire Channel, going as far south as we can along this beautiful route until we're blocked by the ice. We hope at least to go a bit farther south than the expedition here two weeks ago. The sun is very bright today and the clouds have dissipated, again revealing a marvelous snowcapped mountain chain which stretches south along the Antarctic Peninsula at our location here at Port Lockroy, just across the channel from Anvers Island. Anvers is a fairly large island among the long string of them that run parallel to the coast, leaving these marvelous channels between them and the Antarctic Peninsula. The channel is generally about a mile or two wide with fabulous scenery on both sides, mostly ice-covered mountains and endless glaciers. The glaciers are constantly breaking loose and floating out into the channel now that it is springtime. However, the southern end of the channel is blocked with ice, which will limit our southernmost traverse on this trip. We continue to be blessed by marvelous weather, quite unusual here, so perhaps the ice has melted a bit in the past two weeks. We will see this afternoon.

We spent the whole afternoon in the Le Maire Channel. At first, we were just dodging intermittent floes, but as we proceeded up the channel, which is quite narrow, maybe going out a hundred feet on each side of the ship with mountains rising precipitously from the waters, we encountered thicker and thicker ice, so that at the end of the afternoon, we were going through an almost solid mass of ice, broken up into larger and smaller pieces. Occasionally, we would go around icebergs that were as large as a normal house and some as large as a small office building.

The day was extraordinary. Those who have been here before say there has never been a day like it, with clear blue sky, beautiful sunshine, and temperature around freezing, but certainly not below. I'm sure we all got sunburned. There was occasional cloud cover, but not enough to limit our view of the gorgeous mountains on both sides of the passage. Just before entering the Le Maire Channel, we passed the largest mountain on the Antarctic Peninsula, I would gather about 12,000 feet at least, possibly 16,000. We passed another mountain, which was a look-alike for the Matterhorn.

I came down to finish my Breviary in the middle of the afternoon and it was a bit eerie hearing the brash ice crashing along both sides of the ship and the creaking and groaning of our hull, which has been strengthened to handle ice. Actually, we had to cut our way through some floes that were fifteen or twenty feet across and three to four feet thick. We sliced through all right, but then there was this constant cutting noise of the ice against the outer hull. I began to think of the *Titanic*. Anyway, they made this ship very strong, even though it was built twenty years ago. It was originally owned by Linblad and designated for working in the ice. All along the way, there were Weddell, crabeater, and leopard seals on the floating ice floes. Most of them would scoot off the floe as we approached or began to tip it. Occasionally, there were also penguins on the floes and they simply slipped into the water.

It was a wonderful day, such as one can only have once in a lifetime. Ned thought that, all things considered and given all of our travels to the wonders of the world in the past year, he would put it at the head of the line, even before Machu Picchu. That's really saying something. Of course, you must understand that Ned is partial to ice and snow, having grown up in South Carolina.

We are practically running out of night here. Some of our friends were up past midnight last night and others were out on deck at three this morning. They all said it was as bright as it is right now at seven o'clock at night. I recall that when we were 10 or 11 degrees farther south at McMurdo, it never got dark at all. Anyway, today everything conspired for success, fabulous scenery, pleasant temperature, bright sunshine, blue skies, and a good skipper.

I forgot to mention that for the last several days we have been seeing whales almost every day. Today, most of them were minke whales. We learned today that a sailor named Minke was a spotter aboard one of the old whalers. In other words, he was the fellow up in the crow's nest at the top of the mast looking for whales that might be chased and harpooned. Minke apparently didn't have all that great discernment about different whales, because he would get them chasing a small whale that was very fast and did not have very much blubber on it. When they finally caught up with the whale, one of the seamen or the harpooner would say in disgust, "That's one of Minke's whales." As a result, the small whale today is called a minke whale. That's one way to become immortal.

Right now, we are approaching the farthest progress south of the Society expedition voyages this year. On the last trip, they got 65 degrees, 11 minutes, 9 seconds south. Since we are already at 65 degrees, 10 minutes, 7 seconds south, the odds are that we will beat the record of the last trip, since we're still plowing through the ice, which continues to scrape loudly along our sides. At least we'll lose all our barnacles.

At 6:30 tonight, we passed the farthest point south in past expeditions. We are now going a few miles farther through the pack ice to establish our new record. I'll probably know later what it is, and my guess is that it's a few miles farther than where we are now.

It was a few miles and no more. The new record for farthest south was 65 degrees, 12 minutes, 7 seconds. A few went in to shore through the pack ice on the zodiacs and one zodiac got stuck in the ice. However, it was disengaged after a half hour or so. I saw my first movie on board, *Good Morning, Vietnam*. A waste of time.

WEDNESDAY, DECEMBER 21
Antarctic Peninsula

Reveille was at 6:30 this morning. As we raised the porthole cover, once again we were greeted by a beautiful blue sky, sunshine every-where, and in every direction one looked, water, snow, and ice. I don't know how we can be so lucky.

The first trip ashore was at eight and a doubleheader at that. First, there was a landing at González Videla, the site of an unmanned or abandoned Chilean station. It is also a gentoo penguin rookery with plenty of penguins and tons of guano. Again, it's hard to describe the way these rookeries stink. The chicks have not hatched out here, although there were plenty of birds on the nests warming the eggs. Some birds were just coming out of the water after their morning dip and, I assume, a breakfast of krill.

The second sight next door was a small chinstrap penguin rookery perched on high rocks and slippery too. The reason that these rookeries are always on rock outcroppings is that they are sure to be free of snow at this time of year, whereas all around them the snow is still several feet deep. The rocks are blackish, and that attracts the heat of the sun, so they are the first to emerge in the spring as relatively dry places.

The last zodiac was back to the ship at 9:45 A.M., and then we were off to what is billed as one of the loveliest spots in the Antarctic, Paradise Bay. They have a nice custom of serving hot consommé after one of these trips ashore, although ours have not been too rugged since the temperature hovers at 32 degrees Fahrenheit. Of course, the sunshine makes all the difference in the world compared with a damp, overcast day.

While ashore on the first trip this morning, we were able to nose around the Chilean buildings. There were still some groceries in the closet, a puny Christmas tree (no trees on this whole continent), and we even found a January 1988 *New Yorker*, from which we deduced that the Chileans had been down here doing some research on the penguins last year at this time and that an American scientist was with them. I would guess that this station could accommodate a dozen or so people, possibly even a few more. It would not be much fun living here very long with that constant smell of guano, but I guess if you want to study penguins, you've got to be where they are, although I would have pitched my hut some distance upwind.

Incidentally, the farthest south yesterday put us 21 minutes above the Antarctic Circle, which is 66 degrees, 33 minutes.

At 10:30 this morning, we set off to see another supposedly abandoned Argentine research station called Almirante Brown. After visiting, we were supposed to tour the bay in the zodiacs for an hour and a half. It had another attraction in that there was a large snowy hill behind the research station, so people would climb to the top and slide down on their backsides. Great fun.

However, when we arrived there, it turned out that seven Argentinians had been dropped off to recondition the station. Apparently, the last group that was staying here had a crazy man who decided the best way to get home was to burn the place down. Fortunately, they had a few other huts around that they could stay in, but he burned down the main installation. Nothing left but girders. These seven fellows are supposed to clean it up and start rebuilding so that they can reactivate the station. One of them was a real Antarctican, since he had spent fourteen years in Argentinian stations down here as far south as 80-plus degrees. I recall that one, Belgrano.

After meeting the captain and the other men, I asked them if they would like to have Mass for Christmas. They were delighted, so I went back to the ship by myself and picked up the Mass kit, which is in a knapsack, so it is easily carried up and down the gangplank. Back on shore, we cleaned up one of the huts, set up an altar on the table, and proceeded with the Mass. Since our boats were leaving fairly soon, there was no time for Confessions. I took them through the Act of Contrition in Spanish and gave them all general absolution, telling them they could confess later on, but this way they could receive Holy Communion for Christmas. We actually offered the Christmas Mass by anticipation, and they were very pious as they stood around the table blessing themselves and they all received a Christmas Holy Communion.

One other bit of serendipity. Just as I was leaving my room in Corby Hall at Notre Dame, I spotted a Spanish missal and threw it in the Mass kit just in case. It came in handy today since we could have the Mass in Spanish, which made it more meaningful for them. After Mass, I repacked the Mass kit and got suited up again. All the boats and all of the people had gone. However, down the bay was a boat that was leaving this stop for last, so I did get my ride back to the ship after all and was not stranded at the nonabandoned base called Almirante Brown. It seemed like an early Christmas for me too.

Things are a bit confused, but at the same time fairly well organized on this ship. Since we have seven zodiacs operating at once, everyone has a yellow tag at the debarkation door that he turns to red (the other side) when he leaves ship. When we get back, if there are still some unturned cards, we know we're in trouble or else someone has a bad memory for detail and has not turned over his tag on the hook.

Ned was up at the top of the mountain while all of this was happening. Besides, he has the Mass for the regulars this afternoon, so it's a break having two of us here at once. Everybody returned from Paradise Bay somewhat late, so we had a barbecue for a change. It was just like an Argentinian *asado*—pork, beef, chicken, sausages, etc. A fairly quiet afternoon, but always a lot of odds and ends to catch up with. Then Peter Harrison gave another one of his superb lectures, this time on penguins. Everybody mopey at supper tonight because it has been a long day and we always have a session to recap the day just before supper. Now we're out in the Gerlache Channel retracing our trip south, although now we're going north. Tomorrow we have a session on Nelson Island, more rookeries, where we began our arrival down here. Later we go to King George Island (named after King George III, the English king at the time of the American Revolution), where there are research stations of the Russians, Brazilians, Argentinians, and Poles with American assistance. Every nation is trying to make sure that the claims they have made in the Antarctic hold up by virtue of their presence here. In any event, we're hoping to give them Christmas services if they want them, but only tomorrow will tell what the situation is. My guess is that there will be a Polish Christmas Mass. I'm not sure of the Brazilians. It turned out to be just the opposite.

THURSDAY, DECEMBER 22
At Sea, Antarctica

We were just about to turn in last night at 11:30 when suddenly we must have hit an open spot of sea as we came down the Gerlache Channel. The ship began to roll from side to side. Everybody susceptible to seasickness promptly started to get ill. Most of us were in bed, and that's the easiest solution. Somehow you just let it rock you to sleep. We were able to sleep a bit later this morning, although I woke up with a scratchy throat and then, having promptly taken two aspirins, immediately lost it. Let's hope it's gone for good. Just about everyone, including yours truly, has had intestinal disease the last few days. Somewhere along the line we must have gotten some nice bacteria, or some not so nice. Relatively few people went in to Nelson Island, where we landed at our first stop on the Antarctic Peninsula on the way down. This time they are going to another landing to see more gentoo and chinstrap penguin rookeries. I hate to say that if you've seen one, you've seen them all, but that's about what we've come to at this point. I could add that if you've smelled one, you've smelled them all. A number of other birds also nest here, such as kelp gulls, skuas, Antarctic terns, southern giant petrels (a very big bird), pintado petrels, and also Wilson's storm petrels. These petrels are the birds that one mostly sees circling the ship wherever we go in this territory. Some of them are quite large, weighing fifteen to thirty pounds and having a wingspread of six to seven feet. Of course, they are not as big as the albatross. They recently measured an albatross with a thirteen-foot wingspread.

The next stop was King George Island farther north. This one has a lot of research stations, among which are those belonging to the Russians, the Brazilians, and the Poles, with whom a few American scientists also work. We're going to visit the Brazilian station first and then go up the coast to the Polish station, where we'll probably have a Christmas Mass.

We arrived at the Brazilian station, Comandante Ferraz, right on schedule. I went with the advance party in the scout boat to check the landing and see if everything was all right for disembarking passengers from our zodiacs.

This gave me a chance to talk to the young commander who has just taken over this base, Comandante Lisboa. I told him I was a priest and was prepared to offer a Christmas Mass for his people. The problem was that most of them were on station working. He said he would send out the word so that those who could get free could join me for Mass.

I set up in the small library, where, fortunately, there was a Portuguese Bible, so that we could have the Christmas readings in their language. About seven people showed up, including the commander, so I had the commander and one of the doctors do the readings. Also, because of the limitations of time and language, I gave them general absolution so that they could all receive Communion for Christmas. I told them they could confess their sins when they got back home. It was really a three-language Mass—in Spanish for the parts they would easily recognize, English for the Canon, and Portuguese for the Lessons.

This is probably the best known of the Brazilian bases in the Antarctic Peninsula. The installation looks fairly new. Jacques Cousteau stopped here for a while and picked up all of the whale bones on the beach and fit a group of them together into a blue whale skeleton. It's about forty feet long. I took my picture standing inside the mouth so I could be Jonah in the whale's belly, or at least the whale's throat.

Everybody got back on time, so that now we are on our way to the Polish base, Arctowski. Again, if we can get in early and arrange things, Ned will offer the Christmas Mass aboard, and I ashore. At least we're doing a little missionary work down here. When Ned and I arrived at the anchorage for the Polish station of Arctowski, there was, against the large rock formation, a shrine to Our Lady and a crucifix. We were met by one of the four American scientists working here on ornithology, mostly penguins. We walked down a fairly long path to the central headquarters of the Polish station. Once we were inside and took our boots off so as not to dirty their carpets, we met the commander of the station. I simply said that we were priests and we had everything necessary for Mass and we would be happy to offer Mass if that would be convenient to him and his group of twenty or thirty scientists. To our surprise, he told us that this was a Communist state station and that Mass would not be in order. He started to explain with some embarrassment, and I told him not to make a big deal out of it; if it was inconvenient, forget it.

We entered and had some coffee and cakes, and then he insisted on taking us personally all around the station, including a greenhouse they have, where we ate some of their tomatoes, which were very good and, I might add, very unusual.

The curious thing was that when we went into their common room, we saw a large picture of Pope John Paul II on the wall. I am sure all of this was due to some kind of misunderstanding or a fear of what would happen if the commander was reported back home as having allowed Mass at the state station, the state being Communist.

As he conducted us around the base, I explained to him that things were quite different in the Soviet Union today. I said that only two months ago I had been asked to offer Mass, and did so in Moscow, with the vice chairman of the Academy of Sciences, the head of the Russian Space Research Program, and Andrei Sakharov in attendance, plus many other Russians. However, this is thousands of miles away from headquarters, and one can understand the fears that exist in the political order. In any event, we passed the word around that nothing should be made of this and we were utility people to be used if it was feasible and no explanation was necessary if they didn't want to have us provide a spiritual service. I'm sure the majority did not agree with the commander. Three weeks later in Moscow, the former Polish foreign minister told me that the commander was completely out of line in not permitting Mass. So much for *glasnost*.

This is one of the few places in the Antarctic where three of the species of penguins, the Adélie, the gentoo, and the chinstrap, breed together and in peace. The reason they are able to do it is that the Adélie come in early in the season, the chinstraps in the middle, and gentoo later. They also feed at different levels of the ocean to obtain the krill that sustains them. It's a nice accommodation, and all three get along well, despite the fact that they have the same needs.

The Adélie population has doubled down here in the last ten to twenty years, and the chinstrap population has probably tripled. The apparent reason for this is that when most of the whales were killed off, there was an extra supply of krill, the main food of the whales, so the penguins moved in. Now they may be putting too great a burden on krill and the next few years will be interesting to watch. The balance of nature is a marvelous reality. Population numbers are not just a problem for humans, given our total dependence on limited resources.

We had a group from both the Polish station and the Brazilian station join us for a Philippine buffet tonight. After the meal, the Filipinos sang some of their songs and then we had a lecture by the young leader of the American group here. It was interesting to catch up on the levels of research support from the National Science Foundation, since from 1963 to 1966 I was chairman of this activity of the Foundation while a member of the National Science Board. Apparently, the research support is being kept up, and they are even making some long-range plans for research support here. The big fear everybody has is that there will be an influx of national groups looking for oil and possibly ruining this area, which really should be an international park. Life is fragile here and almost anything can threaten it.

As we were winding up the discussion, we were told that reveille is at six o'clock tomorrow morning and that we have two landings during the day. All that being true, I think it's time to go to bed. It's been an interesting day. When we returned to the ship tonight, Ned had Mass in our cabin, attended by our Notre Dame alumni couple and two other of our regular parishioners.

FRIDAY, DECEMBER 23
Antarctica

There was a wake-up call at six this morning, which Ned and I decided to ignore. We had the best sleep since leaving South Bend as a result. We heard that the landing party was fairly small, but they did see elephant seals. They are fairly enormous. We've seen just about every type of seal thus far, so a few more we don't need.

Instead of lunch, they had a brunch in the dining room until 11 A.M. We finally got some laundry out and stopped by the doctor to get a couple of pills for Montezuma's revenge. They seem to come up with different medicines every time. This one was Doxycycline; I believe it's a throw-off from Terramycin. Anyway, it works.

At 11:15 A.M., we have a lecture on Shackleton, since we're approaching Elephant Island, where he left some of his men as he escaped from the ice after his ship was crushed, well south of here. We're stopping at Half Moon Island at one o'clock for another rookery of penguins, blue-eyed cormorants, and Antarctic terns. At four this afternoon, we're heading for Elephant Island and en route we'll have a lecture by Richard Rowlett. He'll talk on whale research in the Antarctic Ocean. Much discussion on this subject. It's hard to believe that tomorrow is Christmas Eve.

Having been faked out by the Polish commander, we had a better break today from the Argentinians. The sea has risen to be quite rough, so we had quite a time getting to shore in the bouncing zodiacs. Some people went to a rookery, but I decided to go directly to the Argentinian camp, about a half mile from there. The camp had been abandoned for the last seven years. A new contingent of

Argentinians arrived here just about two weeks ago. The *comandante* was a nice fellow named Ferrera, who gave me a big welcome and said they would be delighted to have a Christmas Mass. We gathered about a table in their little dining room and had the Mass, mainly in Spanish, with the *comandante* and one of the young seaman doing the readings in Spanish. Again, because we were about to be inundated with tourists in a few moments, I went through the Act of Contrition in Spanish with them and gave them all general absolution so that they could receive Communion for Christmas. They seemed quite happy with the arrangement, but I told them they would have to go to Confession when they returned to Argentina, which would be the next time they would be near a church.

A dozen of them assisted very piously at Mass and afterward took a number of pictures around the altar. This makes three Masses ashore in three days, so we should get overtime for the missionary activity. However, it's been great fun and a delight to be able to bring Christmas to these isolated posts, with a Midnight Mass offered a few days early and in the afternoon.

Some of the Argentinians came back to the ship with us. We had Cokes and beer for those who wanted it, a half-hour conversation in Spanish, and then they were off on the bouncy sea back to the base. They were really a nice group of mainly young men, with one scientist, a biologist, among them. Argentina really wants to keep its claim alive on these lands, having lost the Malvinas, or the Falkland Islands, to the British. When we stepped ashore from the zodiac, the first thing the Argentinian sailor at the dockside said was "Welcome to Argentina."

We had a few good sessions at our debriefing this afternoon. Terry Hughes, a staff lecturer, talked on glaciers in great detail. Nature is a bit more complicated than it seems when you just look at it. Then we started the first leg of our journey to the Falklands by heading toward Elephant Island.

We hadn't proceeded very far when the sea started to kick up, and only about half of the people showed up for dinner tonight. It looks like our good luck on the trip south through the Drake Passage, one of the worst in the world, is giving out on us as we head north again. Anyway, we should be at Elephant Island (named after the elephant seal that lives there) early tomorrow morning. It will be a bit rough and maybe it will flatten out after that. Meanwhile, to bed.

SATURDAY, DECEMBER 24
En Route to the Falkland Islands

When we arrived at Elephant Island about 6:30 this morning, the island was surrounded by pack ice. The scout boat tried to get through, but the zodiac just couldn't cope with the high sea and the heavy hunks of tightly packed ice. There were also several enormous glaciers floating around the island. The island itself is just a series of massive peaks with one small peninsula going out to a small mountain with a bit of beach that would not be overwhelmed by the sea ice. It was here that Shackleton's men gathered under their two overturned lifeboats and managed to survive for 105 days through the Antarctic winter. They arrived here around the middle of April. When Shackleton decided to leave and tried to get to South Georgia by boat in the open sea, an 800-mile trip, he left on Easter Sunday, when the winter was just beginning in earnest. He would not get back here until the last day of August, toward the end of winter. How all twenty-two men managed to go through the whole winter and survive in a place that looks this bad in early summer is beyond imagination. However, Shackleton did not lose a single man, and all twenty-two of them were on the beach cheering as he landed on the Chilean boat *Yelchro*.

Anyway, we didn't land this morning because it would have been impossible in the zodiacs. We had a light breakfast, as befits Christmas Eve, and then a long philosophical talk with Terry Hughes from the University of Maine. He was mainly concerned about why liberals who were so valiant in the fight for civil rights are so totally in agreement with abortion, which violates the most fundamental human right of all, namely life. Not an easy question to answer.

I finally decided it was time to clean up for Christmas. It's not easy to take a shower on a rolling ship, but I accomplished it and I'm clean again. Also, the laundry came back, which is helpful in the cleansing process. Now to the Breviary and to get a Christmas sermon ready.

Because we'll be sailing all day en route to the Falkland Islands, leaving Elephant Island behind, Peter Harrison will lecture this morning on the Totorore Expedition to Cape Horn. Peter was almost killed on that one, but I heard the lecture on the Amazon a year ago, so I'll take that time to work on the sermon.

Another of our lecturers, Jack Child of American University, is talking on the politics of Antarctica at three this afternoon, and later on at five, Terry Hughes will give a lecture entitled "Antarctica, Ice Ages, and the Rising Sea Level." As you can see, we're really getting educated.

We're going to have an early dinner because the staff takes over the only dining room for their Christmas dinner, and while they are eating, we'll see, of all things, *Casablanca*. That will be over about nine o'clock and then we'll have Christmas carols in French, German, and English, followed by our Midnight Mass around 11:30. I suspect we'll have a full house tonight.

The sea is still rolling about as badly as ever because we're crossing the Drake Passage from south to north, just as we did earlier from north to south, although this time we're farther to the east. It doesn't seem to affect the waves, which are just as bad on both sides, east and west. It's really the convergence of Atlantic and Pacific with their different winds and different currents that causes all of this disturbance.

The Christmas carols came off well, with the Filipino crew members singing first, and then Peter Harrison's two little girls, ten and eleven, sang a duet about Jesus and the manger, followed by Micheline Place, our cruise director, and her twin sister singing in French. Then we all chimed in with the secular "Rudolph the Red-Nosed Reindeer" and religious songs for about twenty minutes.

At 11:45 P.M., we went up to the Penguin Lounge for Midnight Mass. It was really starting to get rough. It was all we could do to keep on our feet while hanging on to the little table where we had the altar placed. It had to be the worst Mass we have had at sea for trying to keep one's footing. All the hosts went sailing off the altar early in the Mass, thank God, before we had the Consecration. The hall was quite full. About half of them received Holy Communion. We sang three of the old-time Christmas songs and decided to get people down to their cabins while they could still navigate. I did the homily, but it wasn't all that great, because I spent 60 percent of my energy just to keep standing on my feet and then the other 40 percent trying to think what I was going to say next. I don't recommend it.

We turned in about 1:30 A.M. It was a wonderful Christmas Eve and everybody seems very happy.

SUNDAY, DECEMBER 25
En Route to the Falkland Islands

We rolled and pitched so much last night that everything that wasn't nailed down wound up on the floor—clothes, film, books, glasses, alarm clocks, etc. Toward dawn, they came in to close the porthole because the water was hitting us so hard some of it was coming through the glass.

At 8 A.M., we did a couple of 35-degree rolls and everything in the galley went all over the floor, chairs broke loose from their moorings, and the Christmas tree went over with a loud bang. A lot of people ended up on the floor of their cabin. After sliding up and down the bunk for a few hours since 5 A.M., I decided to get up and see what was happening above. At least I was able to get a cup of coffee and a crust of bread. It wasn't the best Christmas morning breakfast, but better than nothing. It's hard to describe the shambles of the galley, broken crockery everywhere.

After that, I came into our Explorer's Lounge just before one of our passengers, Colonel Carl Buechner, got caught on another 35-degree roll and went sailing across the room and whacked his head on one of the barstools. He is now getting a massage from the ship's doctor, but doesn't seem to have much more than a bump on his head. He's a pretty feisty guy, although he's older than we are. The colonel said he didn't have any idea of what happened, and I guess that's the way it is after a quick accident. One other passenger had to have five stitches in his head after being thrown against the wall in the Penguin Lounge. Everyone seems to be lying low now, and our special Christmas dinner is going to be put off until tomorrow. Today it's sandwiches, which are about all they can manufacture in the galley at the moment. It all adds a little spice to Christmas Day. Here comes the doctor now with her liniments.

We had a lecture this morning, which Ned attended and I skipped because I just didn't feel like struggling up to the top deck. However, Ned said they had a pretty good attendance, considering the bounciness of the ship, which seems to be worse in that lecture hall on the top deck, because it's higher and swings in a larger arc.

A reasonable number showed up for lunch, but they had to put off the Christmas dinner because all of the crockery seemed to have flipped off the shelves and splattered on the floor and it was impossible to cook with this 35-degree roll. We had BLT sandwiches and French fries, which were very good.

During lunch, the captain changed our course a bit to the northeast, away from our destination, so that we would have a following sea rather than broadside waves. After lunch, he said he was going back on course northwest and we had better get ourselves positioned somewhere where we could survive the afternoon. Ned and I came back to our faithful cabin, No. 211, and napped alternately as the ship continued to pitch and roll. We're constantly having things bounce off the table and roll the length of the cabin. I'm glad it isn't us.

About 3 P.M., since the rolling was no better and no worse, we decided to try our last two Christmas Masses. This morning it would have been impossible.

We managed to get through without disaster. I think we could write a new ritual on how to offer Mass on a bouncing ship. It's not easy. However, it is at the heart of our Christmas celebration and we were happy to be able to do it together.

The rest of the day will be reasonably simple. Tea is scheduled, but I doubt that people will face the prospect of having their tea land in their laps. Later there is a get-together for everyone to find out what we're supposed to do tomorrow. The captain still thinks he can land on the southernmost of the Falkland Islands at about 6:30 in the morning and so we'll get an early call. By that time, the sea should have calmed down a bit, especially if we can get into the lee of the island. We'll have dinner of sorts tonight, preceded by champagne from the captain. Ned is certain to attend that one. They say it settles one's stomach too, which is helpful, although we've both been doing pretty well in the seasickness department. If my mother were still alive, she would say, "Knock on wood." There's a long night ahead, and the captain promises more gale-force winds. He also promises the ship won't turn over, and we're happy to take his word for that, although it does come pretty far over on both sides right now. About every twenty seconds, our curtains come right out from the wall and hang at a 45-degree angle and then swing back again. I keep thinking of Shackleton and his men. After depositing the other twenty-two survivors on Elephant Island, he made this whole trip we're now making in an open boat. What's more, he did it in the wintertime, whereas we're in late spring.

One last choice for the day. At 9:15 tonight, they are showing a video of *Raiders of the Lost Ark*, for those who can make it to the top deck again. Merry Christmas. We won't forget this one in a hurry. Last year it was Barbados on the *QE2*. Milder fare.

MONDAY, DECEMBER 26
Falkland Islands

We arrived here just after six this morning. Having picked up a pilot in Stanley, the capital, we came down to the south coast, where there are rookeries, both for Magellan penguins and for king penguins. About 8 A.M., we went to shore on a nice sandy beach for a change. No slippery boulders, no raging surf. Then we started a walk for about a mile or so down the beach, where we saw the Magellan penguins scurrying into their burrows. They cut these burrows in the ground just like rabbits and dwell there. They seem more skittish than some of the other penguins we have seen, for they are quickly into their burrows as soon as you get near to them. If you encounter them along the beach, they jump into the waves and swim away. There was a sheepherder's bright white plaster house nearby, and it was interesting to see the sheep intermingling with the penguins. It's the only place on earth that you'll get that picture.

As we continued to the southern edge of the beach on the other side from where we landed, we met the most impressive penguins that we have seen thus far, the kings. They weigh about eighty pounds and stand about four feet high. They seem a trifle smaller than the emperors that I encountered at McMurdo Sound twenty-five years ago. However, the kings are a great bird in their own right, much larger than the other penguins we have seen on this trip and rather regal in the way they walk and in their red and yellow coloring in addition to their black-and-white tuxedo. They are also quite unafraid and one can walk within a few feet of them without startling them. Ned managed to pet a couple of them.

It seemed good to get a long walk back up the beach to our landing place. We've been cooped up somewhat for the last two days, and everybody was anxious to stretch their legs. The weather was also quite favorable. It was overcast, with a temperature of about 45 degrees. Although down here the windchill factor always makes the red parka feel good, I just wore a regular wool shirt beneath it. And no rubber pants this time. We were back to the ship just before eleven and had Mass at 11:30 with our Notre Dame couple. After lunch, we'll be visiting Stanley, and for the first time on this trip, this afternoon we won't have to wear boots.

Stanley should be interesting because the Falklands war was mainly fought on land around this capital, with the Argentinians inside and the British nipping them off at every point. The naval action took place between this island and the other large island, although there are many smaller islands in this group. All of our penguin watching this morning was done on a place called Volunteer Point. No one seems to know why it's called Volunteer Point, except that Ned says the shepherd who lives in the white house volunteered to go out there and take care of the sheep. Until we get a better explanation, we'll go with that one.

As soon as we were all back aboard, we came around the northern tip of East Falkland Island and into Port Stanley, a trip of about ten or fifteen miles. There we met our sister ship, the *World Explorer*, which is a little larger than ours, carrying 150 rather than 100 passengers. The last time we saw her was in the middle of the Amazon a year ago November when she was going upriver and we down.

As soon as we got to Port Stanley, the weather changed abruptly from fortyish and overcast to a steady sleety rain that made the temperature seem below zero. Also, the wind came up, which added to the cold and chill. Again, we donned our foul-weather gear and boarded a local launch that took us into the jetty.

Right on the harbor front down the main street is the Anglican cathedral, which used to be the bishopric for all of Latin America and everything in the Antarctic. Now it's the parish church for the

Falklands and other surrounding islands and South Georgia, some 300 or 400 miles from here, from which our sister ship, the *World Explorer*, came this morning. Incidentally, she was six hours late because of the foul weather. We were coming into it at an angle and she had it right in the face. In other words, she pitched while we rolled.

We stopped at the cathedral first, saw the crèche, and had a talk with the rector, Father Murphy. He had been a military chaplain and is a good friend of Bishop Robin Woods, who is on our Advisory Board for Notre Dame's Ecumenical Institute in Tantur, near Jerusalem. The cathedral was built ninety years ago and for many years had a bishop here. Now, of course, all of that is changed. There's an enormous battleship flag in the sanctuary that was given to the church by the daughter of the admiral who won a battle against the Germans here during World War I. There was another battle nearby during World War II. This one is generally called the Battle of the River Plate and involved a famous German battle cruiser, the *Graf Spee*, which was dogged all the way to Uruguay by some outgunned British destroyers. They performed with extraordinary valor, such as ours did in the second battle of the Philippines. The British naval squadron returned here after the River Plate engagement.

We continued down the main street a few more blocks, where we found a small shop and a post office. Ned made a few purchases and I bought the local coins. I also purchased some Falkland stamps for our library collection. About the only worthwhile items in these shops are sweaters, since the islands are full of sheep and they do a lot of knitting here. Right across from the post office is St. Mary's, the Catholic church. We knocked on the rectory door and a young priest, whose mother tongue was obviously German, greeted us. He was a member of the Mill Hill Fathers, English missionaries, and his name was Tony Agreiter. When I asked him where he was from, meaning his homeland, he mentioned Sarnes in the southern Tyrol.

It's about one chance in a million that meeting the parish priest in the Falklands turns up a Ladin priest from the town where I spent my first summer after completing my first year at the Gregorian University in Rome. Sarnes is a small village above Bressanone (or Brixen, in German). I don't think one-millionth of the people in the world know where Sarnes is. Father Tony even knew the priest, Herr Ferdinand Plottner, who ran the guesthouse where we stayed that summer of 1938. In fact, he told us a funny story. When the Nazis were inspecting the village, it was at Christmastime. When they saw Herr Plottner's crèche, they tried to embarrass him by asking, "What is this?" He said, "What do you think it is? It's the crèche of Bethlehem, and look closer, here is an ox and here is a donkey. The ox is Mussolini and the donkey is Hitler." The next day they sent him off to a concentration camp, but he survived it, although somewhat broken physically on his return. Good old Father Plottner. He always spoke before he thought, although in this case I think many of us would agree with what he said.

While having some schnapps and a cigar, Father Tony told us that he knew some of our Holy Cross priests in Uganda, where he served some years ago, then Ned and Terry Hughes went out to do some more shopping. I wandered down to the monument of the 1982 Falklands war. The inscription on the monument reads: "To our liberators, 1982." Father Tony told us that there are about 1,800 people in the Falklands, most of them here on East Falkland Island and maybe a few hundred over on West Falkland Island. We'll be visiting a couple of small islands off West Falkland tomorrow to see the rookeries for rockhopper penguins (our sixth and last species) and the giant albatross. Father Tony also told us that he has about 250 Catholics out of some 1,800 people who live on the island and also he takes care of about 300 of the military who happen to be Catholics. He also ministers to the military on Ascension Island, some 2,000 miles from here. He is able to fly up with the military. His assistant is there right now for the Christmas season.

We continue to encounter these "small world" happenings wherever we go in this wide, wide world.

Stanley has a very English look and lifestyle, as one finds throughout the former British Empire. The Anglican church could have come right out of any village in England, although the Catholic church was built, also ninety years ago, by some Norwegian carpenters and it is pretty plain. The houses are Britishy, but in a way more simple. There are practically no trees on the island, so they burn peat in their fireplaces for warmth. Even so, the rooms are quite cold, but I guess that is the British style too.

There are a few wrecks in the harbor. People who had a hard time getting through the Strait of Magellan generally came back here as a place of refuge and were often so battered that their ships sank in the harbor. It was also used a good deal during the California gold rush, when people had to go to California by sailing around Cape Horn. Some just didn't make it and limped back here.

The memory of the invasion of the islands by the Argentinians on April 2, 1982, is still very strong here. The whole island was only defended by about 80 Royal Marines when the Argentinians arrived with 10,000 troops, mainly schoolboys who were told they were going to another part of Argentina where they would be welcomed. The Argentinians were really surprised when the British took them up on their dare and came in here with a force a fourth the size of the Argentinians and whipped them badly and very quickly. Most people felt it was unnecessary to sink the Argentinian battleship *Belgrano* with a loss of life of almost 400, since she was several hundred miles from here at the time and not engaged in the action directly. Argentinian planes flying over from the mainland would arrive here with only five minutes of combat time before returning home because of fuel depletion. The Argentinians used mostly A-4s that they had obtained from us and did manage to sink two or three British vessels, one being the *Sheffield*, which had quite a large loss of life because the aluminum superstructure burst into flames. No more aluminum for British naval ships. They also badly damaged two troopships, which had to be scuttled. All in all, though, the Argentinians fought very badly, even though their air force performed feats of valor. Many fliers didn't make it back because returning to the Argentinian coast found them running out of fuel before they could land. All in all, the Argentinians lost about a fourth of their air force, mostly to British Harrier planes.

From all we could learn, the Falkland Islanders are a rather tight-knit group and are happy to be back in the British fold and don't even want to think about being turned over to Argentina, even though the Argentinians continue to call these islands the Islas Malvinas. From the looks of the weather today, again we can say, as we have in so many other places, this is a nice place to visit but I wouldn't want to live here. They say you can count the sunny days on the fingers of your hand, and when it rains and sleets at the same time, you're really in for a chilling, stinging experience, which was ours today.

Tonight we have the deferred Christmas dinner and the captain's cocktail party. It was too rough for it Christmas Day. The dinner turned out to be about seven courses, all well prepared. Fortunately, they make their courses small so that one can sample almost everything without feeling stuffed.

Ned went to the movie tonight, but quit after the first ten minutes or so. He said it was rubbish. I've been reading three books at once. Ned bought a wonderful book on the Antarctic from the literature stock aboard. It's published by Reader's Digest and is a complete physical, historical, and geological look at the Antarctic continent and the various explorations that took place there. Wonderful photography as well. We're both reading this one. The second book is Barbara Tuchman's new history of the American Revolution, particularly the naval part. It's called *The First Salute* and is extremely well done. She never writes a dull book. The third book is Eugene Kennedy's *Tomorrow's Catholics, Yesterday's Church: The Two Cultures of American Catholicism*. It's an interesting sociological study of the two currents in the Church today. It's too easy to call Catholics liberal and conservative or pre-Vatican II (culture I) and post-Vatican II (culture II). Gene tries to get into the subtleties of the differences, and I think does it quite well. He cites me as an example of culture II and the Cardinal Archbishop of Detroit as culture I. He puts Pope John Paul II in both cultures. He also cites the University of Notre Dame as an example of both cultures existing side by side.

Gene obviously believes that culture II is the culture of the future and culture I must carry all of the baggage of the past. He even believes that both cultures live together in the same Church, pray together, work together, but are simply on different wavelengths in certain matters, mainly how to cope with modern life and reality. The best thing he says about culture II is that it savors the mystery of Catholicism. This mystery, he says, should not be buried under legislation, control, and a too great emphasis on organization. That's where I was when Ned came back from the movie and we both turned in about 11:30.

TUESDAY, DECEMBER 27
Falkland Islands

It was quite rough during the night when we rounded East Falkland Island and continued across the strait between the two islands to West Falkland Island. About six this morning, we anchored off the coast of West Falkland at a little island called Carcass. The island was full of birds, mainly ducks and hawks, albatrosses wheeling on the seaward side, and a lot of little birds they call dickeys. I guess that means small landbirds, like thrushes, as contrasted with the seabirds, which tend to be larger. Anyway, there was a beautiful blue sky and bright sunshine, which is quite a contrast from yesterday. However, the wind is quite high and we got a bit soaked coming to shore and returning in the zodiacs. On shore, we just wandered up and down the beaches at the site of a sheep farm which has about 1,200 sheep here on this smallish island. It's just covered with mossy hills like the moors of Scotland, and the sheep are mainly managed by dogs, directed by men and women on horseback. As in Australia, they claim that one dog can take care of 1,000 sheep and two dogs do much better with 2,000. They work as a team. I guess most of it is instinct with a bit of training.

We all gathered at the farmhouse, where the lady of the house and her husband gave us tea and scones. There was a table with at least ten different kinds of scones on it, all very tasty.

Back to the ship in time for a lecture by Jack Child on the Falklands war. We've already picked up a lot of talk about it from the various islanders we've met. The Argentinians didn't touch this little island, but everything was cut off for the duration of the war and they never knew quite what was going to happen until British commandos finally landed to learn that there were no Argentinians on this small island. They also saw the planes flying overhead from time to time and, of course, there was considerable naval action not too far from here in the channel between the two large islands.

Mass again at noontime. We had a briefing on this afternoon's activities and left for shore about 3:15. Shore happens to be New Island. Before leaving, they put in a new rule. No smoking on the island. They claim it was because of dry conditions, but it looked pretty wet and muddy to me. I think it's once again, as we had experienced on the QE2, just prejudice against cigar smokers.

We arrived at the end of the island in a cove where the two gentlemen who own the island both live with their families. One has been married three times and has had children from each wife. The other is married to the first gentleman's second wife, if you can figure that out. They don't talk to each other, even though they are here on this isolated place living in houses about 100 feet apart. This should prove that isolation is no automatic boon to virtue.

Once ashore, we climbed up a long, sloping hill, mostly spongy heath, with about 2,000 sheep here and there. At the top of the climb, we overlooked an enormous rookery of rockhopper penguins. They are very cute, with weird yellow feather tufts coming out of each side of their heads, generally white against black. They also have unusual eye formations. And hop rocks they do, coming up very steep slopes and even going down with great surefootedness. Mingled with them at the top of the rookery, which was about 100 to 200 yards above a roaring, crashing sea, were the nests of the wandering albatross, almost built up like a chimney. They come from 4,000 miles away to make their nests here each year. They use the same nests and have the same mates. They don't travel together. He goes his way and she goes hers, he to New Zealand and she possibly to South Africa. They are terrific fliers and have an enormous wing-spread. At nesting time, they rendezvous here within twenty-four hours of each other.

We were back to the shore in about an hour and a quarter and then out to the ship. Since we're at anchor and quiet, I decided to take a shower, which is a lot easier in these circumstances than when rolling 35 degrees. It's pretty tough to soap up and wash off while being in proximate danger of losing one's footing at any moment on the slippery floor. Besides, the quarters are very tight in the bathroom. Anyway, the deed is done and now I'm ready to start out clean on our last lap.

We're going to another inlet a few miles up the beach and there we'll have a barbecue on shore. The barbecues are always great, so we look forward to a pleasant evening and maybe even early to bed. Who knows?

When we return to the ship after the barbecue tonight, we begin our long journey over 300 miles from here to Punta Arenas, via the famous Strait of Magellan. We plan to get there about 9 A.M. the day after tomorrow, which means about a day and a half of sailing, if all goes well and the weather behaves.

WEDNESDAY, DECEMBER 28
En Route to Punta Arenas

Not so rough during the night, but a steady roll that one gets used to. We woke up to a moderately bright day with thin, high overcast and the sun breaking through. All around the ship are the enormous albatrosses and the smaller pintado petrels. Just watching them fly makes one envious. They are so graceful and they do it with such ease. Hardly ever moving their wings as they circle the ship, now dipping to the water's edge and then soaring high above us with effortless ease. No wonder they can go thousands of miles at a time.

We should be getting very near to the east coast of South America late this afternoon or evening. Let's hope the calm seas keep up.

This is the day of winding things up. A final talk on penguins by a new birdman who is aboard and will join the other ship, the *World Explorer*, in Punta Arenas, before she heads south on the trip we just took. They call this new lecturer "Mr. Penguin Himself," Frank Todd. I guess Peter Harrison will have to be "Mr. Albatross."

This is the day for cleaning up all of the loose ends, also packing. The nice thing about a sea trip like this is that you only have to pack once. Then there is the matter of tips to a crew that has been wonderful to us, trying to find the tickets where one thought he put them two weeks ago, deciding what to throw away and what to keep, and generally getting some order into the chaos of this cabin.

Our German captain, Ralf Zander, is giving us a farewell cocktail party tonight and the captain's farewell dinner, of course, following that. They then will feature music and dancing in the Explorer's Lounge at 9:30 P.M. There may be music, but I suspect there will be very little dancing, since we'll be arriving at Punta Arenas around six tomorrow morning, all going well.

THURSDAY, DECEMBER 29
Punta Arenas, Chile

We arrived at Punta Arenas at six this morning and we're up at 6:30 for Mass at seven with our Notre Dame couple, Bob and Ruth. Now we're off for a bus tour of the city, which we saw quite thoroughly a year ago when we were down here with Ernie Bartell and George Canepa. It was the farthest south of our Latin American trip. We've gone considerably more to the south this time.

We'll have lunch and a little free time in town before leaving at 5 P.M. for Santiago and then two hours later, to Miami, where we hope to arrive about 5:30 tomorrow morning. At 9 A.M., back to Chicago and South Bend via Midway Airlines.

It's been another great trip, for which we are grateful. I think we did some good as chaplains. At least we tried. I finished the Gene Kennedy book last night and have a couple more I can read en route to Notre Dame. After getting back from the deep south, our biggest desire is to find out what's happened in the world during the past two weeks. News aboard ship is sketchy at best. Anyway, there's always *Time* magazine when we get to Santiago. At least I hope there is.

As we say in Chile, *adiós*.

FRIDAY, DECEMBER 30
En Route Home

The trip home was about what one could expect. We returned this time on Ladeco Airlines from Punta Arenas all the way to Miami. The trip was nice from Punta Arenas to Santiago, where we spent a couple of hours waiting for our flight to Miami. Actually, we used the same airplane, a 727, which meant we had to stop for fuel at Guayaquil, Ecuador. As usual, we didn't get the best seats. I was next to the emergency door, through which cold air was infiltrating. Ned wasn't doing very much better; his seat kept sliding back to full recline, whereas mine wouldn't recline at all. Anyway, it was a long night. We were so crammed in that it was impossible to cut the meat at dinner without being a contortionist. Anyway, we arrived in Miami on time and our bags arrived too, thanks be to the Good Lord.

Then Ned went off to the Fiesta Bowl in Tempe, Arizona, and I came back to South Bend. This time I came on Midway Airlines and arrived on time in Chicago for my short connection to South Bend. When we all boarded the small commuter airplane, the second engine wouldn't start, so we had to take another small plane to Elkhart, where Marty, our faithful chauffeur, was waiting. I was able to call him from Chicago and divert him to Elkhart.

As expected, the pile of mail was very high and I'm still working at it past midnight, but it's mostly under control and all of it is good as befits Christmastime. This time it is really *adiós*. Our Russian-American Foundation for the Survival and Development of Humanity is having a meeting in a few days in Washington and then another meeting in Moscow beginning on January 13. So the New Year gets off to a good start. Amid the large stack of mail tonight was a letter from Andrei Sakharov suggesting how I might collaborate with him and his group in Russia on promoting human rights in both of our countries, as well as in the Third World. All in all, I look forward to a great year. Ned has the responsibility of getting us a victory in Tempe. So does Lou Holtz. And with that, good night and God bless one and all for a great New Year.

AFTERWORD

$\overline{\qquad\qquad\qquad\qquad\qquad}$

And so the yearlong journey (if you take out the in-betweens) came to an end. It had gone exactly as we had hoped: a totally different experience with new and unusual scenes and people, each day a welcome surprise.

Retirement had begun with a bang, not a whimper. We had made a clean break between the old and the new. Looking back, we had to admit that much that had happened was unplanned, but surprisingly welcome and within the span of our previous hopes.

What does one think and do when it—that first clean break—is over? Obviously, especially if one belongs to a religious community, one gets down to work again, and so we have. In the four years that have so quickly passed since the end of our trips, we have both found more than enough to do at the university, as well as beyond, thank God.

We've made clear to all of our associates at the university that we know and understand that we are no longer the president and the executive vice president, nor do we wish to be, either in name or in fact. Naturally, because we continue to live at Notre Dame, some colleagues occasionally try to get us to voice an opinion when a controversy or a crisis arises. We remind them that we have no desire to second-guess our able successors. These fine young Holy Cross priests are going their own good way and our comments are unneeded, even if we were of a mind to comment, which we aren't.

Our friends and associates are still old friends, and associates too,

311

although on a different footing. It takes a little time for this to happen gracefully, but with a little goodwill all around, and especially no hypersensitivity on our part, it happens naturally enough.

News media remain inquisitive. That's natural too, because you can't shut them off completely after years of giving them frequent interviews. However, if one is honest with reporters about one's changed status, they too come to understand. They'll also have to retire someday, and they'll want to do it gracefully.

In a way, it would have been easier if we had retired a few thousand miles away from Notre Dame, but I have this sense that, despite our returning here as ex-this and ex-that, we have been able to be helpful in some ways. We have a fairly open and positive relationship with the alumni of our thirty-five years here. They are always reminding us of wonderful encounters during years past, and we do laugh, reminisce, and thank God together for good years, generous graces, and happy memories.

Then there are the worldwide challenges in the work that the new administration has commissioned us to do through the various Notre Dame international institutes on peace, economic and political development in the Third World, human rights, ecumenism, and ecology. Because I'm free now to become even more involved worldwide, I can help those who direct these institutes by keeping them informed on what is happening in several dozen similar organizations around the world.

Ned has his collateral list of duties, serving on several foundation boards, giving me wise guidance on the Knight Commission on Intercollegiate Athletics, and lending his expertise to fund-raising efforts on a variety of fronts. Somehow the days pass quickly. We never seem to get really caught up on all that needs doing, but we both hope we can continue to be useful—and not be in the way—as the years pass.

I guess we are particularly blessed to belong to such an understanding institutional family in which the old team can find meaningful service without being at cross-purposes with the new leadership. Most retirees don't have it that easy, but the world is very large and the opportunities and the needs are many. I would hope that all retirees could find such a fruitful niche as we have. I also hope that all might have such a wonderful year off as we did. There is nothing like it to give one pause and perspective on the years yet ahead and a determination to make them fruitful.

I began by saying that this is a book about travel, but also about retirement. I would hope that these few notes would reassure fellow retirees that life does go on, and can be all that we want it to be. It's the difference between stopping dead and changing course. May you choose the latter and continue to be both happy and productive. There is a way for everyone, different for each. You just have to find your path and follow it.

Just remember the wonderful final stanza from Robert Frost's poem "The Road Not Taken":

> *Two roads diverged in a wood, and I—*
> *I took the one less traveled by,*
> *And that has made all the difference.* *

The Poetry of Robert Frost, edited by E. L. Latham (New York: Holt, Rinehart and Winston, 1969), p. 105.

INDEX

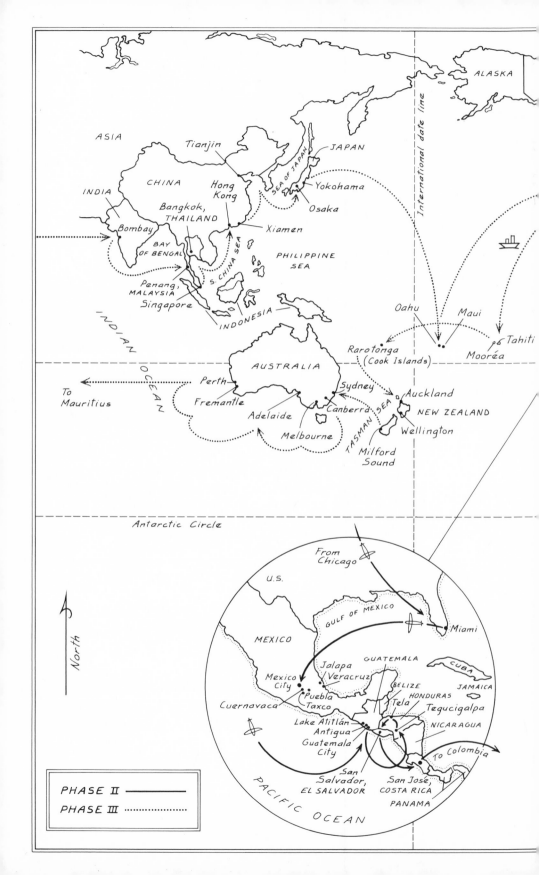